Scorsese on Scorsese

Scorsese on Scorsese

Edited by
David Thompson and Ian Christie

faber and faber
LONDON · BOSTON

First published in 1989
by Faber and Faber Limited
3 Queen Square London WC1N 3AU
This paperback edition first published in 1990
This updated edition first published in 1996

Photoset by Wilmaset, Birkenhead, Wirral
Printed in England by Clays Ltd, St Ives plc

A CIP record for this book
is available from the British Library

ISBN 0–571–17827–8

2 4 6 8 10 9 7 5 3 1

This book is dedicated to the memory of Jacques Ledoux, Curator of the Cinémathèque Royale de Belgique for forty years until his untimely death in 1988: a passionate archivist who believed in the future of cinema as much as in its past; and a rare inspirer of film-makers and film historians alike.

Contents

List of Illustrations

What's Hecuba to him?

The first Martin Scorsese film that I saw – or that saw me – was *Alice Doesn't Live Here Anymore*. The actors were directed with assurance. There was not a frame wasted. I said to myself: Michael Powell, you're going to have a good time – this man knows where he's going and you're going with him. On the screen we were entering a fast-food emporium, with two splendid actresses volleying words and phrases at one another. It was like watching a singles match on centre court at Wimbledon, between two champions. I hadn't seen match play like this since I saw *Pat and Mike*.

We screened *Taxi Driver*. 'Stop! Stop!' I said. 'Who's that devilish actor who plays the Devil in the scene with Robert De Niro?'

'That's Scorsese,' said my friend, who had arranged the screening.

'What! Can he act too?!'

He smiled. 'Want more?'

'Is there more?'

He nodded vigorously. 'Much, much more.'

He arranged a screening of *Mean Streets*. It was in a little projection theatre off Wardour Street, London W1. There were four of us and the projectionist. When the screening ended, we looked at each other, stunned. The five of us crossed the narrow street and went into a pub that was just on the verge of closing. Nobody else was there. Still we said nothing. There was nothing to say.

All art is one, and every artist owes a duty to his art. We can't all be masters, but we can know a master when we see him, because he has something to say to us, and sooner or later imparts it. The difference between these films of Martin Scorsese's is that with *Alice* and *Taxi Driver* he handles the materials like a master; with *Mean Streets* he is in direct contact with his audience, from the beginning to the end. This is the rarest gift given to a movie director. Most directors, however wise, however experienced, however resourceful, however bold, don't have it and never will have it. Marty has always had it.

He has this great, generous gift of creating a situation for an audience, and sharing it with them. He is the ventriloquist and his doll, the singer and the song. In his latest film, *Life Lessons*, Marty performs the same miracle: he is the painter and his palette, he is the pupil and the master, he is the cunning of the fox and the innocence of the child, he is the voice of the tape deck screaming 'A Whiter Shade of Pale'.

When Hamlet sees the tears in the Player's eyes, and asks Horatio:

What's Hecuba to him or he to Hecuba

That he should weep for her?

he is asking the same question that we ask of ourselves when Scorsese, in *The Last Temptation of Christ*, gives us our first glimpse of that hill called Golgotha. For, as the tears spring to our eyes, we know that we shall see that hill again, and then it will be our last sight on earth – and his.

Michael Powell
March 1989

Acknowledgements

This book owes its existence – as does, in part, Martin Scorsese's lifelong fascination with cinema – to the inspiration of Michael Powell. The *Guardian* also played a vital part by generously supporting a unique series of three Guardian Lectures by Martin Scorsese during January 1987, which form the basis of the book's text.

The occasion was a complete retrospective of Scorsese's work under the title 'The Scorsese Album' at the National Film Theatre in London, which was organized by David Thompson, who also chaired the first of the Guardian Lectures. Michael Powell was present in the audience, with his wife Thelma Schoonmaker (Scorsese's regular editor), and he felt that the exchanges gave such insight into Scorsese's formation as a film-maker, and his experiences of the American film industry, that they deserved to be published. Martin Scorsese agreed that the subsequent two Guardian Lectures, at Bradford's National Museum of Photography, Film and Television and at the Filmhouse in Edinburgh, both chaired by Ian Christie, should be planned as complementary to the first. All three were recorded, as was an additional appearance at the Glasgow Film Theatre under the auspices of BAFTA Scotland, and the resulting transcripts provided the skeleton of the book.

As well as additional interviews conducted by the editors, flesh and blood have been added to this by the ready response of many friends and colleagues, who have kindly given permission for their original interview material to be incorporated to amplify those lectures and to bring the book up to date. Particular thanks are due to: David Pirie, editor of *Anatomy of the Movies* (1981), and its publishers, Barrie and Jenkins Ltd and Macmillan; to Melvyn Bragg and Steve Jenkins of *The South Bank Show*, produced by London Weekend Television; to Barry Norman and Judy Lindsay of the BBC TV series *Talking Pictures* (1987); to Anthony Wall and *Arena*, produced by the BBC; to Chris Rodley and Lucida Films; to Gavin Smith and *Film Comment* magazine; to Graham Fuller and *Interview* magazine; and to Jonathan Romney and the *Guardian*.

The British Film Institute Information Library and the Stills, Posters and Designs collection were invaluable resources for this book, as was Martin Scorsese's personal archive. Walter Donohue has throughout been a sympathetic and knowledgeable editor. Thanks are especially due to Thelma Schoonmaker, Raffaele Donato, Julia Judge, Margaret Bodde, Kent Jones, Deanna Avery, and of course Martin Scorsese himself, for supporting this volume from its original conception through to its current revision.

Martin Scorsese – Storyteller, Illusionist, Smuggler and Iconoclast

Since the first edition of this book appeared in 1989, in the aftermath of the controversy provoked by *The Last Temptation of Christ*, Martin Scorsese has become for many the greatest film-maker still working at the height of his powers – the king of American cinema, even if as yet uncrowned by the Academy of Motion Picture Arts.

It's a title that Scorsese himself would be quick to dispute since, more than most film-makers or critics, he is deeply conscious of what has gone before. For the centenary of cinema that is being widely celebrated in 1995–6, he has made a three-part history of American cinema which pays eloquent tribute to the masters – and the mavericks – who taught him his craft and made the movies both America's essential art and industry. While being a very contemporary director, he has always felt a mission to celebrate the memory of cinema through archival and promotional work. Indeed it is fundamental to Scorsese's concept of cinema that present and future are, and must be, nourished by the past, and if this has to be experienced today through other media such as the videocassette and the laser-disc, let these be the agents of such an education. While expressing this desire through his *Personal Journey through American Movies*, Scorsese was also able to reflect precisely on how the directors of the past have dealt with the artistic dilemma posed by Hollywood.

To be an American film-maker today is to command extraordinary power, as well as running the risks that accompany such power. And Scorsese has few illusions. As he said in 1987 at one of the public question-and-answer sessions which formed the basis of this book, 'I am an

American director, which means I am a Hollywood director.' Having just seen *The Color of Money*, some of his audience queried whether by making a star vehicle for Paul Newman and the then up-and-coming Tom Cruise, the director of *Mean Streets, Taxi Driver* and *Raging Bull* had not sold out to the studio system. Wasn't he really a sophisticated East Coast film-maker, doomed to humiliation or compromise among the fleshpots of Hollywood? In fact, as Scorsese argued, *The Color of Money* had rehabilitated him with the people who controlled film-making in America. And just at that moment, unknown to him and his audience, he was about to find a studio – Universal – willing to back the project whose recent collapse had caused him so much pain, *The Last Temptation of Christ*.

That film would, through the controversy of its reception, make its director virtually a household name. He subsequently went on to win many critical accolades for *GoodFellas*, which was made for Warner Brothers. But in return for their risk, Universal would require from him a 'commercial' project as his next feature. *Cape Fear* was his answer, and indeed it proved to be his biggest box-office hit yet. The director has argued that the film remains in many ways 'A Martin Scorsese Picture' despite the requirements of fitting a readily marketable genre. But more importantly, *Cape Fear* highlighted the director's plight in Hollywood, that the large budgets now required for even a 'personal' project will come at a certain price.

The fascination of Scorsese's career, as well as his films, is that of a parable of cinema itself after the Golden Age. Scorsese emerged too late to belong to the great post-war European movements of Italian Neo-Realism or the French New Wave, much less the Hollywood studio system which had nurtured his home-grown heroes. But he was fortunate to find himself part of the first American generation of film-school students who were inspired equally by what they studied and by what was happening around them in the early sixties.

He witnessed American daily life etched for the first time on American screens in unsanitized, ethnically diverse images by the New American Cinema documentarists. He experienced the excitement of the European 'art cinema' explosion – Fellini, Antonioni, Visconti, Resnais, Godard, Truffaut, Bergman – as it burst on to no-nonsense American screens. And he belonged, briefly, to the resulting vanguard: to the radical Newsreel movement, and to the international independent cinema, winning a prize at one of its most eclectic festivals, Knokke. It was a baptism which now seems as remarkable as anything in the cinema's legendary past; and it left a permanent trace on his ambition.

As the example of John Cassavetes had shown him, and in particular the extraordinary impact of *Shadows* in 1960, film-making must be *personal*, and this most of all when it commands the greatest technical and industrial resources. Only with this insistence on coherent authorship will it be *authentic*, demanding that the film-maker test every gesture and line-reading against personal experience and emotion. Its techniques must be, above all, *expressive*, bending the spectator's eye and emotion to the film-maker's vision, however bizarre or removed from normal experience. And the resulting beauty will follow the Surrealist André Breton's definition: it will be convulsive, or it will not be.

But, unlike his European contemporaries – and heroes, like the Bertolucci of *Before the Revolution* – for him, there was also Hollywood. Not merely as a nostalgic mythology, or a source of eclectic influences, but as a living, bustling reality – the 'Mecca of cinema', as the French poet Blaise Cendrars called it. Mecca, Babylon, Burbank, the Dream Factory – whichever frame of reference, it drew the young Scorsese towards his destiny: to be a Hollywood film-maker. He would enter it through the last available apprenticeship scheme, making exploitation movies for Roger Corman, and would find in this latter-day *atelier* the freedom to test his radical, aesthetic ambitions against the discipline of genre imperatives and audience reaction.

And throughout the first triumphant decade of his career, spanning the seventies, he succeeded better than any other American director of his generation in combining the personal and the mythic, the visceral and the classic. The great trajectory that runs from *Who's That Knocking at My Door?* to *Raging Bull* is simultaneously a journey through the Italian–American psyche, through the founding myths of America, and through the previous forty years of cinema. The cost, in personal and professional terms, was enormous; and there were many inclined to regard Scorsese as a spent or compromised force in the aftermath of the early eighties.

But he fought back, remaining true to first principles. While *The Color of Money* revealed him as a serious 'player', *The Last Temptation of Christ* was vital to his survival in a more personal sense. Not only did the Gospel story evoke some of his most potent childhood experiences, oscillating between the magical poles of church and cinema, but it represented a challenge: to his own imagination and resource, and to the industry that wanted to tame him. The controversy that continued through its making and release still simmers on (in Britain, a nervous BBC cancelled its planned screening in 1991, and it finally received its television première on Channel 4 in 1995). And while *GoodFellas* identified Scorsese not only as the supreme documentarist of the Italian-American gangster lifestyle but also as a virtuoso of film-making craft, it plunged him into the ongoing debate on violence in the cinema. *Cape Fear*, a remake of a film that had itself encountered censorship problems in its day, was also greeted with charges of excess, though this did not detract from its success with a wider audience than he had hitherto enjoyed.

Controversy has flared up frequently in Scorsese's career. One instance was of his own making: in 1981 he led a campaign to awaken an uncaring industry to the problem of fading colour film, an act of aggression that led to Eastman Kodak eventually producing a more permanent film stock, as well as raising the whole question of methods of preservation. But in the same year, one John Hinckley Jr claimed that seeing *Taxi Driver* fifteen times had been the source of his obsession with Jodie Foster, as well as the inspiration behind his attempted assassination of President Ronald Reagan. In the trial, the film was shown to the jury, who subsequently acquitted Hinckley on the grounds of insanity.

The extreme 'realism' that some critics had reacted against in Scorsese's films had apparently come full circle. Scorsese's answer, conscious or not, came in the supremely satirical *The King of Comedy*, in which the world of obsessive fans crossed over into the protected unreality of superstardom, and both were found wanting. But Scorsese's is a thoroughly modern conception of 'realism', one that combines total authenticity *and* expressivity. The visual and aural realization of this deeper authenticity encompasses an eclecticism that is rarely self-advertising, but applied with a singular passion. Michael Powell once said in an interview with Bertrand Tavernier, 'I am not a film director with a personal style, *I am cinema.*' What was true for Powell seems also to be true of Scorsese, as his own testimony will demonstrate.

The life of a Scorsese protagonist is essentially expressed through emotion, be it the experience of growing up in a Mafia-dominated society (*Mean Streets*), the psychosis induced by urban loneliness (*Taxi Driver*), the despair of a man who lives only through violence (*Raging Bull*), or the confusion of one who feels a special calling (*The Last Temptation of Christ*). Frequently Scorsese deals with people in severe crisis, men and women in the grip of ambition, and his portraits of human relationships only occasionally suggest that fulfilment also brings happiness. More likely, his characters will emerge, as they say, sadder but wiser – an everyday redemption. Scorsese's own life has known its share of vicissitudes (more than one critic has sought to interpret his films through the maker's turbulent career), and the autobiographical element in the early features came back into focus when he finally realized his youthful ambition to film a life of Christ.

From that moment, Scorsese's films took on a certain detachment with regard to their protagonists. *GoodFellas* was less a portrait of one individual's dealings with mob life than a vibrant, bustling canvas exploring a whole society at play with guns, money, food, drugs and unwritten codes of conduct. *Cape Fear* showed the vulnerability of a family in conflict with each other as well as with an outside force. But *The Age of Innocence* revealed that the director could now identify closely with a character seemingly far removed from his own social experience – a member of New York's aristocracy in the late nineteenth century – simply because the primary emotion involved was the universal one of the pain of unfulfilled love. As Scorsese himself feels, the film seemed to mark a new maturity in his work, while also demonstrating his unparalleled skills in breathing life into the period picture, a genre fraught with potential stiffness. It was a bold undertaking, and an expensive gamble – the kind that Hollywood is less and less inclined to make.

Even with *Casino*, another project based on real characters, Scorsese has taken the narrative chances he took with *GoodFellas* a stage further, utilizing two principal voice-overs, as well as continuing the technical experimentation of *Cape Fear*. If in the past his narratives have rarely satisfied the Hollywood norm – a musical that was more *film noir* than MGM gloss, a life in boxing without a grand climactic bout, a mobster who simply vanishes into anonymity – these can be attributed to the inspiration of those formative years of the sixties, when dreams of a personal cinema came true. The freedom of the seventies, when the studios were more indulgent with large budgets and long schedules, are over – or at least for anything other than the summer blockbuster. Even for a director as readily acclaimed as Scorsese, it's a tough market-place that he has to operate in. Furthermore, he has yet to win huge audiences and the accolade of an Oscar. As he said in a particularly frank press conference given at the Berlin Film Festival in 1992, 'I think the Academy to a certain extent is an organization which adheres to the values of Hollywood's "Golden Age". My films represent something just the opposite, I guess. Yes, I'd like to be like John Ford and win four of them. But I come from a different place, every which way. Whether I want to win one or not, I have to accept that, because I'd rather have the films.'

CHAPTER I

Childhood in Little Italy – New York University

'I love movies – it's my whole life and that's it.' Martin Scorsese in 1975

Martin Scorsese was born on 17 November 1942 in Flushing, Long Island, the second son of Charles and Catherine Scorsese. His parents were both children of Sicilian immigrants who had settled in New York around 1910. As recounted in Italianamerican, *Charles first sold men's clothes and lit gas stoves for Jews on the Sabbath, Elizabeth Street being mostly Jewish at this time, with only a few Irish and Italian families. Charles's father worked in the shipyards, and in the fruit and vegetable business. Catherine's father had been a cavalryman, before persuading her mother to emigrate with him to America. He enjoyed making wine, while she was good at sewing. Charles and Catherine were married in St Patrick's Old Cathedral on 10 June 1934. He worked as a presser and she as a seamstress. Both have appeared frequently in their son's movies.*

The centrality of the family in Italian immigrant culture, its emphasis on the struggle for success, its close ties with the Roman Catholic Church and the everyday proximity of organized crime – these were to dominate Martin Scorsese's formative years. The alternative to remaining, like his older brother Frank, within this closed society with its strong sense of pride, yet equally deep feeling of isolation, was, for the young Martin, to immerse himself in the fantasy world of cinema.

My parents were born on Elizabeth Street, in the Lower East Side of Manhattan, and worked in the garment district. But until I was seven or eight years old we lived in a place called Corona in the suburb of Queens. It was a nice area and we had a back yard with some trees. Then my father ran into business problems and we had to move back to a tenement

1 Elizabeth Street from Scorsese's window in 1961.

building on the block where he was born. I stayed for four or five months with my grandparents until we could find some other rooms, and this was a terrifying experience because I was old enough to realize that there were some tough guys around. You might be playing in a sandbox and something would fall behind you – not a bag of garbage, as you might expect, but a little baby that had fallen off the roof!

At this time the Italian–American community lived in a series of about ten blocks, starting from Houston Street down to Chinatown at Canal Street. The three main blocks were on Elizabeth Street, Mott Street and Mulberry Street. Little Italy was very sharply defined, so often the people from one block wouldn't hang out with those from another. Elizabeth Street was mainly Sicilian, as were my grandparents, and here the people had their own regulations and laws. We didn't care about the Government, or politicians or the police: we felt we were right in our ways.

We'd sometimes go up to 42nd Street to see a movie, or visit Staten Island or Queens, where there were similar immigrant communities. But until I went to New York University, on the west side of Greenwich Village, I'd only ever been there once before! When friends said to me, 'I can imagine you guys really wanting to get out,' I would reply, 'Oh no, we were all right, it's you who didn't dress properly and drove the wrong cars.' In *Mean Streets*, Charlie is stuck there: he doesn't think about getting a restaurant in the Village, because it's his soul that's really stuck there. And the idea that I would be making pictures one day was quite inconceivable then.

As a child I wanted to be a painter, so I started trying to draw. But I was also fascinated by films and, having asthma, I would often be taken to movie theatres because they didn't know what else to do with me. Most of all I was amazed by the size of the images on the screen, and I would come back and draw what I saw. I made up my own stories, taking my cue from newspaper comic strips and books, and although I didn't realize it at the time, I soon started using close-ups just like they did. Eventually I became decadent and actually copied the comics, but I was also really fascinated by aspect ratios and would do little drawings in 1:1.33.[1] Usually these were war films, almost always made by United Artists, with Hecht and Lancaster in the credits.

And of course I loved biblical epics – only mine weren't just in 70 mm, they were in 75 mm! I planned a gigantic Roman epic, but it only got as far as a gladiatorial fight at the beginning to mark the Emperor's homecoming after a war, painted in watercolours. I still have these strips and when they're framed they look very like the traditional Sicilian puppet shows of knights fighting.

The first image that I remember seeing on a cinema screen was a Trucolor trailer for a Roy Rogers movie, in which he was wearing fringes and jumped from a tree onto his horse. My father asked me if I knew who Trigger was and I imitated firing a gun. 'No,' he said, 'it's the horse's name. I'll take you to see it next week.' Which is why I still like trailers a lot and at the age of three I dreamed of becoming a cowboy. Westerns remained my favourite movies until I was about ten.

After I was three my asthma became worse, so my father took me to see a lot of movies. He had been a big film buff in the thirties and movies were a luxury he could always afford, even when there was no money for anything else. We were one of the first families on our block to get a television set in 1948. I recall I was playing in the back yard and my cousin Peter rushed out shouting, 'Come and see a television screen that's bigger than the whole house!' Of course it was only a sixteen-inch RCA Victor. I guess my father was well connected, since he always found work in the garment district. When he retired, he used to sit around at home and drive my mother crazy. 'Get him out of the house!' she would say, and it was her idea that I should ask him to work on costumes for my movies. This was perfect, because he knew all about clothes between 1941 and 1964, the period of *Raging Bull*.

But I remember it was my mother who took me to see *Duel in the Sun*, which had been condemned by the church. I couldn't watch the end, it was all so frightening – the sun beating down, the woman's hands bleeding and these two people who were so much in love they had to kill each other. I think the music by Dmitri Tiomkin also made it all seem like a horror film, but my mother kept yelling, 'Look at it, you took me here to see it, now watch it!' Of course, the first thing I wanted to do in movies was to act in them. I had no idea that anything happened behind the cameras.

Because the big studios didn't want to sell to television at this time, many of the films shown were British. So I saw *The Thief of Bagdad* when I was six – the perfect age – and a lot of the other Alexander Korda films, like *The Four Feathers* and *Elephant Boy*. They also showed early Westerns and, on Friday nights, Italian films such as *Bicycle Thieves*, *Rome Open City* and *Paisa*, which our families found very upsetting and had them all crying.

There was one programme in the fifties called 'Million Dollar Movie', which would show the same films twice on weekday evenings, at 7.30 and 9.30, and three times on Saturday and Sunday. There were four of us

2 Alexander Korda's fairytale *Thief of Bagdad* (1940).
3 Former ballerina Ludmilla Tcherina in *The Tales of Hoffmann* (1951).

living in a small four-room flat and when I wanted to watch the same film over and over, it was like an assault on them – my mother would yell, 'Is that film on *again*? Turn it off.' I remember seeing Powell and Pressburger's *The Tales of Hoffmann* on this programme: it was in black and white, cut and interrupted by commercials (it wasn't until 1965 that I saw it in colour). But I was mesmerized by the music, the camera movements and the theatricality of the gestures by these actors who were mostly dancers. There's a lot that can be said against *The Tales of Hoffmann*, yet I've always said that those repeated viewings on television taught me about the relation of camera to music: I just assimilated it because I saw it so often. Even now there's hardly a day when the score of the picture doesn't go through my mind, and of course it had an effect on the way I handled the musical sequences in *New York, New York* and the fights in *Raging Bull*. There was another lesson I learned from it too: when we were doing the close-ups of De Niro's eyes for *Taxi Driver*, I shot these at 36 or 48 frames per second to reproduce the same effect that I'd seen in the Venetian episode of *The Tales of Hoffmann*, when Robert Helpmann is watching the duel on a gondola.[2]

I remember the first time I saw Powell and Pressburger's Archers logo – the arrows hitting the target – in colour, was when my father took me to see *The Red Shoes* at the Academy of Music on 14th Street, and of course I was hypnotized. I don't think anything had struck me as that powerful in movies up to then, except perhaps another film I had seen in the same theatre with my father, Renoir's *The River*, which also had a dance sequence.

But *The Red Shoes* dance sequences were extraordinary; and I remember being intrigued to know how they made Robert Helpmann turn into a scrap of newspaper during the fantasy ballet. But mainly I was drawn to the mystery of it, the hysteria of the picture, which was quite shocking at the time for me. When it came on television, in black and white, I watched it again and again; then later, when I saw it in colour again, I became fascinated by Anton Walbrook's character, the impresario Lermontov, whose dedication destroys everything around him. What appealed to me was the cruelty and the beauty of his character – especially the scene where he smashes the mirror, filled with self-hate. I even had a cossack shirt made up by Berman's & Nathan's in the same style as his, and I wore it for the opening of Michael and Emeric's retrospective at the Museum of Modern Art in 1980.

A lot of the films on 'Million Dollar Movie' were cut: *Citizen Kane*, for instance, had no 'March of Time' sequence at the beginning, though I

4 Fantasy ballet in Powell and Pressburger's *The Red Shoes* (1948).
5 *The Seventh Seal*, directed by Ingmar Bergman in 1956.

didn't realize this was missing. But the opportunity to see them repeatedly was very important for me. I think it was also seeing *Citizen Kane* about the age of fourteen or fifteen that made me aware for the first time of what a director did. I already liked Welles as an actor – especially the way Carol Reed used him in *The Third Man*, with his cuckoo-clock speech – but now I was struck by how dynamic and ambitious this film he had directed was. Then I discovered it was playing at the Thalia Theater on 96th Street along with John Ford's *The Informer*. I'll never forget that occasion: it was a rainy night and there was a mob trying to get in. The screen was small, but it didn't matter – I was overwhelmed again. Subsequently both films played all over New York and I dragged all my friends, my parents – anyone – to see them. Before this, I suppose I was mainly aware of directors like Ford and Hawks through the stars who appeared regularly in their films, like John Wayne.

At first it was fantasy that appealed to me: George Sidney's *The Three Musketeers* was a real childhood favourite and I loved anything set in the distant past, with costumes and elaborate sets. It wasn't until the mid fifties that I saw anything that really related to my own situation. *On the Waterfront* made a big impression and I must have seen it twenty times; then came *East of Eden*, which also reflected some of my own emotions and experience.

But, for the most part, I didn't expect films to relate to what I saw around me and of course in my working-class neighbourhood we didn't treat them with any particular respect. We would just walk in, in the middle of the double feature, stay through the second picture and see the first one up to where we came in. This was how I saw films up to the age of fifteen or sixteen. Then came another revelation.

Every summer on 96th Street, there would be two 'classic' films showing every day, along with all the other stuff. I noticed they were showing *Alexander Nevsky*, which I had read about in a magazine, and I walked in half-way through, as usual. It was like being in a time machine, as if I was there watching the battle on the ice in 1242! Seeing the design of the film, I fell under the spell of Eisenstein and his style of editing. In my first years at film school, it really wasn't so terrific if you went around liking Nicholas Ray movies or John Wayne. American films were considered no good, except 'serious' ones like *Wuthering Heights* or *A Place in the Sun*, and most of those that were coming out in the fifties were embarrassing, because it was the end of the studio system. You really had to look to foreign films like Ingmar Bergman's *Wild Strawberries* and *The Seventh*

Seal to find something impressive and different. And having gone to a Catholic school, *The Seventh Seal* affected me very deeply in religious terms.

Life on the streets of Little Italy was to shape the style as well as the narrative content of Scorsese's own films. Neighbourhood stories, mingled with real-life experiences, were to become the prime sources of his overtly autobiographical first features. Mean Streets opens with the San Gennaro Festival, a noisy annual event which involves the whole Italian–American community; and the film gathers its momentum from the conflict and friendship of disparate characters based on Scorsese's contemporaries.

I used to hang out with a guy named Joey, on whom *Mean Streets* was partly based – he was a sort of combination of Charlie and Johnny Boy. We went to see practically everything together. Whenever there was a fight, everyone would shout, 'Come on over, quick!' We'd say, 'Right,' and then we'd take our time walking so that when we got there it'd be all over. Guys at one end of a block weren't too friendly with guys from the other end, and naturally there was always one man controlling the whole area, but you never knew who or where he was. So you had to develop a sense of survival. For a long time, wherever I went, I tried to sit with my back against a wall!

Joey and I had a very close brush one night, and I based the ending of *Mean Streets* on it. It was three in the morning and we were sitting in the back of a guy's red convertible, which was a big deal, since none of us had cars. He already had a young teenage kid sitting in the front seat with him and he said he'd drive us around for a while, but we thought he was acting a little too wise. He might have been a cop – in that area there wasn't much difference between them and the hoods! Eventually, since there wasn't much going on, we got bored and he dropped us off in Elizabeth Street. Three minutes after we left there was a shooting. The wise guy in the convertible got angry with another driver blocking his path and flashed his gun. A few blocks later, the other driver pulled alongside them and fired a load of bullets. The teenage kid was hit in the eye, though he lived. It could very easily have been us. Just two months later, as it happened, President Kennedy was killed.

In my neighbourhood, the people in power were the tough guys on the street, and the Church. The organized crime figures would tip their hats to a priest and watch their language, and they would have their cars and pets blessed. This may have had something to do with my decision, when I was

6 First Communion: 26 May 1951.

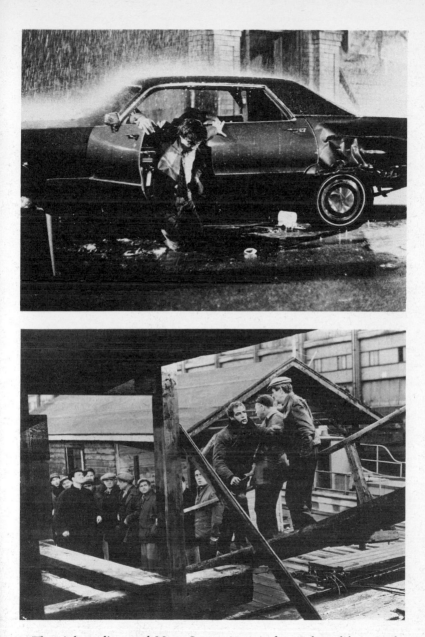

7 The violent climax of *Mean Streets* (1973), drawn from life in Little Italy.

8 Brando's Calvary in *On the Waterfront* (1954).

eight or nine, that I wanted to become a priest. At any rate, it lasted right up until the time I made my first movie. The first Mass I attended, in St Patrick's Cathedral, just after I entered the Catholic school, made a deep impression, with its pageantry and theatre, and all those old Italians singing hymns in Latin. I learned to write script at St Patrick's School, and the Irish nuns seemed to like me because I wanted to be a missionary. I remember a visiting missionary who told us how he had exorcized a boy possessed of devils in the Philippines. The main thing, we learned, was the vocation: 'Many are called, few are chosen.' There was no specific way of going about it; they just nurtured a few of the students who had a fascination with the trappings of religion.

Listening to the story of Father Damien, who had devoted his life to lepers and died of leprosy himself, it was difficult for us to grasp that these were real people who tried to live their lives according to God's word and were approaching sainthood. I thought a lot about salvation, and it seemed that the best guarantee of being saved was to become a priest, which would be like being able to pick up a phone any time and talk to God.

Around 1953 a young priest, in his early twenties, came into the neighbourhood and played classical music to us, took us to the movies and involved us in sports. I wasn't too keen on sports, but I began to pattern my life on his and he became a stronger role model than the local gang chiefs. Of course, he was against rock'n'roll – we'd try to play records to him and he'd get angry and put on Tchaikovsky or Beethoven – but the main thing was my getting an insight into his views, which was a new experience. He felt that *On the Waterfront* was a very important film, because of the scene where Karl Malden, as the priest, tries to force Brando to get up and walk that last stretch up to the fellow who says, 'All right, let's go to work.' It's a kind of Calvary, except that Brando doesn't die; and the priest believed that, while it wasn't at all realistic in terms of how the docks were run, it was important that a film like this should be made, because life does continue. This strongly influenced my sense of what could be done in a film, as did hearing my family say, 'Yes, but it doesn't happen like that; in reality the guy would do such and such.'

At the age of fourteen, I went to Cathedral College, a junior seminary on the Upper West Side. But I was expelled after a year, because I didn't really have my mind on my work: I had met a young lady with whom I fell in love, and I was extremely distracted. Celibacy was really setting yourself aside from the people, forcing yourself to live in an unnatural way. The old Italian people in the neighbourhood didn't take it seriously at all, in fact they were constantly debunking it. They'd say, 'He's a priest, he's a man, so he needs a woman; but that's nothing special.'

Rock'n'roll was another big distraction – Little Richard, Elvis Presley and all those guys. I used to listen to the radio constantly and buy all the records (some of which I've had to use in my films because I couldn't find new copies). This period was the height of gang warfare and black leather jackets. I wore a leather jacket, but I was made fun of because the gangs in our area wore sharkskin suits! The one thing you couldn't wear was the colour red. I remember wanting a red jacket, and my father said, 'Only pimps wear red, you're not having one and that's that.' Wearing red was also a sure way to attract police attention.

By this stage, I was a real film buff: I even remember saving up ten dollars to buy Paul Rotha's *The Film Till Now*. I went to Cardinal Hays, a high school in the Bronx, for the rest of my schooling and I planned to go to the Jesuit University at Fordham, where my friends were. But I couldn't make it because of my grades: I was in the lowest quarter of my graduating class.

Before he could lay hands on professional equipment, Scorsese began making amateur films with his close friends. One such was Vesuvius VI, *a miniature epic set in Ancient Rome and 'inspired' by the then popular television series* 77 Sunset Strip. *The soundtrack featured the song 'Does Your Chewing Gum Lose Its Flavour on the Bedpost Overnight?', and the end credits included 'Directed by Martin Scorsese' going up in flames.*

I went to New York University specifically because they had film classes there, along with the more general courses. I read the catalogue and realized that I could just afford to take Film as a major and English as a minor. I had started to read a lot, beginning with Thomas Hardy, and I even had some idea of going back to the seminary afterwards, until I saw Professor Haig Manoogian, who took the first film class. It was a three-hour course, once a week, called 'The History of Motion Pictures, Television and Radio'. Most of the kids took the class because they thought they wouldn't have to do anything much except watch films and get two credits for it. But Haig was brutal! He would talk so fast – even faster than me – and he described everything in great detail from the very beginning. He wasn't the head of the department because he hated administration, but he really inspired the film-makers.

You can learn how to use a camera in two minutes from anybody, but Haig would come on stage, hit you with a lecture for onc-and-a-half hours, and then show a film. Once he showed Stroheim's *Greed* and a student asked why there was no music. Back came the answer, 'Do you think this is a show? Get the hell out!' He would weed people out, semester after semester. The idea was to be as serious about it as possible – serious in the sense that you could argue, laugh and joke about the films, but you really had to be there for the love of cinema.

In the second year there were courses that involved making a three-minute film of your own in 16 mm, learning about side-lighting, back-lighting, lenses, fast motion, stop motion and so on. We had very little equipment at that time, only a 16 mm Arriflex and a Cine-Special. By the third year you were allowed – if you wrote your own script and if Haig liked you – to direct a five- or six-minute film. There was a lot of politicking going on, which made it like a mini-studio. Out of thirty-six students there was only enough money for six films, so it was tough. But Haig really inspired us: he had this almost religious zeal, so that if you had an idea, before you knew it you were out on the streets and in the middle of filming!

Although Haig produced my first feature, we didn't agree on films. When I had to write a little treatise on a film, I chose *The Third Man*. He gave me a B+ and said, 'Forget this, it's just a thriller.' But we did agree that films should be personal. In fact, when kids would come to him and say, 'I know I can be a great director, I just need a script,' he would tell them they had to write their own scripts if they wanted to direct – no one was going to do it for them.

I was a film student from 1960 to 1965, during the height of the French New Wave, the international success of the Italian art cinema and the discovery of the new Eastern European cinema. What these movies gave us as film students was a sense of freedom, of being able to do anything. For me, the first two minutes of *Jules et Jim* were the most liberating of all; I still use it as an example to writers I am working with. Resnais had an enormous impact: what he did with cuts in *Hiroshima mon amour* and *Last Year at Marienbad* just freed you completely. Now you no longer had to shoot a film in the traditional manner, which required a master shot, medium shot and close-up, with the camera tracking or panning to follow a character. In Godard's *Vivre sa vie*, Anna Karina is reading a letter and suddenly there's a jump-cut to a man folding it up; he's got up and taken it out of her hand. By jumping someone out of a chair, there was a sense of breaking the dramatic narrative of the Hollywood films of the thirties, forties and fifties that we had been raised on. In my first movie, not one shot was a matched cut. At the same time, Cassavetes had used a lightweight 16 mm camera for *Shadows* in 1959, so there were no more excuses. If he could do it, so could we!

While a student at NYU, Scorsese photographed Inesita, *a nine-minute film of a flamenco dancer directed by Robert Siegel. He later observed that this short anticipated the editing techniques used in* New York, New York.

What's a Nice Girl Like You Doing in a Place Like This?, *his first real film, made in 1963, was inspired by Mel Brooks's collaboration with Ernest Pintoff on the animation short,* The Critic. *Almost continuous voice-over narration accompanies a fast-paced montage of still photographs, animated objects and occasional live action to tell the story of Algernon – called Harry by his friends – who is obsessed by a picture of a boat on a lake. Described by Scorsese as a tale of 'pure paranoia', it was made in 16 mm with funding from the Edward L. Kingsley Foundation, the Screen Producers' Guild and Brown University Film Festival.*

At the beginning of the sixties there were two camps: those who liked Antonioni's *L'Avventura* and the others who championed Fellini's *La Dolce Vita*. I was on the *L'Avventura* side because it was slow and anything slow must be serious! But it *is* a great film. *La Dolce Vita* doesn't stand up nearly as well as Fellini's *8½*. I saw *8½* just two weeks before shooting my first short film at NYU, *What's a Nice Girl Like You Doing in a Place Like This?*, and the impact was overwhelming because of the fluidity of the camerawork and the beauty of the black and white. I fell in love with the moving camera so much in that film that I also fell for everything about Italy – the cafés and the fashions. So I paid homage to *8½* with my second short, because I just couldn't figure out how to end it!

Scorsese's second student short, It's Not Just You, Murray!, *made in 1964, used real stories from the neighbourhood, and its narrative of two friends, incompetent small-time criminals called Joe and Murray, looks forward to the buddy relationships of* Who's That Knocking at My Door? *and* Mean Streets. *A police raid on their gin still, shot in long takes with a hand-held camera, anticipates the pool-room scene in* Mean Streets; *as well as references to gangster movies, there is an optically processed (to make it seem grander) homage to the Hollywood musical. Italian cinema joins this mix of influences in the shape of Joe's blonde wife, who looks distinctly like Antonioni's star Monica Vitti, and a circus finale in which Joe takes the megaphone, recalling the flamboyant finale of Fellini's 8½.*

9 Directing *What's a Nice Girl Like You Doing in a Place Like This?*
(1963).

10 The final scene of *It's Not Just You, Murray!* (1964).

*But the quick-fire dialogue, playful editing and eclectic sound mix show
an original talent emerging, while the subject-matter is also fresh and
personal. It's* Not Just You, Murray! *won the Jesse L. Lasky Inter-
collegiate Award. In the same year, Scorsese received his B.Sc. in Film
Communications.*

*While still an undergraduate, he had married a fellow student, Laraine
Marie Brennan, and their daughter Catherine was born on 7 December
1965. Scorsese meanwhile became friendly with other young New York
film-makers, Brian De Palma, Michael Wadleigh, Jim McBride and
Mardik Martin.*

At this time the new American Underground was emerging, and since our
campus was in Greenwich Village we had access to all these films.[3] Jonas
Mekas was writing his *Village Voice* column every week, while Andrew
Sarris was deploying the *politique des auteurs*, imported from the French
Cahiers du cinéma, in *Film Culture* magazine. Then *Movie* magazine
appeared from Britain with its list of great directors, and there were
Hawks and Hitchcock at the top. The professors were totally against these
critical views, but what we learned was that the new critics liked John
Wayne films too – except they weren't just John Wayne movies, but John
Ford and Howard Hawks working through him. What had impressed us
as good when we were young had impressed other people too.

This was when I first became aware of another Michael Powell film,
Peeping Tom. I remember it opening in 1962, while I was at NYU, and it
showed at only one theatre, the Charles on Avenue B and 12th, in that
part of Manhattan that's known as Alphabet City. This was a neighbourhood where you really had to be armed to see the film – to get into the
theatre, stay close during it and fight your way out to get a bus or taxi
afterwards. Being a New Yorker, I didn't risk it myself, but other students
from out of town went to see it. Jim McBride told me about this amazing
film in black and white, about a guy who films his son and makes a film
diary all about fear itself;[4] and from his fascination with it came *David
Holzman's Diary*, which he was working on when we were editing
alongside each other in 1966–7. When I moved to California in 1970,
through Fred Weintraub I met Phil Chamberlain, who had his own 35 mm
print, and that was when I saw it for the first time, complete and in colour.
The next time I saw it was in 1973, on the day that John Ford died – I
remember hearing the news while Jay Cocks and I were screening it.

Fred Weintraub had wanted to do a remake, but felt that he couldn't

11 The philosophy and danger of film-making: Powell's *Peeping Tom* (1960).

top it. I'm glad he didn't try. It was extraordinary: at first, I just couldn't believe it had been made by one of the team who'd made *The Red Shoes* and *The Tales of Hoffmann*. What struck me was its precision about the mechanics of film-making, as in the opening sequence when Mark approaches the prostitute and you see her through the viewfinder. This isn't at all like a Hollywood movie about film-making, where the film they're making looks more professional than the one you're watching. *The Bad and the Beautiful* and *Two Weeks in Another Town* only deal with film production, not making. Here you get a sense of the actual nuts and bolts of film-making, and it's very shocking because of how it relates to the gruesome subject-matter. What remains unspoken in, for instance, Hitchcock's *Vertigo* is explicit here. It's as if the process of film-making becomes an accessory to the crime and makes us all feel guilty.

I remember Michael Chapman, who shot *Taxi Driver* and *Raging Bull* for me, was watching *Peeping Tom* on television one night and he phoned me about one line in the film: 'All this filming, it's not healthy.' He was laughing because it reminded him of me. 'That's the beauty of it,' I said. I have always felt that *Peeping Tom* and *8½* say everything that can be said about film-making, about the process of dealing with film, the objectivity and subjectivity of it and the confusion between the two. *8½* captures the glamour and enjoyment of film-making, while *Peeping Tom* shows the aggression of it, how the camera violates. These are the two great films that deal with the philosophy and the danger of film-making. From studying them you can discover everything about people who make films, or at least people who *express* themselves through films.

I didn't get to meet Michael Powell until 1975, when I was coming back through London from the Edinburgh Film Festival, but I told him then about the cult that had developed around *Peeping Tom*. And in 1978, I was approached by a New York distributor, Corinth Films, who needed some money to re-release the film with a brand-new print. I agreed to put up $5,000 on condition that the poster and print said 'Martin Scorsese presents . . .', because I wanted to have this honour – and get my own 35 mm print.

Back in 1960, another important stimulus to would-be film-makers of my generation was the first of Roger Corman's Edgar Allan Poe films, *The Fall of the House of Usher*, which had a beautiful atmosphere in its use of colour and CinemaScope. We loved this blend of English Gothic and French *grand guignol*, mixed together in an American film. There was something of the same atmosphere in Mario Bava's films, like *Black*

Sunday, which started to arrive from Italy. Everything was very alive in a way that it's not today – every day there seemed to be an exciting film coming from another country.

In 1969 I went back to NYU as an instructor – Haig gave me the job because I was broke – and at this time there was a film criticism class in which the teacher would give the students a film like *Wild Strawberries* or *Nights of Cabiria* and a book to read that complemented it. The students got angry with the teacher and there was a kind of uprising, so we revamped the schedule and said, 'Now look at these American films by Ford and Hawks, they're wonderful!'

Vernon Zimmerman, who later made *Unholy Rollers* and *Fade to Black*, had a loft in the Village where he showed us *Scorpio Rising*. It had been banned, but the shocking thing about it wasn't the Hell's Angels stuff, it was the use of music. This was music I knew, and we had always been told by our professors at NYU that we couldn't use it in student films because of copyright. Now here was Kenneth Anger's film in and out of the courts on obscenity charges, but no one seemed to be complaining that he'd used all those incredible tracks by Elvis Presley, Ricky Nelson and The Rebels. That gave me the idea to use whatever music I really needed. But I held back some of the music I wanted for my first feature, *Who's That Knocking at My Door?* There was a thing in America that you had to direct your first picture while you were still under twenty-five, just like Orson Welles! Then I saw Bertolucci's *Before the Revolution* at the New York Film Festival, and, realizing that we were the same age, this was a further inspiration and incentive to me.

Notes

1 1:1.33 or 3:4 defined the standard shape of the film image as a ratio of height to width until the introduction of CinemaScope (1:2.35) and other wide-screen processes in the 1950s.
2 Filming faster than the normal 24 fps produces a slow-motion effect when the film is projected. *The Tales of Hoffmann*, like many of Michael Powell's films, used a wide variety of camera speeds for effect.
3 Properly speaking, 'underground' refers to the avant-garde film-making of visual and experimental artists, which was an international movement by the late fifties and, in America, by no means confined to New York. However, in 1960 a number of underground film-makers joined other New York independents who worked in documentary and low-budget narrative to form The New American Cinema Group. According to their manifesto, dated 28 September: 'We don't want false, polished, slick films – we prefer them rough, unpolished, but alive; we don't want rosy films – we want them the color of blood.' A key figure in this, and in the foundation of the New York Film-makers'

Cooperative in 1962, was Jonas Mekas, a film-maker himself, publisher of the journal *Film Culture* and also critic for *The Village Voice*.

Throughout the early sixties in New York, 'Independent Cinema' excited lively controversy. The fourth New York Film Festival, in 1966, mounted a special parallel programme of twenty-seven events devoted to 'independent film-making in the United States today'. This provoked Andrew Sarris, a regular contributor to *Film Culture* – where he had applied the French *politique des auteurs* evaluation to American cinema in a landmark 1963 special issue – but also guardian of traditional values, to challenge the 'journalistic fiction' of Independent Cinema. Interestingly, this is where he located the young Scorsese; the context makes intriguing reading today:

The collectivity of Independent Cinema is not worth writing about. Only individual films. I have liked Kenneth Anger's *Scorpio Rising*, Andy Warhol's and Ronny Tavel's *The Life of Juanita Castro*, Adolfas Mekas's *Hallelujah the Hills*, Peter Goldman's *Echoes of Silence*, several works by Stan VanDerBeek, Carmen D'Avino, and Robert Breer in the more abstract categories. Martin Scorsese's short films reveal a wit capable of talking features. Robert Downey has his moments of hilarious satire. Shirley Clarke and Lionel Rogosin have given us some candid moments in the more depressed areas. (*Movie*, November 1966; reprinted in *The New American Cinema*, ed. Gregory Battcock, 1968.)

4 *Peeping Tom* is predominantly in colour, with only the 'home movie' sequences in black and white. It appears, however, to have been first released in America in a completely black and white version – presumably because, as Scorsese recalls, it only 'made the grind houses on 42nd Street' – which was also cut.

CHAPTER 2

Who's That Knocking at My Door? – Boxcar Bertha

'I'm going to die behind a camera.' Martin Scorsese in 1975

What eventually became Scorsese's first feature, Who's That Knocking at My Door?, *was originally intended to be the second part of a trilogy dealing with the experience of his own generation growing up in Little Italy. He had written a forty-page script entitled* Jerusalem, Jerusalem, *about a group of eighteen-year-old boys brought together by a three-day religious retreat at a Jesuit house. The central character was called J.R., who would reappear in* Who's That Knocking at My Door? *and again in* Mean Streets, *as Charlie, played on both occasions by Harvey Keitel.*

J.R. was very much an autobiographical projection. The story of Jerusalem, Jerusalem *deals with religious doubt and the temptations of sexuality as Scorsese himself was experiencing these, and it includes a contemporary visualization of Christ's passion. The third part of the trilogy, initially titled* Season of the Witch, *was greatly modified to become* Mean Streets.

In Who's That Knocking at My Door?, *J.R. is a neighbourhood boy who makes conversation with the blonde WASP girl of his dreams by telling her how much he loves John Wayne westerns. In spite of his strong attraction, he cannot bring himself to have sex with her and the revelation that she isn't a virgin disgusts him. Having recovered from the shock, he decides to forgive her and proposes marriage, only to be rejected. The structure of the film is loose and its style aggressive, with an authentic depiction of the tempo of street life interrupted by lurid religious and erotic fantasies.*

12 Harvey Keitel and Zina Bethune in *Who's That Knocking at My Door?* (1969).

Haig Manoogian became my first producer with *Who's That Knocking at My Door?*, which was a very long time in the making. We started in 1965, when I tried to make it as my graduate film at NYU. There was no real graduate department at the time, just myself, Mike Wadleigh and a few others who started this film. My father raised $6,000 from a student loan and it must have been the first student film shot in black and white 35 mm on the East Coast, although it was never really completed. We were over-ambitious, until we found that we couldn't move the camera and get the angles that we wanted. However, it was accurate about the way we were when nothing was going on, just sitting or driving around. On one level, that's what the film was about; on another it was about sexual hang-ups and the Church. Finally, we made a version called *Bring on the Dancing Girls* which didn't quite work: it was 65 minutes long and just confounded everyone. We held a big screening and it was a disaster.

By 1966 I was back on the streets, desperately trying to make some money, while my marriage was breaking up. I teamed up with a writer named Mardik Martin, who had worked his way from Baghdad to New York, attending the university and working as a waiter. Neither of us had any money and we were killing ourselves. I had won some awards for my student films, but they were forgotten because *Bring on the Dancing Girls* was universally hated. The worse things became, the less I felt like giving in. Mardik and I would often end up writing in his car in the snow, shivering and thinking we were crazy, because the apartment I lived in was so small and our wives were so angry at us. Skinflicks were very popular at the time, and Mardik had the idea of making a film called 'This Film Could Save Your Marriage' – which is what they all used to claim at the time. But we were going to give all the wrong advice!

Haig and Joe Weill, another student who was a lawyer, somehow got $37,000 together to finance the rest of the picture, which involved scenes with a young girl. This meant we needed an actress and would have to shoot with an Eclair 16 mm camera, cutting the new material into the 35 mm scenes we had already shot. I had previously tried to shoot sequences without dialogue, telling the story through images – after the New Wave, we were trying all kinds of things – but they didn't work. So we pulled them out, found a new actress, Zina Bethune, and called Harvey Keitel back. He was very upset. He was working as a court stenographer and we were wasting his time. He kept having his hair cut at inappropriate times, so the scenes we shot never matched! I would say, 'Harvey, how can you do this?', and back came the answer, 'But I have a life too.'

While work continued intermittently on the feature, Scorsese received financial support from Jacques Ledoux, Curator of the Cinémathèque Royale de Belgique in Brussels and a noted patron of avant-garde cinema, to make a six-minute short. The Big Shave *emerged from a spell of deep depression (when Scorsese apparently had difficulty shaving!) and, although conceived quite seriously, it turned out humorously macabre. To the sound of Bunny Berigan's 1939 recording of 'I Can't Get Started', a handsome young man cuts himself while shaving and keeps on doing so until he is covered in blood. The setting is an ultra-white bathroom and a final credit reads 'Whiteness by Herman Melville', while another states cryptically 'Viet '67'. Scorsese thought of* The Big Shave *as a film against the Vietnam War and considered at one point ending it with stock footage from that war. The film won the Prix L'Age d'Or (named after Buñuel's 1930 Surrealist masterpiece) at Ledoux's Festival of Experimental Cinema, held in the Belgian seaside town of Knokke-le-Zoute in December. Meanwhile, earlier that year, another version of the feature was completed.*

It was screened at the Chicago Film Festival under the title *I Call First* and Roger Ebert of the *Sun-Times* gave it a great review, but we still couldn't get it released. I went to Europe on the advice of a friend who was making commercials in Amsterdam, and I spent some time in London, researching at the British Film Institute, where I discovered a lot about Italian directors like Cottafavi.[1] Then when I was in Paris in 1968 someone told me that Joseph Brenner Associates, who were a soft-core porn distributor, would handle it if one nude scene was added. Everything was opening up in America at that time; Brenner was going legitimate and just one scene with nudity would be enough to get the film distributed.

He was literally on 42nd Street – the seediest place in the world – and he had my film and *The Birth of a Nation*! I had to send a storyboard to show what I was going to do, then we brought Harvey Keitel over and, because of the fighting in the streets of Paris, we ended up shooting the scene in Amsterdam, though it looks like a loft on 3rd Avenue. It was really fun, putting The Doors on the soundtrack: we used the Freudian part of 'The End' just to hammer it home.[2] However, there was no way of getting it back through customs, so I stuck the film in one pocket of my raincoat and the soundtrack in the other, and I shaved on the plane to look respectable. I got through, spliced in the scene, and then the film was released. It was the first film to show what Italian–Americans really were like and that was what was good about it.

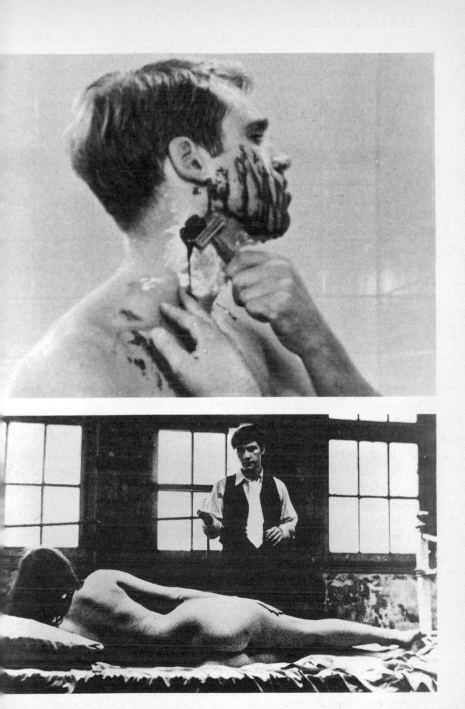

13 *The Big Shave* (1967).
14 Fantasy sequence in *Who's That Knocking at My Door?*.

In many ways the main thing was the experience of music. I was living in a very crowded area where music would be playing constantly from various apartments across the street, from bars and candy stores. The radio was always on; a juke box would be playing out over the street; and in the tenement areas you'd hear opera from one room, Benny Goodman from another, and rock'n'roll from downstairs. I remember one time looking out of the window, a block away from a bar, seeing two bums staggering down Elizabeth Street, one so drunk the other's stealing his shoes, and while this fight was going on I could hear from somewhere 'When My Dream Boat Comes Home' by Fats Domino. That was just how crazy this world actually was, and it made me think, why don't they do that in films? A love scene with love music is just mediocre. So *Who's That Knocking at My Door?* was like a grenade, throwing all this music at the audience.

Who's That Knocking at My Door?, *completed on a final budget of $75,000, was shown at the 1969 Chicago Film Festival and subsequently opened at the Carnegie Hall Cinema in New York. It also went on to win the Golden Siren at the Sorrento Festival in the following year. Despite such welcome public recognition, this was a difficult period for Scorsese.*

He was fired from The Honeymoon Killers *in 1968 after only a week of shooting. A highly ambitious project on the history of soldiering floundered for lack of money. From his European contacts came a request to supply 'tough' American dialogue for Pim de la Parra's and Wim Werstappen's Dutch thriller in homage to Republic Pictures,* Obsessions. *Scraping together a living in New York from occasional editing work, Scorsese was appointed artist in residence at local high schools by the Film Society of Lincoln Center, the organization responsible for the New York Film Festival.*

In 1969 he also began teaching at NYU as an Assistant Instructor, covering basic technique and film criticism, and supervising the making of students' three-minute films. In May 1970, he acted as production supervisor and post-production director for the New York Newsreel Collective's largely student production, Street Scenes.[3] *This begins with a rallying call for the United States to pull out of Indochina, end political repression at home, especially as directed against the Black Panthers, and remove the 'war machines' from college campuses. It goes on to cover a demonstration on Wall Street and the march on Washington, interspersing these with interviews, confrontations with the media and occasional bursts of acid rock.*

15 Keitel and Scorsese in *Street Scenes* (1970).
16 Mike Wadleigh, Scorsese and Thelma Schoonmaker working on
Woodstock (1970).

Though he clearly was the major influence on the editing, the only sequence that Scorsese admits to directing is a final, heated discussion about the efficacy of demonstrations – and the role of movies – set in a room in Washington. The participants include a largely silent Scorsese, Harvey Keitel, Jay Cocks and Verna Bloom. Among the then students who took part in this production were the future directors Jonathan Kaplan and Oliver Stone.

With his old friend Michael Wadleigh, who had photographed the 16 mm sections of Who's That Knocking at My Door?, *Scorsese worked on the editing of* Woodstock, *an epic record of the 1969 rock festival. His most notable contribution was the Sly and the Family Stone sequence and the addition of the 'bouncing ball' sing-alongs. But entry into the mainstream industry still eluded him.*

At that time there was no recognized way to get into the film business. I had a young man just stand next to me all the way through *The Color of Money*, for which he got three credits. But when I tried as a student to get on the crew of a film being made by a major director in New York, the unions wouldn't allow it. The best post-graduate training you could get in America at that time was to work for Roger Corman. But it was easier for all those kids coming out of USC and UCLA in California because they were out there already. They could just walk up Sunset Boulevard, go into his office and say, 'I'm a film-maker.' In fact, Roger Corman saw *Who's That Knocking at My Door?* in 1970 on the West Coast under the title *J.R.* It had been retitled because the manager didn't like the original and preferred to use the main character's name! Charles Champlin gave it a good review in the *L.A. Times*, which helped things along.

I was taken out to California by Freddie Weintraub, then a vice-president of Warner Brothers and one of the guys responsible for buying *Woodstock* when we were actually on site. He somehow got a certified cheque dropped off by helicopter, and we said 'OK – it's a Warner Brothers film' and went ahead and shot it! Freddie had another rock film called *Medicine Ball Caravan*, which François Reichenbach had directed, and there was nine hours of footage. Some of it was on 8 mm, most of it on 35 mm Techniscope and the rest on 16 mm. He brought me out as an editor to put it in some kind of order; it was meant to be a two-week job. So when I got to Hollywood I bought a poster of Minnelli's *Two Weeks in Another Town* and hung it over my bed. In the end it took nine months and this was a very, very unpleasant time for me because of the adjustment between New York and California, which is very hard to make if you're a strong New Yorker.

Everyone was in Los Angeles at that time. George Lucas was having a hard time at Warners: they wanted to cut *THX 1138* down, which he thought was terrible, and he swore that directing was the worst job in the world and that he'd never do it again! I'd first met Francis Coppola in September 1970, at the American Film Festival in Sorrento in Italy. We'd become friendly there and would meet up again when he came to visit George. He'd built an incredible screening room at his house in San Francisco out of the proceeds from *The Godfather* and we'd look at films there sent over from the Pacific Film Archive.

Brian De Palma was already a close friend from New York and he was also at Warner Brothers, where they were in the process of taking him off *Get to Know Your Rabbit*. Then Fred Weintraub left Warner Brothers. I was struck by an asthma attack while cutting this monstrosity. So we would all just sit and complain, hanging together out of misery. We also got to know Steven Spielberg, who was doing television shows for Universal. As a generation, we seemed to be more cine-literate than our predecessors, who came from many different backgrounds, like literature, the theatre or live television. For example, Michael Powell could quote from literature in a way that's quite amazing to me; it's from a different age entirely.

During the first month I was out there, January 1971, the William Morris Agency got me together with Roger Corman, who asked if I'd be interested in doing a sequel to *Bloody Mama*. I asked, 'Does it have costumes and guns?' He said, 'Yes'; so I said, 'All right.' It was called *Boxcar Bertha*, the script would be ready in six months and he said he'd call me then, as he was off to get married. I said, 'Sure' – I'd heard this story before.

But six months later he called me with a script. I had finished work on *Medicine Ball Caravan* and I'd begged John Cassavetes, who had become a friend, to give me some work. He put me on *Minnie and Moskowitz* as a sound editor at $500 a week for doing nothing! I even lived on his set for a week and, when he required sound-effects for a fight, I held John while someone punched him! When my agent called his office, looking for me, John's secretary took the call and asked if it was anything important. 'Important?' my agent said. 'It's the biggest break of his life. He's gonna make a film. The script just came in.' To which she said, 'Oh, don't be silly,' and hung up.

Boxcar Bertha belonged to a new genre, begun by *Bonnie and Clyde*, which I think had a regular audience at the time. The genre has gone now because exploitation has moved into 'slasher' films like *Halloween* and *Friday the Thirteenth*, which are more graphically gory. *Bonnie and Clyde* had incredible violence in it, as did *Boxcar Bertha*, but there was more of a story round it, not just going from one murder to the next. *Bonnie and Clyde* became an amazing success, although it received some very bad criticism. Bosley Crowther of the *New York Times* attacked it. But within a week, he had written a second review that was more favourable, because of the audience response, and then left his job. Remember the tag line – 'They're young, they're in love, and they kill people'? We loved them, they were terrific, and they just wore the greatest clothes.

It was a similar experience watching Hawks's *Scarface* for the first time, on 16 mm with Jay Cocks. There's a wonderful scene where all these cars line up outside a coffee shop, the guys get out, kneel down and fire into the shop with machine guns, wrecking everything. This goes on for a long time. Then Paul Muni says to George Raft, 'What are they shooting with?', and he replies, 'Tommy guns.' Muni then says, 'Great, I'll go get one,' and he comes back with a gun and starts firing with it! Jay and I looked at each other and both said, 'We really love these guys.' It's strange that we don't normally like people who are killing other people, but the way they're presented in these films is extremely glamorous. I believe that's why they had that little section in *Scarface*, directed I believe by someone else, where a real Italian–American says that these people are giving us a bad name – they had to give the movie some sort of temperance.

It was Julie Corman who had discovered Bertha Thompson's autobio-graphy, Sister of the Road, *and American International Pictures bought the rights. But the eventual script had little to do with the book and used only a few characters from it. Provided that he stayed within the exploitation genre rules, and the budget of $600,000, Scorsese had considerable freedom to inject personal and classic movie references – especially to* The Wizard of Oz, *with Barbara Hershey's hair-style clearly modelled on Dorothy's. Barry Primus's character was rewritten to become almost a Scorsese alter ego from New York. And there are even two characters called Michael Powell and Emeric Pressburger! But above all, Scorsese stressed the David Carradine character, Big Bill Shelley, as an heroic, incorruptible union man, allied with his black supporter, who blasts the sadistic lawmen at the end of the film. The love scenes also have*

17 The glamour of guns in Hawks's *Scarface* (1932).

a special warmth, no doubt partly due to the close relationship between Carradine and Hershey at the time.

Roger just told me, 'Read the script, rewrite as much as you want, but remember, Marty, that you must have some nudity at least every fifteen pages. Not complete nudity, maybe a little off the shoulder, or some leg, just to keep the audience interest up.' This was very important for the exploitation market, so it was what he had to have. Roger had all these little ideas about how films should be made. For example, in the sound mixing, he said, 'Remember you're mixing the entire film in three days: nine reels, three days. The first reel has to be good because people coming to the drive-in have to hear what's going on. Forget the rest of the film until you get to the last reel, because they just want to know how it turned out.' And he said it with a straight face. In New York we had this image of him being very tough, pounding the table and smoking cigars like Sam Arkoff, who called us all 'intellectuals' on *Unholy Rollers*. Roger, however, is very tall, thin and quietly spoken. Very sweet and very suave.

I was insecure at first because I had been fired from *The Honeymoon Killers* in 1968 after one week's shooting, and for a pretty good reason too. It was a 200-page script and I was shooting everything in master shots with no coverage because I was an artist! Since the guys with the money only had enough for a $150,000 black and white film, they said we just couldn't go on; there would have to be close-ups or something. Of course, not every scene was shot from one angle, but too many of them were, so that there was no way of avoiding a film four hours long. That was a great lesson. From 1968 to 1972 I was very much afraid I would get fired again. So when I started on *Boxcar Bertha* I drew every scene, about 500 pictures altogether.

Roger came into the hotel room one morning asking to see my preparation, and I started to show him the drawings. He said, 'Excuse me, do you have these for all the rest of the film?' I admitted that I did. He said, 'OK, don't show me any more, that's fine,' and just walked away. This didn't mean I was going to shoot exactly what I had drawn. But it meant that if something went wrong I could go back to the blueprints and rework them. Suppose I was still missing two or three angles, maybe I could somehow combine what I had into one shot. It just means being prepared: *Boxcar Bertha* was twenty-four days' straight shooting, with no time for the actors to go and get a haircut or anything – a professional production.

Roger came down to the location in Arkansas. Believe me, it still looked

18 Crucifixion in *Boxcar Bertha* (1972).

like the Depression in the areas where we shot. He told me, 'I'm going to scowl. It's not for you, it's for the crew.' So he walked around scowling and the crew shaped up immediately. He took me aside at one point and said, 'Martin, you know the audience will expect a chase scene and we don't have one in the script. It's *Bonnie and Clyde* that we're doing and I think we should put in a chase scene with the cars.' I said, 'Well then, Roger, give me an extra day's shooting.' And he replied, 'Oh no, it's twenty-four days, we can't go any extra on that. But you can work out something, draw the shots the way you normally do and we'll put the chase in somehow.' He would have a way of doing that kind of thing to you. But it was a refreshing experience and I really learned a lot from it.

I had nothing to do with the final scene in which the main character was crucified. It was in the script that was given to me, and I thought it was a sign from God. I liked the way we shot it, the angles we used, and in particular the way you saw the nails coming through the wood, though they were never seen piercing flesh.

Scorsese was later to point out that he filmed the crucifixion scene in The Last Temptation of Christ *using precisely those shots again.*

Notes

1 Vittorio Cottafavi (b. 1914) became a cult figure among young critics and film-makers, especially in France during the sixties, for such distinctive contributions to the 'Peplum' genre as *Goliath and the Dragon* (1960), and *Hercules Conquers Atlantis* (1961). What seemed like conventional muscleman epics to many were provocatively hailed by the 'new critics' as witty parodies, which also, as in *The Hundred Horsemen* (1964), could become bizarrely expressive, even experimental.

2 The Doors were a leading rock group of the late sixties, primarily because of their lead singer, Jim Morrison (1943–71), whose poetically conceived lyrics and dynamic, sensual stage presence have created a myth around him (he also, incidentally, majored in film technique at UCLA). The section of the song 'The End' featured in the sex scene is as follows:

> The killer awoke before dawn
> He put his boots on
> He took a face from the ancient gallery
> And he walked on down the hall
>
> He went to the room where his sister lived
> And then he paid a visit to his brother
> And then he walked on down the hall
> And he came to a door
> And he looked inside

'Father'
'Yes, son?'
'I want to kill you
Mother I want to . . .'

Come on baby take a chance with us
And meet me at the back of the blue bus

3 'Newsreel started in America, and is the model for similar projects throughout the world. Born of the convergence between "the underground" and the domestic student opposition to the war in Vietnam, Newsreel became the filmic arm of the movement. Young, committed film-makers like Robert Kramer and Norm Fruchter shot, collected, supervised and assembled material on the manifold happenings throughout the United States . . . Stylistically, Newsreel owes much to the New American Cinema: pop music tracks, superimpositions, images rather than structured narrative, foggy focus, wobbles.' (Simon Hartog, 'Newsreel', *Afterimage* 1, April 1970.)

CHAPTER 3

Mean Streets – Alice Doesn't Live Here Anymore – Taxi Driver

'You don't make up for your sins in church – you do it in the streets.'
Charlie in *Mean Streets*

Boxcar Bertha, as Scorsese predicted, was a film aimed at 'the guys on 42nd Street'. It earned him membership of the Directors' Guild and, even if it proved to be not exactly a sequel to Bloody Mama, *Roger Corman was pleased.*

I showed *Boxcar Bertha* in a rough-cut of about two hours to John Cassavetes. John took me back to his office, looked at me and said, 'Marty, you've just spent a whole year of your life making a piece of shit. It's a good picture, but you're better than the people who make this kind of movie. Don't get hooked into the exploitation market, just try and do something different.' Jay Cocks, who was then the *Time* film critic, had shown him *Who's That Knocking at My Door?* and he had loved it. He said I must go back to making that kind of film and was there anything I had that I was really dying to make. I said, 'Yes, although it needs a rewrite.' 'Well, rewrite it then!'

I dug it out and showed it to Sandy Weintraub, who was my partner at the time. She said she thought a lot of the stories I told her about Little Italy were far funnier than anything in it. So I took out a lot of religious stuff – it was still called *Season of the Witch* at this stage – and put in things like the pool-hall scene. After rewriting the script, I started sending it out to everyone – and that was *Mean Streets*. After all the different titles it had had over the years, this was suggested to me by Jay Cocks, from Raymond Chandler's 'Down these mean streets a man must go.' I thought it a little pretentious, but it turned out to be a pretty good title.

I was working now as an editor at MGM on *Elvis on Tour*, as well as on Vernon Zimmerman's *Unholy Rollers*, which Roger Corman produced for AIP. *Unholy Rollers* was the rip-off of the Raquel Welch movie about roller derbys, *Kansas City Bomber*, but it came out afterwards and was destroyed. Roger offered me *I Escaped from Devil's Island*, which was a rip-off of *Papillon*. The idea was that if you shot it fast enough, you could release the film before *Papillon*. I was still very keen on genre films, and I could have made a picture on gladiators, *The Arena*, that Roger had set up in Spain.

Jay Cocks's wife, Verna Bloom, was in Los Angeles at that time doing *Old Times* on stage, and she told me about a young man (he was twenty-six) named Jonathan Taplin who wanted to meet me. I had dinner with him and he turned out to have been road manager for Bob Dylan and The Band, and now he wanted to produce movies. So I gave him the script of *Mean Streets*, thinking that would be the end of it. However, he liked it, so I showed him *Who's That Knocking at My Door?*, which he also liked, and then I took him to a preview of *Boxcar Bertha* at the Pantages Theater. The audience loved the film and applauded it; Roger Corman came out smiling; and even Sam Arkoff looked at me and said, 'I've gotta tell you, it's almost good. That's the best preview we've had since *The Wild Angels*.' I said, 'That's pretty good.' But he warned me, 'No, don't get too excited, it's almost good.'

Well, Jon came up with some financial backing for *Mean Streets* from a twenty-three-year-old who had just come into an inheritance, which promptly fell through. Then we all met at another dinner, at which we just talked about how Venice was sliding into the water! The next thing I knew was that the money was back in. Before this, I'd shown the script to everyone – I'd even sent it to Francis Coppola, who passed it on to Al Pacino, but I never got an answer. Eventually Roger Corman got hold of it. His reader Frances liked it, and assured him it had sex, violence, gangsters and a lot of action.

Now, Roger's brother Gene had just had a big hit with a film made in Harlem called *The Cool Breeze*, a black version of *The Asphalt Jungle*. So Roger said to me, 'If you want to make *Mean Streets*, and if you're willing to swing a little' – I'll never forget that phrase – 'and make them all black, I'll give you $150,000 and you can shoot it all with a non-Union crew in New York.' I asked for time to think about it. But I soon realized that I just couldn't see those black guys in church, or at confession. It just wouldn't work. The plot wasn't really anything, it was the characters that mattered, so I stuck to my guns. But Roger helped by saying he would distribute the

19 Scene from Corman's *Tomb of Ligeia* (1965) quoted in *Mean Streets*.

film and I put the clip from *The Tomb of Ligeia* in because he really got it started.

So *Mean Streets* was produced by Jonathan Taplin, and I shot it with the Corman crew from *Boxcar Bertha*. The only way we could do it, he thought, was to shoot everything in Los Angeles. I said, 'What about four days in New York?', and he said, 'Well, maybe.' I eventually improvised on the budget and swindled eight days. I did ten days of rehearsals in New York; shot all the interiors in Los Angeles, as well as most of the exterior stuff including the final car crash; then we did hallways and the beach in New York to get the authentic look. Charlie's apartment was a set in an office building on Hollywood Boulevard, and the bar was in the Chicano section – a very rough area, where the everyday violence was far worse than anything we showed in the film.

An important man on the film was Paul Rapp, who had been Roger's associate producer, quite a tough guy who guided me in the same way he had Francis Coppola, Jack Nicholson, Monte Hellman and Peter Bogdanovich. He would look at my drawings for a conversation scene and tell me to shoot everything that was lit in one direction first, so *Mean Streets* was all shot backwards, as the master shot would be left until last to save time waiting for lights. We were doing twenty-four set-ups a day sometimes – thirty-six for the big fight scene in the pool room – which was a lot even for a non-union crew.

Mean Streets revisited the milieu of Who's That Knocking at My Door?, *with Harvey Keitel as Charlie, the ambitious Scorsese alter ego, anxious to please his uncle, a local Mafia boss, while also troubled by two important relationships in his life. One is his strongly sexual affair with Teresa, a cousin who suffers from epilepsy, which causes him social and religious guilt. The other is his friendship with the wild, unpredictable Johnny Boy, who constantly plunges further into debt and eventually drags Charlie into a terrible, climactic shooting. This character was based on a neighbourhood friend of Scorsese's, Sally GaGa, who had undergone a nervous breakdown after accidentally killing a drunk, and who had previously been unable to sit through a screening of* Who's That Knocking at My Door? *For the part of Johnny Boy, Scorsese cast an actor whose dynamism in De Palma's early features,* Greetings *and* Hi, Mom!, *had shown great promise.*

Robert De Niro was introduced to me by Brian De Palma, who'd discovered him in the early sixties and cast him in *The Wedding Party*, at a

Christmas dinner given by Jay Cocks and his wife Verna. Bob had worked with Verna in a play. He'd heard that I had made a film about his neighbourhood – *Who's That Knocking at My Door?* – though he used to hang out with a different group of people, on Broome Street, while we were on Prince Street. We had seen each other at dances and said hello. He recognized me first at the dinner and mentioned several names of people I used to hang out with. He had liked *Who's That Knocking at My Door?* and felt, like many, that it was the only accurate representation of life on the Lower East Side to date.

My training in handling actors came from watching a lot of movies and being thrilled by them. That's how a lot of mirror scenes in my movies came about. I used to fantasize in front of the mirror, playing all my heroes. I remember trying to do Alan Ladd in *Shane* and I liked Victor Mature a lot – he was great, for me he had real emotion! Then I saw *On the Waterfront* and *East of Eden* and those two boys, Marlon Brando and James Dean, changed my life completely. Now I was emulating those actors. But I still didn't know anything about technique. When I made my first film, *What's a Nice Girl Like You Doing in a Place Like This?*, in 1963, it was inspired by Mel Brooks's comedy and Ernie Pintoff's animation, and the lead actor was a mime. So it was like anti-acting rather than acting; more to do with the way the film looked and was cut than anything else. And I'll never forget that actor saying to me, 'Marty, you don't know a fucking thing about acting.'

So I decided I had better do something. I listened to everything they told me and learned from them. Very often I would let them do what they wanted. When I cast Harvey Keitel in my first feature, I found him to be very much like me, even though he's a Polish Jew from Brooklyn. I became friends with him, got to know him, and found we had the same feelings about the same problems. Both our families expected us to achieve some sort of respectability. But there were other actors on that film who were very difficult to be with, very mean people. I learned to deal with that, too.

I certainly never took any acting courses, or went down to the Actors' Studio. I would just listen to their voices on earphones during shooting, and if I believed what they were saying, that was OK. A lot of the time on *Mean Streets* I couldn't even look at what they were doing, because the camera was flying around and I had to duck! I believe the hardest thing for two actors to do is just sit down and talk. The hysterics, the screaming, the yelling and the fighting – you can get two or three good takes of that; but talking, communicating, is the hardest thing. Because we were shooting so quickly and cheaply, I couldn't let the actors go crazy and improvise.

I really had to cut it down and keep pounding into them, 'Don't forget to come back to this. Don't forget to get to this or that line, because if you don't there's no point to the scene.' What's difficult is that you all have to agree on what you're doing, what film you're making. You have to get that out of the way immediately, because the worst thing that can happen is for an actor to get on the set and ask, 'What does this scene mean?' You have an answer, but it's not his answer and he doesn't want to hear it.

Much of the improvisation in the film was taped at rehearsal and then scripted from those tapes. A few scenes, like the one in which De Niro and Keitel fight each other with garbage pails, were improvised during shooting. I remember that at the end of one take, Bobby threw the thing at Harvey and Harvey threw it right back and I said, 'Great, we'll do that in the next take.' In the scene in the back room between De Niro and Keitel after they meet in the bar, I thought it would be fun to improvise and show more of the characters. We realized that we liked Abbott and Costello a great deal, their language routines with inverted word-meanings done with wonderful timing. We tried to keep as much of that as possible, although it had to be shot very quickly. And the result is so structured that if you only see that one scene you know more about their way of life from it than from anything else in the film. We see the shifting of trust, how Johnny trusts Charlie but, God, he's got his problems; and Charlie trusts Johnny, but he's using him. The scene was Bob's idea, and since he and Harvey are not afraid to try things, I said, 'Why not?' When I shot it, it was about fifteen minutes long, hilarious and clarified everything totally. It's like the betrayals of trust, one character taking advantage of the other, that I enjoy in the Hope and Crosby movies.

We did the climactic scene where Bobby suddenly pulls a gun on Richard Romanus on the next to last day of shooting. Something had happened between Bobby and Richard because the animosity between them in that scene was real, and I played on it. They had got on each other's nerves to the point where they really wanted to kill each other. I kept shooting take after take of Bobby yelling these insults, while the crew was getting very upset.

While we were in the Lower East Side, a slate[1] would come up saying *Mean Streets*, and people would get angry and say, 'There's nothing wrong with these streets!' And I'd say, 'No, it's only a preliminary title,' and I kept on hoping to change it, but it turned out to be known as that. *Mean Streets* had a little more violence and night life in it than *Who's That Knocking at My Door?* and at the same time as giving this accurate picture

20 De Niro as Johnny Boy in *Mean Streets*.
21 William Wellman's *The Public Enemy* (1931): a stylistic influence.

of Italian–Americans, I was trying to make a kind of homage to the Warner Brothers gangster films.

Actually I slipped in a clip of Fritz Lang's *The Big Heat*, a Columbia film from the fifties, but that was like a new gangster film in the same tradition. We grew up with *The Public Enemy* and *Little Caesar*. I found *Little Caesar* to be vulgar, very overdone and heavily acted. But even though they were Irish gangsters in *The Public Enemy*, which was a little odd to us, we understood the thinking behind it. I was influenced by the way William Wellman kept popular tunes playing in the background, no score but source music. And that blend of different kinds of music became the soundtrack of *Mean Streets* and later *Raging Bull*.

Mean Streets featured the music I grew up with and that music would give me images. One of the things I have against rock videos is that they specify certain images in your mind for each song. I would rather make up my own imagery for the music. With *Mean Streets* we got caught out on rights: people came out of the woodwork years later and Warner Brothers would have to pay them, though we often tried finding them at the time and failed. But for me, *Mean Streets* had the best music because it was what I enjoyed and it was part of the way we lived. Suddenly a piece would come on and we'd stay with it for two or three minutes. Life would stop, so I wanted the film to stop and go with the music. *Mean Streets* has that quality, whether it's rock'n'roll, opera or Neapolitan love songs. In our neighbourhood you'd hear rock'n'roll playing in the little bars in the back of the tenement buildings at three in the morning, so that was 'Be My Baby', when Harvey's head hits the pillow. For me, the whole movie was 'Jumping Jack Flash' and 'Be My Baby'.

Despite the restrictions of budget, schedule and location, Mean Streets *at last allowed Scorsese to achieve much more expressive and experimental camerawork than he had been able to realize previously. The celebrated opening tracking shot, when Charlie enters an infernal red-hued bar, used slow-motion cinematography and slowed-down sound. A prolonged fight in a pool room was filmed in long, hurtling shots and cut to the Marvelettes' 'Please, Mr Postman'. Probably the key influence on his use of such a mobile and 'involved' camera was Sam Fuller.*[2]

I was moved emotionally and psychologically when I first saw Sam Fuller's films, then I went back to figure out how he made them. *Park Row* – which is Sam's favourite, by the way – is a very important movie to me for the use of tracking shots and the staging of action and violence – how

22 The long bar-brawl take in Samuel Fuller's *Park Row* (1952).
23 Opening scene of Fuller's *The Naked Kiss* (1964).

the camera tracking implies more violence than there really is.[3] Doing that one long take creates so much in emotional impact, giving you a sense of being swept up in the fury and the anger, that you begin to understand more why it is happening. What Sam always says is that emotional violence is much more terrifying than physical violence.

For me, there's no such thing as 'senseless' violence. In the fight in the pool room, I held it long because of the sense of helplessness, the silliness of the whole thing. In the opening of Fuller's *The Naked Kiss*, when Constance Towers fights with her pimp, he slaps her, and her wig flies off to show she's bald. For this sequence, Sam strapped the camera on to their chests, so you actually go with the hit. In *Mean Streets*, in the drunken scene, Harvey had an Arriflex body brace under his jacket, with a piece of wood made by a grip joined to the camera.[4] As Harvey walked forward, the grip would move backwards with him, and when Harvey went down to the ground the grip just went sideways with him holding the contraption – which was just a jerry-built thing, nothing special. And when Harvey got up to dance with the strippers, we put him on the dolly.

I used a lot of hand-held camera for the sense of anxiety and urgency, to have that surreptitious camera sliding around corners. I remember Robert Altman seeing the film at the New York Film Festival and saying he liked it, but he would have done the hand-held shots on tracking. I said if we'd tracked every one of the shots, we'd still have been there shooting! So the economics dictated the style, and the style just happened to work.

Mean Streets dealt with the American Dream, according to which everybody thinks they can get rich quick, and if they can't do it by legal means then they'll do it by illegal ones. That disruption of values is no different today, and I'm interested in making a couple more pictures on the same theme. These guys' idea of making money, maybe a million or two, is by stealing, beating or cheating someone out of it. It's much sweeter, much better than actually earning it. At the beginning of the script of *Mean Streets* there was a quote from Bob Dylan's 'Subterranean Homesick Blues': 'Twenty years of schooling and they put you on the day shift'. Or, 'forget it, we're not going to do it'. Of course Dylan meant something else. But I wanted to delineate that attitude, to understand how these people suddenly find themselves in a quandary, where the only way out is very often death.

They begin by hijacking cigarettes, selling them for a little less than the normal price, not hurting anybody really, and then it gets a little higher. Selling dope would be another level altogether. Very often the leaders of these different groups and mobs don't like the younger guys selling dope –

not for moral reasons, but because it draws attention to them. In my own case, in my neighbourhood, if it had come to the point where I'd have to pull a gun and kill somebody, I wouldn't have been able to do it. I wouldn't even get into a brawl and ruin my suit at that time; I'd smile and walk the other way. But the people who received the most respect in the area where I grew up were not the working people, they were the wise guys, the gang leaders, and the priests. And that was what inclined me towards the priesthood, which was a tougher profession, I'm afraid!

Mean Streets was an attempt to put myself and my old friends on the screen, to show how we lived, what life was like in Little Italy. It was really an anthropological or a sociological tract. Charlie uses other people, thinking that he's helping them; but by believing that, he's not only ruining them but ruining himself. When he fights with Johnny against the door in the street, he acts like he's doing it for the others, but it's a matter of his own pride – the first sin in the Bible. My voice is intercut with Harvey's throughout the film, and for me that was a way of trying to come to terms with myself, trying to redeem myself. It's very easy to discipline oneself to go to mass on Sunday mornings. That's not redemption for me: it's how you live, how you deal with other people, whether it be in the streets, at home or in an office.

Mean Streets *was acclaimed at the 1973 New York Film Festival and subsequently in the Directors' Fortnight at Cannes. Reviews were distinctly more enthusiastic than for Scorsese's previous features. Robert De Niro was now a hot property, as was Scorsese, who had amply confirmed the wisdom of his mentor, Cassavetes.*

John Cassavetes saw the first rough-cut of *Mean Streets* and said, 'Don't cut it whatever you do.' I said, 'What about the bedroom scene?' and he replied, 'Oh yeah, you could cut that,' because John didn't like nudity. I learned a lot from him and the way he dealt with people. Especially how to treat actresses. He told me how Judy Garland had acted up on *A Child is Waiting*, until finally he tried to attack her and they had to be separated. Then she said, 'Get me away from all these people – you I like.' She took him into her dressing room and began to cry, and he asked why she was crying. She replied that she'd been working on the film for a week and you'd have thought they'd have sent her flowers by now. It was then he realized how vulnerable she was.

In Hollywood they liked *Mean Streets* a lot, but on the strength of it they thought I could only direct actors, not actresses! Ellen Burstyn, who was riding a wave on account of her success in *The Exorcist*, was looking for a young director for *Alice Doesn't Live Here Anymore*, a script which had previously been with Diana Ross. She had dinner with Francis Coppola and he told her to see *Mean Streets*. He'd just seen it himself and as a result cast Bob De Niro in *The Godfather Part II* and apparently he recommended me. John Calley, who was head of production at Warner Brothers, told me about the script and he thought it was a good one for me to do: nobody would expect it from me. Because I was receiving a lot of scripts now, Sandy Weintraub read it first and said it was really interesting. I thought it was a good idea too, dealing with women for a change, only I wanted to improvise some of it and change the third part dealing with the farmer. I was only partly happy with the result, as we really shot a three-and-a-half-hour picture and then had to cut it down to less than two hours.

Alice Doesn't Live Here Anymore was a complete departure from the male-dominated worlds of Scorsese's autobiographical films. Now he had a budget three times that of Mean Streets, *and a script by a writer new to him, Robert Getchell. The story follows a widowed woman on the road in Arizona, travelling with her precocious young son and determined to make a new life for herself as a singer. Conscious of its old-fashioned Hollywood optimism, Scorsese worked with Getchell and the actors on improvisation to give it a sharper edge.*

He wanted it to begin like a Douglas Sirk melodrama – although Sirk is not a director to whom he responds emotionally – and then shift into a different world when Alice is suddenly bereaved. The means to achieve this was a highly stylized $85,000 set, seen only in the pre-credits sequence, which portrays the mental landscape of Alice's dreams.

Alice Doesn't Live Here Anymore was the first time in my movie career that I was able to build a proper set. It was also the last picture to be shot on the old Columbia sound-stages on Gower Street. We even had the set decorator from *Citizen Kane*, Darrell Silvera. Russell Metty shot the tests for me – he happened to be on the set.[5] In the opening sequence, showing Alice as a little girl, we tried for a combination of *Duel in the Sun* and *Gone with the Wind* in the William Cameron Menzies style of *Invaders from Mars*.[6] We painted a red sunset that went 180 degrees around the entire stage, and we made up this little girl to look like Dorothy in *The Wizard of Oz*, to stand in front of this incredible backdrop and sing

24 Ellen Burstyn in *Alice Doesn't Live Here Anymore* (1974).
25 Set for the opening sequence of *Alice Doesn't Live Here Anymore*.

'You'll Never know'. In a way, the songs that Alice sings are inspired by the old Betty Grable pictures.

It was a challenge for me to work with a young boy who was a non-actor. Things would be happening between him and Ellen Burstyn on the set that would happen again at night between her and her own twelve-year-old son. She would tell me about these things and we'd include them, so the picture was constantly changing. I also enjoyed working with Kris Kristofferson, though at first we kept making each other nervous. In rehearsal he would ask, 'Where do you want me to stand?' and I would say, 'I don't know.' Then he'd say, 'You've *got* to tell me where to stand.' The poor guy had just done *Pat Garrett and Billy the Kid*, which I loved, but a lot of people hated. So one day we went off on our own to rehearse and I kidded him, shouted stupid things and looned around, saying, 'I look funny in front of you and you look funny in front of me. So what? We'll look funny in front of each other.' It broke the tension and after that our relationship was great. I had learned something from him.

Another important idea on *Alice Doesn't Live Here Anymore* was to use women in the crew – Sandy Weintraub was associate producer, Toby Rafelson our art director and Marcia Lucas my editor – to help us be as honest as possible. But we never intended it to be a feminist tract. It was a film about self-responsibility and also about how people make the same mistakes again and again. There was even thought of her getting divorced and running away from her husband at the beginning, but we decided to make it very different, that he died and she was left with no choice.

There was some criticism of the ending, with Burstyn getting the handsome man in the end. But in fact the film doesn't finish with them, it finishes with Alice and her son walking away and the boy saying she's smothering him. Maybe Burstyn and Kristofferson would be together for the rest of their lives, but it was going to be rather stormy. There was a key line, when he said about his first wife, 'She said "I'm leaving", and I held the door for her.' I tried to play it so that this was realistic in terms of their relationship: he was obviously holding some things back and it wasn't going to be pretty when he let them out.

Ellen Burstyn's strong central performance won her an Oscar for Alice Doesn't Live Here Anymore, *which was collected by Scorsese, now wearing his familiar beard. Robert Getchell received a nomination, and a commission for a television series based on the characters. Scorsese meanwhile plunged back into the world of Little Italy by making a documentary about his parents,* Italianamerican. *Financed by a Bicenten-*

26 Charles and Catherine Scorsese in *Italianamerican* (1974).
27 Paul Schrader, Scorsese and Robert De Niro on *Taxi Driver* (1975).

nial Award from the National Endowment for the Humanities, this was intended by its sponsors to become part of a series entitled Storm of Strangers *about immigrants and ethnic minorities.*

Filming took place in the Scorsese family apartment on Elizabeth Street, where his parents talked informally about their early life in New York and their Sicilian roots. When the film was first presented at the 1974 New York Festival, its final credits – which include Catherine Scorsese's personal recipe for spaghetti sauce – received a standing ovation. Scorsese has subsequently regarded the film as a documentary counterpart to Mean Streets.

On 30 December 1975 Scorsese married Julia Cameron. This was following the filming of Taxi Driver, *a project which proved difficult to finance. The original screenplay was by Paul Schrader, who had quickly established himself as a screenwriter, following a spell as a critic after leaving university and the publication of his thesis,* Transcendental Style in Film: Ozu, Bresson, Dreyer.

Brought up in a strict Dutch Calvinist home in Grand Rapids, Michigan, Schrader had not been allowed to see any films until the age of seventeen. Thereafter, he made up for lost time – and claimed that this deprivation had protected him from the self-indulgent nostalgia of 'normal' childhood viewing. His third script, The Yakuza, *was bought by Warner Brothers for the notable sum of $350,000 and directed by Sidney Pollack.* Taxi Driver *came partly out of personal experience of living rough in New York and a passion for guns; from Sartre's first 'existential' novel,* La Nausée; *and from studying the diaries of Arthur Bremer, the man who tried to assassinate Governor George Wallace. Originally considered by Robert Mulligan, with Jeff Bridges intended for the title role, it was eventually acquired by the producers Michael and Julia Phillips.*

Brian De Palma introduced me to Paul Schrader. We made a pilgrimage out to see Manny Farber, the critic, in San Diego.[7] I wanted Paul to do a script of *The Gambler* by Dostoevsky for me. But Brian took Paul out for dinner, and they contrived it so that I couldn't find them. By the time I tracked them down, three hours later, they'd cooked up the idea of *Obsession.* But Brian told me that Paul had this script, *Taxi Driver*, that he didn't want to do or couldn't do at that time, and wondered if I'd be interested in reading it. So I read it and my friend read it and she said it was fantastic: we agreed that this was the kind of picture we should be making. That year, 1974, De Niro was about to win the Academy Award for

The Godfather Part II, Ellen Burstyn won the Award for *Alice Doesn't Live Here Anymore*, and Paul had sold *The Yakuza* to Warner Brothers, so it was all coming together. Michael and Julia Phillips, who owned the script, had won an Award for *The Sting* and figured there was enough power to get the film made, though in the end we barely raised the very low budget of $1.3 million. In fact, for a while we even thought of doing it on black and white videotape! Certainly we felt it would be a labour of love rather than any kind of commercial success – shoot very quickly in New York, finish it in Los Angeles, release it and then bounce back into *New York, New York*, on which we'd already begun pre-production. De Niro's schedule had to be rearranged anyway, because he was due to film *1900* with Bertolucci.

Much of *Taxi Driver* arose from my feeling that movies are really a kind of dream-state, or like taking dope. And the shock of walking out of the theatre into broad daylight can be terrifying. I watch movies all the time and I am also very bad at waking up. The film was like that for me – that sense of being almost awake. There's a shot in *Taxi Driver* where Travis Bickle is talking on the phone to Betsy and the camera tracks away from him down the long hallway and there's nobody there. That was the first shot I thought of in the film, and it was the last I filmed. I like it because I sensed that it added to the loneliness of the whole thing, but I guess you can see the hand behind the camera there.

The whole film is very much based on the impressions I have as a result of growing up in New York and living in the city. There's a shot where the camera is mounted on the hood of the taxi and it drives past the sign 'Fascination', which was on Broadway. It's that idea of being fascinated, of this avenging angel floating through the streets of the city, that represents all cities for me. Because of the low budget, the whole film was drawn out on storyboards, even down to medium close-ups of people talking, so that everything would connect. I had to create this dream-like quality in those drawings. Sometimes the character himself is on a dolly, so that we look over his shoulder as he moves towards another character, and for a split second the audience would wonder what was happening. The overall idea was to make it like a cross between a Gothic horror and the New York *Daily News*.

There is something about the summertime in New York that is extraordinary. We shot the film during a very hot summer and there's an atmosphere at night that's like a seeping kind of virus. You can smell it in the air and taste it in your mouth. It reminds me of the scene in *The Ten Commandments* portraying the killing of the first-born, where a cloud of

28 Original drawings by Martin Scorsese for the climactic scene of *Taxi Driver*

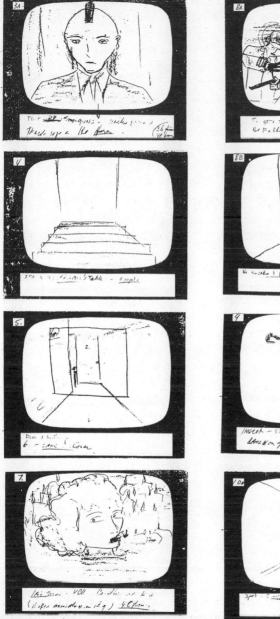
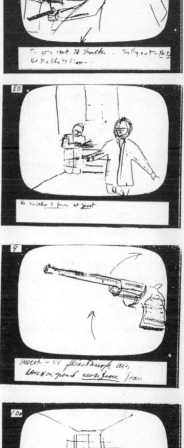

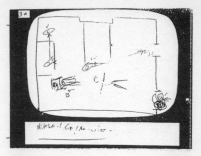

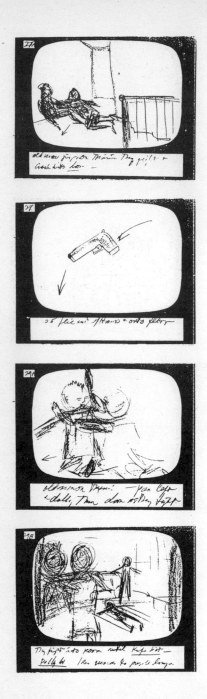

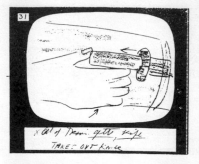

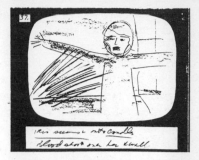

33

In pale tonic Hix ——— ....

37

Iris recesses into candle
Blood shot over her dwell

34

IA, Rec. sld now to wall — Iris come
one yell. — Fr. yes Hoja people

35

Bob sits into back — Reach to Cap —
put his to him, etc. — sleep bash

35

Pain. Yeles superimmin. 38

41

start on hand (blood) Tilt up
to Face fm quad-shit — the mile
the camp out

40

tits and to Face — fires into wall — Iris scam
jumps back house shout out

42

green smoke seeps along the palace floor and touches the foot of a first-born son, who falls dead. That's almost what it's like: a strange disease creeps along the streets of the city and, while we were shooting the film, we would slide along after it. Many times people threatened us and we had to take off quickly. One night, while we were shooting in the garment district, my father came out of work and walked by the set. The press of bodies on the pavement was so thick that, in the moment I turned away from the camera to talk to him, it was impossible to get back. That was typical.

As in my other films, there was some improvisation in *Taxi Driver*. The scene between De Niro and Cybill Shepherd in the coffee-shop is a good example. I didn't want the dialogue as it appeared in the script, so we improvised for about twelve minutes, then wrote it down and shot it. It was about three minutes in the end. Many of the best scenes, like the one in which De Niro says, 'Suck on this,' and blasts Keitel, were designed to be shot in one take. Although every shot in the picture had been drawn beforehand, with the difficulties we encountered, including losing four days of shooting because of rain, a lot of the stuff taken from the car had to be shot as documentary.

We looked at Hitchcock's *The Wrong Man* for the moves when Henry Fonda goes into the insurance office and the shifting points of view of the people behind the counter.[8] That was the kind of paranoia that I wanted to employ. And the way Francesco Rosi used black and white in *Salvatore Giuliano* was the way I wanted *Taxi Driver* to look in colour. We also studied Jack Hazan's *A Bigger Splash* for the head-on framing, such as the shot of the grocery store before Travis Bickle shoots the black guy.[9] Each sequence begins with a shot like that, so before any moves you're presented with an image like a painting.

I don't think there is any difference between fantasy and reality in the way these should be approached in a film. Of course, if you live that way you are clinically insane. But I can ignore the boundary on film. In *Taxi Driver* Travis Bickle lives it out, he goes right to the edge and explodes. When I read Paul's script, I realized that was exactly the way I felt, that we all have those feelings, so this was a way of embracing and admitting them, while saying I wasn't happy about them. When you live in a city, there's a constant sense that the buildings are getting old, things are breaking down, the bridges and the subway need repairing. At the same time society is in a state of decay; the police force are not doing their job in allowing prostitution on the streets, and who knows if they're feeding off it and making money out of it. So that sense of frustration goes in swings

29 De Niro as avenging angel in *Taxi Driver*.
30 Insurance office scene in Hitchcock's *The Wrong Man* (1956).

of the pendulum, only Travis thinks it's not going to swing back unless he does something about it. It was a way of exorcizing those feelings, and I have the impression that De Niro felt that too.

I never read any of Paul's source materials – I believe one was Arthur Bremer's diary. But I had read Dostoevsky's *Notes from Underground* some years before and I'd wanted to make a film of it; and *Taxi Driver* was the closest thing to it I'd come across. De Niro had tried his hand at scriptwriting on the subject of a political assassin, and he'd told me the story. We weren't very close at this time, I'd just worked with him on *Mean Streets*, but he read the script and said it was very similar to his idea, which he therefore might as well drop. So we all connected with this subject.

Travis really has the best of intentions; he believes he's doing right, just like St Paul. He wants to clean up life, clean up the mind, clean up the soul. He is very spiritual, but in a sense Charles Manson was spiritual, which doesn't mean that it's good. It's the power of the spirit on the wrong road. The key to the picture is the idea of being brave enough to admit having these feelings, and then act them out. I instinctively showed that the acting out was not the way to go, and this created even more ironic twists to what was going on.

It was crucial to Travis Bickle's character that he had experienced life and death around him every second he was in south-east Asia. That way it becomes more heightened when he comes back; the image of the street at night reflected in the dirty gutter becomes more threatening. I think that's something a guy going through a war, any war, would experience when he comes back to what is supposedly 'civilization'. He'd be more paranoid. I'll never forget a story my father told me about one of my uncles coming back from the Second World War and walking in the street. A car backfired and the guy just instinctively ran two blocks! So Travis Bickle was affected by Vietnam: it's held in him and then it explodes. And although at the end of the film he seems to be in control again, we give the impression that any second the time bomb might go off again.

It wasn't easy getting Bernard Herrmann to compose the music for *Taxi Driver*. He was a marvellous, but crotchety old man. I remember the first time I called him to do the picture. He said it was impossible, he was very busy, and then asked what it was called. I told him and he said, 'Oh, no, that's not my kind of picture title. No, no, no.' I said, 'Well, maybe we can meet and talk about it.' He said, 'No, I can't. What's it about?' So I described it and he said, 'No, no, no. I can't. Who's in it?' So I told him and he said, 'No, no, no. Well, I suppose we could have a quick talk.'

Working with him was so satisfying that when he died, the night he had finished the score, on Christmas Eve in Los Angeles, I said there was no one who could come near him. You get to know what you like if you see enough films, and I thought his music would create the perfect atmosphere for *Taxi Driver*.

I was shocked by the way audiences took the violence. Previously I'd been surprised by audience reaction to *The Wild Bunch*, which I first saw in a Warner Brothers screening room with a friend and loved. But a week later I took some friends to see it in a theatre and it was as if the violence became an extension of the audience and vice versa. I don't think it was all approval, some of it must have been revulsion. I saw *Taxi Driver* once in a theatre, on the opening night, I think, and everyone was yelling and screaming at the shoot-out. When I made it, I didn't intend to have the audience react with that feeling, 'Yes, do it! Let's go out and kill.' The idea was to create a violent catharsis, so that they'd find themselves saying, 'Yes, kill'; and then afterwards realize, 'My God, no' – like some strange Californian therapy session. That was the instinct I went with, but it's scary to hear what happens with the audience.

All around the world people have told me this, even in China. I was there for a three-week seminar and there was a young Mongolian student who spoke some English following me around Peking; and he would talk about *Taxi Driver* all the time. He said, 'You know, I'm very lonely,' and I'd say, 'Yes, basically we all are.' Then he said, 'You dealt with loneliness very well,' and I thanked him. Then he'd come round again and ask me, 'What do I do with the loneliness?' He wasn't just weird, he was a film student who was really interested. I said, 'Very often I try to put it into the work.' So a few days later he came back and said, 'I tried putting it into the work, but it doesn't go away.' I replied, 'No, it doesn't go away, there's no magic cure.'

People related to the film very strongly in terms of loneliness. I never realized what that image on the poster did for the film – a shot of De Niro walking down the street with the line, 'In every city there's one man.' And we had thought that audiences would reject the film, feeling that it was too unpleasant and no one would want to see it!

I wanted the violence at the end to be as if Travis had to keep killing all these people in order to stop them once and for all. Paul saw it as a kind of Samurai 'death with honour' – that's why De Niro attempts suicide – and he felt that if he'd directed the scene, there would have been tons of blood all over the walls, a more surrealistic effect. What I wanted was a *Daily News* situation, the sort you read about every day: 'Three men killed by

31 Wayne as the embittered Ethan Edwards in Ford's *The Searchers* (1956).

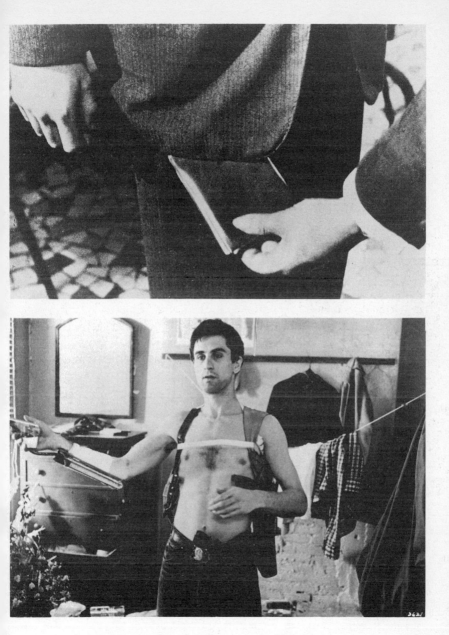

32 Robbery as ritual in Bresson's *Pickpocket* (1959).
33 De Niro training before the mirror in *Taxi Driver*.

lone man who saves young girl from them'. Bickle chooses to drive his taxi anywhere in the city, even the worst places, because it feeds his hate.

I was thinking about the John Wayne character in *The Searchers*. He doesn't say much, except 'That'll be the day' (from which Buddy Holly did the song). He doesn't belong anywhere, since he's just fought in a war he believed in and lost, but he has a great love within him that's been stamped out. He gets carried away, so that during the long search for the young girl, he kills more buffalo than necessary because it's less food for the Comanche – but, throughout, he's determined that they'll find her, as he says, 'as sure as the turning of the Earth'.

Paul was also very influenced by Robert Bresson's *Pickpocket*. I admire his films greatly, but I find them difficult to watch. In *Pickpocket* there's a wonderful sequence of the pickpockets removing wallets with their hands, a lot of movement in and out, and it's the same with Travis, alone in the room practising with his guns. I felt he should talk to himself while doing this, and it was one of the last things we shot, in a disused building in one of the roughest and noisiest areas of New York. I didn't want it to be like other mirror sequences we'd seen, so while Bob kept saying, 'Are you talking to me?' I just kept telling him, 'Say it again.' I was on the floor wearing headphones and I could hear a lot of street noise, so I thought we wouldn't get anything, but the track came out just fine.

I was also very much influenced by a film called *Murder by Contract* (1958), directed by Irving Lerner, who worked on *New York, New York* as an editor and to whom the film was dedicated following his death. I saw *Murder by Contract* on the bottom half of a double bill with *The Journey*, and the neighbourhood guys constantly talked about it. It had a piece of music that was like a theme, patterned rather like *The Third Man*, which came round and round again. But above all, it gave us an inside look into the mind of a man who kills for a living, and it was pretty frightening. I had even wanted to put a clip of it into *Mean Streets*, the sequence in a car when the main character describes what different sizes of bullet do to people, but the point had really been made. Of course, you find that scene done by me in *Taxi Driver*.

Notes

1 'Slate' is normal slang for the clapperboard which is included in every shot for identification and bears at least the working title of the film.
2 Sam Fuller (b. 1911) was a juvenile crime reporter and country-wide traveller before he began writing pulp stories and film scripts in the mid-thirties. After distinguished service in

the Second World War, he began to produce and direct his own scripts in 1949, with *I Shot Jesse James*. Other notable films include *The Steel Helmet* (1950), *Park Row* (1952), *Pickup on South Street* (1953), *Run of the Arrow* (1956), *Forty Guns* (1957), *Underworld USA* (1960) and *Shock Corridor* (1963). Described by Sarris as 'an authentic American primitive', Fuller has a graphic – if not tabloid – style, making much use of bizarre point-of-view shots, long identificatory tracks and energetic cross-cutting.

3 *Park Row* (1952) was Fuller's very personal tribute to the spirit of the early American newspaper business, for which he built a lavish studio replica of New York's 'Fleet Street'. This film also features some of his most bravura tracking shots: for one which follows a running fight in and out of many taverns he greased the seat of the operator's trousers so that he could slide smoothly along the bars!

4 A grip is the handyman on the film set, with such duties as laying tracks and moving heavy camera equipment.

5 Russell Metty (1906–78) worked with many major directors in a long career as cinematographer, including Hawks (*Bringing Up Baby*) and Welles (*The Stranger*, *A Touch of Evil*). He also photographed Douglas Sirk's three great Technicolor melodramas: *Magnificent Obsession*, *Written on the Wind* and *Imitation of Life*.

6 William Cameron Menzies (1896–1957) was one of Hollywood's most respected art directors (*The Thief of Bagdad*, 1924) before he took up direction as well in the thirties. His most prestigious projects of the thirties were Korda's spectacular *Things to Come* (1936), which he directed and part-designed, and *Gone with the Wind* (1939) for which he was art director. But his later low-budget science fiction movies have a cult following – especially *Invaders from Mars* (1953), in which both the adult world and a flying saucer invasion are seen from a child's point of view.

7 Manny Farber coined the phrase 'termite art' to cover the unselfconscious action cinema that he valued highly, alongside avant-garde work, as a critic working against the grain of respectability. One of the first to celebrate Fuller among other genre- and B-movie-specialists, he is also a painter and teacher and has latterly given up writing criticism in favour of allusive 'movie paintings'.

8 Hitchcock's *The Wrong Man* (1956) has a rare documentary-style quality and sense of real New York locations amid his more flamboyantly theatrical works and is also one of his most overtly Catholic. An innocent man (Fonda) falsely accused of homicide is eventually vindicated after a religious experience in prison.

9 Jack Hazan's *A Bigger Splash* (1975) took its title from the painting by its subject, David Hockney. A kind of fantasy documentary on Hockney, his work and his life, the film's lush colour photography and precise, clean framing reflected the artworks which, on occasion, it reproduced exactly.

CHAPTER 4

New York, New York – The Last Waltz – Raging Bull – The King of Comedy

'It's a goddamned impossible way of life.'
Robbie Robertson in *The Last Waltz*

Taxi Driver *won the Golden Palm at the 1976 Cannes Film Festival. It had cost only $1.9 million. But to avoid an 'X' rating for its American release, which would have reduced its box-office earning potential, Scorsese had to agree to putting a red tint over the final bloodbath. He was subsequently invited to play Charles Manson in* Helter Skelter *and Sam Fuller asked him to act in* The Big Red One, *but he turned down both offers. He did, however, play a* mafioso *in Paul Bartel's exploitation movie* Cannonball (1976). *Unrealized projects from this period included* Haunted Summer, *about Mary Shelley, and a film to have been made with Marlon Brando about the massacre at Wounded Knee and the destruction of American Indian culture. But* New York, New York *was already in view before the Cannes Golden Palm further boosted Scorsese's reputation.*

Before we began *Taxi Driver*, I read in *The Hollywood Reporter* that Irwin Winkler had bought the rights to the script *New York, New York*, and no director was yet announced for it. I felt it would be an interesting movie to make, since the big band sound of the forties was the music I had grown up with. We thought it would be a commercial picture – meaning it had the potential to be an across-the-board hit. I wanted to make it in the style of the forties films, with all their artifice and the idea of no reality. The sets would be completely fake, but the trick would be to approach the characters in the foreground like a documentary, combining the two techniques. So there would be a different story in the foreground, not boy meets girl, boy loses girl, boy gets girl, or even *Meet Me in St Louis*.

Anyway, *Taxi Driver* intervened, then Bob finished *1900* with Bertolucci and he was available to do it.

However, after winning the Cannes Golden Palm for *Taxi Driver*, we got big heads and felt that no script was good enough. For example, we shot for weeks on the opening scene where De Niro picks up Liza Minnelli, and the original cut of this alone ran one hour. This was before *Heaven's Gate*, when it was a case of giving the director everything he wanted – two brilliant actors, a thousand extras behind them, and ending up with a one-hour sequence![1]

Since the old Hollywood sets didn't exist any more, I had Boris Leven, who was the designer of *The Shanghai Gesture*, *Giant*, *The Silver Chalice* and *West Side Story*, build them. In the city streets I'd seen in MGM and Warner Brothers musicals, New York kerbs were always shown as very high and very clean. When I was a child, I realized this wasn't right, but was part of a whole mythical city that they had created. Now I wanted to re-create that mythical city, as well as the feeling of the old three-strip Technicolor with lipstick that was too bright and make-up even on the men.

I tried to follow the example of Vincente Minnelli's films in moving the camera and then took it further. First the camera would track in on the band for a few bars of music before the first cut, with no master shot, which would run for 24 bars.[2] Next the camera would track at one angle for 12 bars, then another way for 12, and so on back and forth until this became a style. I applied it to the studio sequences in *The Last Waltz* and to the boxing scenes in *Raging Bull*, where every fifteen or twenty punches there was a different angle with no coverage, and even to the pool games in *The Color of Money*.

Marcia Lucas, who was then married to George, cut *Alice Doesn't Live Here Anymore*, *Taxi Driver*, and then *New York, New York* for me. Not that we ever really finished cutting the film, since it keeps being released in different versions! George Lucas came down to look at the rough-cut and said we could add $10 million to the box-office receipts if we'd give the film a happy ending and have the man and the woman walk away together. He was right, but I said it just wouldn't work for this story. I knew that he was going for something that was extremely commercial, but I had to go another way.

I guess it's a good picture, though I think it's good only because it's truthful. It's not a film about jazz, therefore it wasn't necessary to have someone, like in *Round Midnight*, to pick up a sax and actually play it. It could have been a film about a director and a writer, or an artist and a

34 Directing Liza Minnelli and De Niro in *New York, New York* (1977).

35 'Two people in love who are both creative': *New York, New York*.

composer. It's about two people in love with each other who are both creative. That was the idea: to see if the marriage would work. We didn't know if this marriage was going to work, because we didn't know if our own marriages were working. So we were just doing it – rewriting, improvising, improvising, improvising until finally twenty weeks of shooting had gone by and we had something like a movie.

At the same time, we were trying to keep the technique of improvisation and documentary approach in the foreground, with the artifice of the fake sets in the background. But you have to build the sets in advance, which means you're not being practical, because once you start improvising in one set you soon improvise your way out of that set into another situation. In the meantime, they're building a different set because it's in the script! So you have to go back and shoot some more to get yourself back in line to use that second set – and that's one of the reasons why the scenes are so long.

It was an experimental situation and, in retrospect, I don't think we should have been given that free a hand. It was a mess, and it's a miracle that the film makes any kind of sense. At times I think it became brilliant, but for the sake of the little brilliant pieces we lost too much of the whole. As I said, it's a film about two creative people and the impossibility of a relationship of that kind. The kind of music they make doesn't matter. He loved jazz so much, but he could only go so far: he's white and he wants to be black. She had this show-business, Las Vegas type music. But we don't take sides on the music, we go with the characters.

I was extremely disappointed when the movie was finished because I had had a really bad experience making it. But over the years I've been able to see that it has truth to it. I still don't really like it, yet in a way I love it. Some people understand the ending, others just don't get it. I didn't make it quite clear enough that they both reconsidered: why should they go to dinner together? You know, the pain, the trouble – forget it, it's just not going to work. That's why both of them decide not to show up at the same time.

Scorsese reduced New York, New York *from an initial cut of four-and-a-half hours to a commercially acceptable 153 minutes (which was cut even further for the European release to 136 minutes). The final cost was more than $9 million, which amounted to $2 million over budget. Although it did respectable business, the film was nonetheless widely regarded as a failure. Not until 1981 was it re-released at 163 minutes, with some important scenes restored – notably the 'Happy Endings' musical fantasy,* *which had cost $350,000 to stage – when it reaped wide critical praise for its evocative celebration of, yet ironic distance from, the classic Holly-wood musical.*

During the last week of shooting *New York, New York*, I was asked by Jonathan Taplin, who had been the road manager for The Band years before, if I would like to shoot *The Last Waltz*, which was going to be The Band's last concert with some great people as guests.[3] I said that I didn't know, but that the event should at least be photographed for the archives, even if only in 16 mm. We were all out of our minds at that time and had trouble sorting out our plans, but Jonathan thought it was a great idea, so I said, 'All right.' But this was in September, and the concert was to be on Thanksgiving Day in November!

In any event, I came up with the idea of shooting it in 35 mm, with full sync sound and seven cameras. The Band were paying for the raw stock, while the cameramen and I would get a percentage if the picture was ever made, and in the meantime we'd enjoy the show. I prepared a 200-page script, so that when a camera ran out of film I could tell which other camera should pick up where. But of course I hardly got any of my planned moves, because once The Band started playing you couldn't hear anybody. But eventually, in spite of all the screaming, the cameras picked it up and once I saw the rushes I realized we had a movie.

For some reason, Bob Dylan was concerned that *The Last Waltz* would conflict with his own picture, *Renaldo and Clara*.[4] All I know is that he was the last act after seven hours, and just before he went on we were told we could only shoot two songs, 'Forever Young' and 'Baby, Let Me Follow You Down'. I asked if we'd get a signal when he was going to do these two, and I was told, 'Well yeah, kind of.' But when he came on, it was so loud on the stage that I didn't know what to do. Bill Graham was next to me saying, 'Shoot him! He comes from the same streets as you. Don't worry, don't let him push you around, shoot him.' But as I said to the guys later, we had a seven-hour concert and I didn't want to press it. Nevertheless, we got our cues right, and we shot the two songs that were used in the film.

Then I had to begin editing *New York, New York*. In fact, the producer Irwin Winkler became very upset when he discovered that I was in San Francisco shooting the concert. So now I had two features to cut and that's why *The Last Waltz* took two years to come out. During this time, Robbie Robertson would keep coming back with new ideas, saying we should have a 'Last Waltz Suite' comprising 'Evangeline', 'The Last Waltz' and

'The Weight', because the footage of the stage version of 'The Weight' was incomplete. And for 'Evangeline', he said we could get Emmylou Harris, the Staple Singers and Ray Charles, and all this sounded good to me. By this time the movie was sold to United Artists, who gave us more money to do ten days' shooting at night on a sound-stage.

A few months later Robbie felt he wanted some interviews in it, so we got some more money from UA and he decided *I* should interview them, which was not a good idea. They were very quiet, very formidable – especially Levon who didn't want to talk about anything to anybody, no how! So I had two 35 mm cameras all the time on these guys, and I just didn't know what they were going to do next. Robbie was all right and got into it; and Rick was fun, but he'd get up and walk down the hall, and I had to walk with him. Eventually he told me he was going to do just that, so I lit the hallway, but I didn't know what he was going to do at the end of it! Finally the movie came out in 1978.

Soon after the filming of New York, New York, *Scorsese's second daughter, Domenica, was born on 6 September 1976. Scorsese was invited by one of the stars of the film, Liza Minnelli, to direct her in a show in which she played a former musical comedy star intent on making a comeback.*

I was doing a stage play – the only one I'll ever do, I think – called *The Act*, with Liza Minnelli, and I was having a very, very bad time. I realized that I was out of my element, but I thought I'd stay with it, until I discovered that I really didn't like it. This was a difficult and painful situation. Then I was allowed to take three days off, to go to the Telluride Festival up in the Colorado mountains, where Tom Luddy had asked me to present their award to Michael Powell. I remember arriving at Telluride, and Jim McBride driving an open car with Brooks Riley and my co-writer Mardik Martin, and we passed Michael – who had no idea I was there to hand over the award – so I had to duck down when they stopped to say hello to him.

That night I put on a white suit to go to the Opera House, and when I appeared on stage Michael was very touched. He said, 'My dear boy, what are you doing here? You should be back with your play.' Then I realized he was right – and there must have been a reason why I was allowed to leave for three days. Next day I went back to LA and I left the play two weeks before it opened in New York. Michael came and talked to me about it.

36 The Band performing in a studio for *The Last Waltz* (1978).
37 Shooting *American Boy* in a jacuzzi.

Gower Champion, the former dancer and Broadway star, took over direction of The Act. *Scorsese announced a new project,* Gangs of New York, *about the Irish street gangs of the late nineteenth century. In June 1978, he received in Florence the David de Donatello Award for his contribution to cinema.*

During this year he also made a low-budget documentary about his friend Steven Prince, who had appeared as the gun salesman in Taxi Driver. American Boy *cost only $155,000 and was shot in a living room where many Scorsese associates are gathered to hear Prince recount his experiences as an army brat, a sometime junkie and Neil Diamond's road manager. Prince's vivid recollections of violent incidents and his fascination with guns make* American Boy *something of an objective correlative to* Taxi Driver, *just as* Italianamerican *had been to* Mean Streets.

Scorsese began working on a new script with Jay Cocks entitled Night Life, *about a fraternal rivalry. But by the end of 1978 his marriage had broken up, he was in poor health and in a severe state of depression. It was at this juncture that* Raging Bull, *the life story of former boxing champion Jake La Motta, offered a way out of his creative and personal impasse. It became, as Scorsese later acknowledged, a means of redemption.*

When I was doing *Alice Doesn't Live Here Anymore*, De Niro gave me the book *Raging Bull*. The book isn't really an autobiography; it was written by Jake La Motta, with Pete Savage and a guy named Joseph Carter. We never met Carter and for a while we didn't believe he existed, though somebody got the money! But Pete was a good friend of Jake's, and Jake's brother Joey and Pete were combined together in the script. Pete also became one of the co-producers of the film. In the book, they tried to give a reason for everything Jake did in his life, for his guilt and for his violence. It was very bad. But there were incidents in the book that were extremely interesting and we said we would make the film on that basis.

Right after *New York, New York*, during those two-and-a-half years from 1976 to 1978, I went through a lot of problems. The film was not successful, and I was very depressed. I finally came out of it when I was in hospital on Labor Day weekend in 1978, and De Niro came to visit me and he said, 'You know, we can make this picture.' There were three or four scripts which had been written in the meantime, and they had all been rejected. I didn't like any of them and didn't pay much attention, because I was in pretty bad shape. And Bob said, 'Listen, we could really do a great job on this film. Do you want to make it?' I found myself saying, 'Yeah.' I understood then what Jake was, but only after having gone through a similar experience. I was just lucky that there happened to be a project there ready for me to express this. The decision to make the film was made then.

I was fascinated by the self-destructive side of Jake La Motta's character, his very basic emotions. What could be more basic than making a living by hitting another person on the head until one of you falls or stops? Bob and I then decided to take Paul Schrader's script, with Paul's blessing, to an island – which is hard for me, because as far as I'm concerned there's only one island, Manhattan. But Bob got me through it, he'd wake me up in the morning and make me coffee, and we spent two-and-a-half weeks there rewriting everything. We combined characters and in fact rewrote the entire picture, including the dialogue. When we got back we showed it to Paul, who didn't care for it all that much but, as he wrote in his telegram to us when we began shooting, 'Jake did it his way, I did it my way, you do it your way.'

I put everything I knew and felt into that film and I thought it would be the end of my career. It was what I call a kamikaze way of making movies: pour everything in, then forget all about it and go find another way of life.

We had a version of Paul's script in which the 'Evening with Jake La Motta' came at the beginning and the end, making the whole film circular. Jake recited bits of Shakespeare, Tennessee Williams, a speech from *On the Waterfront*; and I thought it would be interesting if he did a scene from *Richard III*. You can still see the billboard in the film which lists this whole string of authors. Anyway, we had already shown the script to Michael Powell and his reaction was that it would be wrong. 'You can't have him doing that, whether he did it in reality or not, for this film it's just wrong.' So on the island Bob and I were looking at each other, and he said that *On the Waterfront* was *our* iconography, not Shakespeare, so why don't we use it?

I pointed out that this would mean De Niro playing Jake La Motta playing Marlon Brando playing Terry Malone! The only way to do it was to make it so cold that you concentrate on the words and you feel him finally coming to some sort of peace with himself in front of that mirror. And that's the way we did it, in nineteen takes. Sometimes Jake himself would really act it out in a very strong way which was quite heartbreaking, and Bobby did it that way three times. It was the last day of shooting, and I think we used take 13 in the end. One reviewer in America wrote that it's the most violent scene in the film. When he says in the mirror, 'It was you, Charlie,' is he playing his brother, or putting the blame on himself? It's certainly very disturbing for me.

Bob got to know Jake well and he worked with him a great deal just to be with him. I think he actually took care of Jake. When we shot the boxing scenes we had Jake there for ten weeks. After they were completed, Bob looked at him and Jake said, 'Yeah, I know, goodbye.' Bob said, 'That's right.' The dramatic scenes bear little relation to what actually happened. Mardik Martin's original script had various versions of the truth, rather like *Rashomon*, from which Bob and I extracted what was the essence of these characters, what made them interesting to us.[5] Jake wasn't around for the filming of those scenes.

I always find the antagonist more interesting than the protagonist in drama, the villain more interesting than the good guy. Then there's what I guess is a decidedly Christian point of view: 'who are we to judge, to point out the speck in our brother's eye, while we have a beam in our own eye?' Jake La Motta acted much tougher in real life than he appeared in the film. The script originally showed much worse things about him, but I felt it was impossible to show them – you could over twenty years, but in the space of two hours there is a risk of forcing them out of context. Nevertheless, I find these characters fascinating. Obviously, I find elements of myself in them and I hope people in the audience do too, and can maybe learn from them and find some sort of peace.

Force of Evil was a great influence on me, because of the relationship between the brothers, showing what happened in the course of betrayal, and that strange dialogue written in verse.[6] I showed Bob *Body and Soul* on 16 mm during our preparation for *Raging Bull*, then he looked at *Force of Evil* and said that he found it more interesting. The numbers racket, which is the basis of the story, was going on around us all the time and here was a film which dealt with it honestly and openly and had a crooked lawyer with whom we could identify.

Kiss of Death I found fascinating for the wonderful look of the film – Twentieth Century-Fox under the Italian Neo-Realist influence – and, of course, Richard Widmark being so hysterical and totally uncontrolled.[7] But it was told from the 'law side', with Victor Mature becoming an informer – well, where I grew up, the worst thing you could be was an informer, so I couldn't really sympathize with that character. The tough guys downtown really liked Cagney in *The Public Enemy* and *White Heat*. Certainly, I loved *White Heat*, although I don't particularly care for the Edmund O'Brien character.[8]

There were a number of boxing movies coming out at that time: *Rocky II*, which was a blockbuster movie in bright colours, strong reds and blues; *The Main Event*, *The Champ* and even one about a boxing

38 De Niro with Jake La Motta on the set of *Raging Bull* (1978).
39 The brothers in Abraham Polonsky's *Force of Evil* (1948).

kangaroo called Matilda!⁹ All naturally in colour. But the one use of colour in a fight sequence that had really impressed me was the flashback in John Ford's *The Quiet Man*, when Wayne looks down and realizes he's killed his opponent, and I'll never forget the vibrance of his emerald green trunks.

During preparations for *Raging Bull*, we shot some 8 mm while Bobby was training in a gym and I remember we were looking at this, projected on the back of a door in my apartment on 57th Street, and Michael Powell was sitting on the floor watching it with us. Suddenly Michael said, 'There's something wrong: the gloves shouldn't be red.' Back in 1975, he'd written to me after first seeing *Mean Streets* to say that he liked it, but I used too much red – this from the man who had red all over his own films, which was where I'd got it from in the first place! But he was right about the boxing footage, and our cinematographer Michael Chapman also pointed out how colour was detracting from the images. A man named Gene Kirkwood, who worked with Chartoff–Winkler at the time and was associate producer on *Rocky*, used to walk into our offices and he talked about how much *The Sweet Smell of Success* and *Night and the City*, both in black and white, had to do with *Mean Streets*.¹⁰ We said, no, it's too pretentious to use black and white now. But then it clicked in my mind that colour wasn't going to last anyway – the film stock was subject to rapid fading.

There were so many boxing pictures being made in the seventies that I dreaded that moment in the future when I wouldn't be able to sleep and the only thing on TV would be the poorest of them and nothing else, and I'd be forced to look at it! A real nightmare. I was never a fight fan. I saw two fights at Madison Square Gardens for research and the first image I drew was the bloody sponge. Then the second time I went, I was in the fifth row from the front, and I saw the blood coming off the rope. As the next bout was announced, no one took any notice of it. In *Raging Bull*, the camera almost always stays in the ring with Jake. When I'd seen boxing matches between double features on Saturday afternoons as a kid, it was always from the same angle, and that's why I became so bored. The only person who had the right attitude about boxing in the movies for me was Buster Keaton.¹¹

I felt that Jake used everybody to punish himself, especially in the ring. When he fights 'Sugar' Ray Robinson, why does he really take that beating for fifteen rounds? Jake himself said that he was playing possum. Well, that may be Jake in reality, but Jake on the screen is something else. He takes the punishment for what he feels he's done wrong. And when he's

40 'Jake takes the punishment for what he feels he's done wrong.'

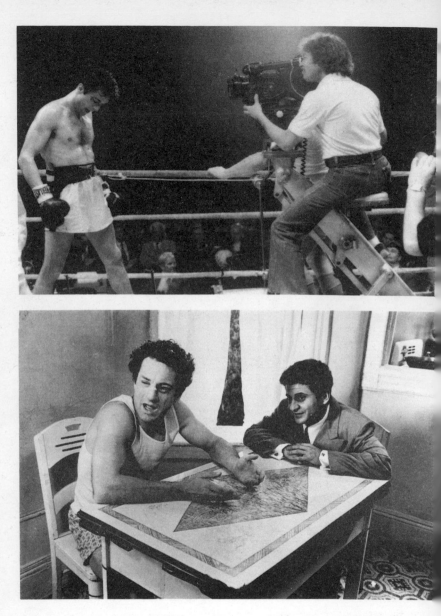

41 'In *Raging Bull* the camera stays in the ring with Jake.'
42 Robert De Niro and Joe Pesci in *Raging Bull*.

thrown in jail, he's just faced with a wall, and so with the real enemy for the first time – himself. Jonathan Demme gave me a portrait of Jake made by a folk artist and around the edge of this piece of slate was carved, 'Jake fought like he didn't deserve to live.' Exactly. I made a whole movie and this guy did it in one picture!

The sound on *Raging Bull* was particularly difficult because each punch, each camera click and each flashbulb was different. The sound-effects were done by Frank Warner, who had worked on *Close Encounters of the Third Kind* and *Taxi Driver*. He used rifle shots and melons breaking, but he wouldn't tell us what many of the effects were; he became very possessive and even burnt them afterwards so nobody else could use them. The fight scenes were done in Dolby stereo, but the dialogue was recorded normally, and that caused us something of a problem. We anticipated about eight weeks of mixing and I think it took sixteen weeks. It was murder, mainly because each time we had a fight scene, it had to have a different aura.

One of the best things we did, though, was to drop the sound out completely at certain moments. Silence, then suddenly the punch goes flying – whack! It became like scoring music and that took the extra period of time. For the actual music heard in the film, I was able to use the songs that I grew up with and draw on my own collection of 78s. Each scene is set at a certain date and there's not a song in the background of the film that wouldn't have been played on the radio at that time. In the mix, I could also slip lyrics that I liked in between dialogue.

Bob is a very generous actor and he will be even stronger when the other guy's in close-up. Often I steal lines from the speeches we film over his shoulder, because some of them are so good. And he really gets other actors to act in his scenes. For example, when Jake asks Joey, 'Did you fuck my wife?' I had written a seven-page scene, the only full-length dialogue scene in the film. When he asks the question, you see Joey asking him back, 'What, how could you say that?' I told Bob I wasn't getting enough reaction from Joe Pesci. He told me to roll the camera again, and then said, 'Did you fuck your mother?' When you see the film again, look at Joe's reaction! I like that kind of help. You have to throw your ego out of the door: you can't take it into the rehearsal room and you can't take it on the set.

Bob and I would work together in our own way. One morning we would rehearse, then the rest of the day would be spent looking at clothes. Or else I'd be checking out locations and he'd rest, or be writing a scene. De Niro's not really a student of any particular method of acting. He took what he liked best from different teachers, from Stella Adler to Lee Strasberg and others. Actors scare you by going off into a corner to get into a scene and then beginning to scream. But I don't see Bob doing those kinds of things, except of course in a physically demanding role like Jake La Motta. In the fight scenes we would have a punch bag in the middle of the ring. Off-camera you would hear him punching at this thing, then he'd come flying into the frame, all sweated up and ready to kill. When I acted in *Round Midnight*, I found it a humiliating experience, but it has to be done to understand what the actor goes through. Even though I have a good time with it, I find it humiliating because I don't like the way I look or sound. Even though people might appreciate the performance, I still find it personally disturbing.

Raging Bull took a long time because Bobby wanted to put on all that weight.[12] We had to shut down and pay the entire crew for about four months while he ate his way around Northern Italy and France. He said it was hard to get up in the morning and force yourself to have breakfast, then lunch, then dinner. After a while it became really uncomfortable for him. In the meantime Thelma Schoonmaker and I cut the whole film except, of course, for the fat scenes. We had to shoot those around Christmas 1979.

It had taken a lot out of me emotionally. I decided to go on tour with the film around the whole world. At the same time, we decided to take on the film preservation programme about fading colour. I would do two nights on the film, and one on film preservation with Thelma. Bob and Harvey Keitel came along too, even though Harvey wasn't in the film. And we wound up really overdoing it again. We were exhausted and I ended up catching pneumonia in Rome, which kept me in bed for six or seven weeks.

Raging Bull *was dedicated to Haig Manoogian, who died before its completion, 'with love and resolution'. It opened the Berlin Film Festival in February 1981 and won Oscars for De Niro as Best Actor and Thelma Schoonmaker for Best Editing. Before its release the previous year, Scorsese issued a declaration on 5 April that 'Everything we are doing now means nothing!' So long as the colour film stock used in virtually all film-making since the eclipse of three-strip Technicolor around 1950 remained so vulnerable to rapid fading, he felt that film-makers had no guarantee their work would last. He now toured festivals and cinémathèques, following the theatrical opening of* Raging Bull, *using the occasion to give an illustrated lecture on the problem of colour fading.*

43 De Niro after putting on weight for 'the fat scenes' in *Raging Bull*.

44 Scorsese lecturing on colour film fading at Filmex, Los Angeles, 1981.

Eastman Kodak, the main suppliers of film stock both in America and world-wide, have since made available at no extra cost a stock considerably less prone to fading – while, ironically, certain forties three-strip Technicolor productions, like those of Powell and Pressburger and Ford, have proved more restorable than films made later on Eastman Color.

During the shooting of Raging Bull, *Scorsese had married Isabella Rossellini, the daughter of Roberto Rossellini and Ingrid Bergman, on 30 September 1979. He also made a brief appearance as a TV director in the Italian comedy* Il Pap'occhio *(English title,* In the Eye of the Pope, *1981), a parody of John Paul II in which Pope Woytila sets up a Vatican television station. A comedy vehicle for Roberto Benigni which also starred Isabella Rossellini, its release led to a court battle over alleged 'offence to the state religion'.*

We decided to do *The King of Comedy* and there was an imminent directors' strike looming. If you didn't start shooting by a certain date and have four weeks of important scenes – not just a character crossing the street – in the can, then the film would be stopped while you were shooting. On this film we had a first-time producer, Arnon Milchan, who was really a terrific guy, but he insisted that we had to start shooting on 1 June. This was four weeks before we had planned and I told him we wouldn't be ready. He replied that we were going to have to start. I looked at Bob and said, 'Do you think we can do it?' He said 'Yes', but physically I didn't feel ready. I shouldn't have done it and it soon became clear that I wasn't up to it. By the second week of shooting I was begging them not to let me go on. I was coughing on the floor and sounding like a character from *The Magic Mountain!*[13]

Finally it got so bad that some days I wouldn't get there until 2.30 in the afternoon. One day we managed to shoot the whole scene in Sardi's between 2.30 and 7 p.m. Then the whole picture slowed down – and this was the big time now. We were shooting in New York and there were maybe five trailers, which you had to park in a certain way because the teamsters wanted this and the police wanted that. Finally, if you wanted to move, the entire company had to go along like a caravan through the city streets in the daytime.

We didn't get one break from anybody there, or at least that's how it felt. If we wanted something, we had to pay for it and pay a lot. It was like making a film with a dinosaur: the tail was so big it was wagging and slamming into everything, perhaps not intentionally, but destroying things as in a *Godzilla* movie. Both Bob and I were tired and we just had to wait all the time.

By this stage we were shooting every day from 4 to 7 p.m., for three intensive hours. The whole film took twenty weeks to shoot. The director always sets the pace and maybe a faster cameraman would have got me moving. But I didn't do it, so what went wrong is really all my responsibility. But I don't feel anything went wrong in front of the camera. I always felt that between 'Action' and 'Cut', I was there enjoying it and we had a great time. Rehearsals were good, Jerry Lewis was great and everybody else was terrific. But it was a very strange movie. The scene when Rupert Pupkin turns up uninvited at Jerry's house was extremely difficult for everyone. It took two weeks and it was just so painful because the scene itself was so excruciating.

Scorsese later commented that although The King of Comedy *was very funny, it was not a comedy. Certainly the embarrassment generated by Rupert Pupkin, the crazed mediocrity with delusions of talent, determined to become a star even if he has to kidnap a real one, was very different from the fear and/or sympathy associated with previous Scorsese–De Niro anti-heroes. Scorsese's shooting style, too, was disconcertingly plain after the striking experimentation of earlier films.*

People had reacted in such a way to *Raging Bull*, saying it was a beautiful film – like *Days of Heaven*, you could take every frame and put it on the wall – that I decided my next picture was going to be 1903 style, more like Edwin S. Porter's *The Life of an American Fireman*, with no close-ups. So in *The King of Comedy* that's what I tried to do.

When it was shown on the first night at the Cannes Festival, I went backstage with Sergio Leone and he looked at me and said, 'Martin, that's your most mature film.' I don't know if it was his way of saying he didn't like it. I guess that comes to mind because over the years my friends and I have had a running joke about slow movies, where the camera doesn't move, as being 'mature'. I read in the *Village Voice* that Jim Jarmusch, who made *Stranger Than Paradise* and *Down by Law* said something like, 'I'm not interested in taking people by the hair and telling them where to look.' Well, I *do* want them to see the way I see. Walking down the street, looking quickly about, tracking, panning, zooming, cutting and all that sort of thing. I like it when two images go together and they move. I guess it may not be considered 'mature', but I enjoy it.

Paul Zimmerman had written the script about fourteen years before

45 Pupkin gate-crashes Jerry's house in *The King of Comedy* (1983).
46 Sandra Bernhardt tries to seduce Jerry in *The King of Comedy*.

with, I believe, Dick Cavett in mind for the part of the chat-show host. Of course, we really wanted Johnny Carson, but a lot of people felt that Carson wasn't right because the phenomenon of his talk show wasn't that well known outside America. Besides, Johnny wouldn't do it. He said, 'Listen, you know one take's enough for me.' I said it would be one or two takes at the most, but he knew what filming would be like. So I thought, 'My God, Sinatra would be the best.' And if we went that way towards the Vegas crowd, there was Joey Bishop, Sammy Davis Jr, that whole *Ocean's Eleven* group – I just love that crowd and their clothes![14] We even considered Orson Welles, but he wasn't 'show business' enough. Then I thought – well, Dean Martin and then, of course, Jerry Lewis.

Now Lewis is not only a stand-up comic and a director, but also a philanthropist, because of his incredible telethon for cerebral palsy, which with its combination of money pouring in for charity and its Vegas sensibility, seems at times to verge on nervous breakdown. Also the thin line between reality and drama seems to be shattered constantly during this telethon. Anyone who could conjure up and sustain this atmosphere is quite extraordinary. I'd never met Jerry, but he turned out to be terrific to work with. I was just recovering from pneumonia and I found it difficult to deal with the usual problems that constantly arise on a set. He said, 'I know I'm Number Two in this picture. I won't give you any difficulty and I'll do what you want. I'm a consummate professional. I know where I stand. If you want me to wait around, you're paying for my time, I'll do that.' Feeling the way I did then, it was very liberating to hear that. He was very funny between takes and when he started cracking jokes I'd get asthma attacks from laughing. It got to the point of being maniacal, you had to shake him to stop it! But he also really got into the dramatic stuff. In the scene where he's talking to Bobby, and says, 'I'm just a human being, with all of the foibles and all of the traps, the show, the pressure, the groupies, the autograph hounds, the crew, the incompetents' – that was improvised by him. I think he's a wonderful actor.

The King of Comedy had very little improvisation, just wall-to-wall dialogue, which is not surprising since the screenwriter, Paul Zimmerman, speaks even faster than me! We couldn't fit the music in, and though Robbie Robertson put together a terrific soundtrack you can't hear it in the film because it would have drowned out the dialogue. What improvisation there was came mainly from Sandra Bernhard in the sequence in which she tries to seduce Jerry. Sandra is a stand-up comedienne and I used a lot of her stage performance in that scene. The sexual threat to Jerry was very important, but he used to crack up laughing. Then it became

47 De Niro as Rupert Pupkin on television in *The King of Comedy*.

difficult to deal with, and his comments and jokes became edgier, throwing Sandra off for a little while. Finally he worked it all out and helped her with the scene.

People in America were confused by *The King of Comedy* and saw Bob as some kind of mannequin. But I felt it was De Niro's best performance ever. *The King of Comedy* was right on the edge for us; we couldn't go any further at that time.

Notes

1 The cost overrun on Michael Cimino's super-western *Heaven's Gate*, which took the eventual budget up to $36 million from an intended $12 million and created an epic film of 219 minutes' length, has been credited with crippling United Artists as a production entity and marking a watershed in director–studio relations. After the disaster of its first release in a shortened version of 148 minutes, *Heaven's Gate* was reissued in 1983 in a 'complete' version, which also inaugurated a trend that would later benefit *New York, New York*.

2 Traditional American editing syntax requires a 'master shot', showing the general layout of a scene's space, either at the beginning of the scene or soon after an introductory closer shot. Economy, plus an earlier sense of 'modern' style, had led Scorsese to shoot entirely in masters – which got him fired from *The Honeymoon Killers*. Now he had swung to the other extreme, making more use of the moving camera and substituting 'rhythmic' for strictly narrative editing.

3 The Band, consisting of Robbie Robertson (whose association with Scorsese would continue), Rick Danko, Richard Manuel, Garth Hudson and Levon Helm, formed around 1960 in Canada, first as Ronnie Hawkins's backing group The Hawks, then as Levon and the Hawks (all were Canadian apart from Helm) and, most famously, toured internationally in the mid-sixties as Bob Dylan's occasional backing group. Their own recording and performing career continued in parallel, increasingly under the leadership of Robertson, who wrote the majority of their original songs and nourished movie ambitions.

4 The only commercial film directed by Dylan to date (released in 1977 in two versions, of 235 and 112 minutes respectively) ostensibly chronicles his 'Rolling Thunder' Tour of 1975–6, which was intended to publicize the plight of the Tuscarora Indians and the jailed boxer 'Hurricane' Carter. However, it dwells most on the mythology of being 'on the road' and the aura of mystery cultivated by Dylan himself. His then wife Sara, Joan Baez, Ronnie Hawkins and many others also appear, but The Band do not.

5 In Kurosawa's *Rashomon*, which became world-famous after winning the Golden Lion at Venice in 1951, four different accounts of the same incident are given by different protagonist–observers, each according to their own interests.

6 *Force of Evil* (1948) was screenwriter Abraham Polonsky's first film as a director (he had written the boxing movie *Body and Soul* for Robert Rossen the year before), but he soon fell foul of the McCarthy witch hunt, was blacklisted and did not work again in Hollywood under his own name until 1968, when he wrote *Madigan* for Don Siegel. In 1970 he directed *Tell Them Willie Boy is Here*. *Force of Evil*, now widely regarded as one of the greatest post-war American films, deals with the web of corruption surrounding the numbers racket and has stylized dialogue which dispenses with punctuation and plays upon repetition.

7 *Kiss of Death* (Henry Hathaway, 1947) was one of the late-forties wave of crime films, based on actual cases and filmed on location, of which the most famous was probably the same director's *Call Northside 777* (1948). Richard Widmark made his screen début in *Kiss of Death* with a memorable performance as a giggling psychopath, while Victor Mature played the informer Nick Bianco. Psychoanalytic perspectives on the criminal personality were another influence, alongside the gritty authenticity of Italian 'Neo-Realist' films, on the post-war American crime movie.

8 William Wellman's *The Public Enemy* (1931) launched Cagney as a star and linked him permanently with the new tough gangster genre: it contains the famous scene in which he smashes a grapefruit into Mae Clarke's face. *White Heat*, directed by Raoul Walsh in 1949, marked the explosive climax of the Warners' gangster cycle, with Cagney as the mentally ill Cody Jarrett. Edmond O'Brien plays the undercover agent Hank Fallon who has infiltrated Cody's gang as 'Vic Pardo', pretending to be his friend.

9 *Rocky II* (1979), written and directed by its star, Sylvester Stallone, followed the immense success of *Rocky* in 1976. *The Main Event* (1979) was a Barbra Streisand vehicle, co-starring Ryan O'Neal, directed by Howard Zieff. *The Champ* (1979) was a lachrymose remake of King Vidor's sentimental 1931 *The Champ*, with Jon Voight in the title role.

10 *The Sweet Smell of Success* (1957) was the US début of Ealing comedy director Alexander Mackendrick, a brilliant anatomy of media corruption. *Night and the City* (1950) was made in Britain by Jules Dassin after he had been forced to leave Hollywood by a denunciation before the House UnAmerican Activities Committee.

11 Probably Scorsese is thinking of *Battling Butler* (1926), Keaton's seventh feature, in which he plays a spoilt young man who pretends to be a champion boxer to impress the girl of his dreams, and receives a brutal beating for his deception.

12 To appear convincing as the older, shockingly overweight La Motta, De Niro forsook the fakery of prosthetics and put on an additional 55 pounds himself.

13 Thomas Mann's novel is set in a tuberculosis sanatorium.

14 *Ocean's Eleven* (Lewis Milestone, 1960) provided the definitive screen image of Sinatra's hard-playing 'Rat Pack'.

CHAPTER 5

After Hours – The Color of Money

'I'm back.' 'Fast' Eddie Felson in *The Color of Money*

The King of Comedy ended up costing $20 million and was premièred at the Cannes Film Festival in 1983. Although a commercial failure – it appeared on British television at Christmas that same year, after a perfunctory cinema release – it attracted five BAFTA nominations and considerable critical speculation. Scorsese acknowledged in interviews that the characters of Rupert and Jerry were close to him: the ambitious outsider who will stop at nothing to achieve his goal, and the successful celebrity who is essentially lonely and vulnerable (his own marriage to Isabella Rossellini had ended).

His next project was to be The Last Temptation of Christ. *But there was time for a brief, exotic cameo appearance as the director of the Metropolitan Opera House in* Pavlova – A Woman for All Time, *an Anglo-Soviet co-production initiated by Michael Powell's then partner Frixos Constantine and originally intended to be directed by Powell. This would lead to a more substantial acting role in Tavernier's* Round Midnight *in 1984.*

The King of Comedy was going to be followed by *The Last Temptation of Christ.* I had read Kazantzakis's novel *The Last Temptation* some years before and it had been in my mind a long time to make that picture.[1] Paul Schrader had condensed the 600 pages of the novel into a 90-minute film, which Jay Cocks and I then rewrote, adding another twenty pages. In 1983, Paramount – which then consisted of Barry Diller, Michael Eisner (company president) and Jeff Katzenberg (head of productions) – decided to go ahead with the film.

From January that year we began nine months of casting and checking out locations in different countries, finally choosing Israel. Arnon Mil-chan, my producer on *The King of Comedy*, even got us the use of a military helicopter there. The producers were to be Bob Chartoff and Irwin Winkler from *New York, New York* and *Raging Bull*. But already this had the aura about it of becoming a film which was going to go out of control in terms of money – and not in New York, or Los Angeles, but in the Middle East!

All the executives at Paramount felt that the furthest away from Hollywood you could make a film was San Francisco, because it's only an hour by plane. Look at *Star Trek IV: The Voyage Home*, where the story conveniently lands the film in San Francisco! Paramount's policy at the time was to be wary of 'name' directors going way over budget and shooting outside of Hollywood, basically because they were all extremely frightened by the *Heaven's Gate* affair.

After all, Paramount had spent very little on *Flashdance*, which was a big hit, and had kept control because it was shot in Los Angeles. If something went wrong, they could go right on to the set and stop the production or fire the director. As Katzenberg told me, 'I have a picture right here on the lot that's a week over schedule. If anything goes wrong on yours, if there's a war, we'll have to fly over there to get you people out.' To which I said, 'We've got to shoot in Israel.' It went on and on like this until the budget of the film was about $12 million and the schedule was ninety days.

It wasn't going to be a big spectacular or a real epic. It was to be a film about people. But to get to certain locations would take a day and then everything would have to be set up and shot. At that time I was totally convinced that any film I made in future would take at least twenty weeks to shoot (about ninety working days) and require a budget of at least $15–16 million. At this rate, it wasn't going to be a film a year any more but one every three years, and that film would have to make a lot of money. Not just a measly $40 million, but $150 million. Take *Aliens*, for example: this was going to be the big 'hot' picture of the summer in America, but after five weeks Hollywood was glum. They reckoned it was only going to make $80 million! A movie has to make the profit of a *Beverly Hills Cop* or a *Crocodile Dundee* to be a true success – that is $150 or $180 million.

So in September, the ninth month of our preparation, Irwin Winkler said that we would need another ten days' shooting and a further $2 million. I think that was the final blow, together with the campaign being mounted by the Moral Majority. The religious fundamentalists in America were sending letters to Gulf and Western (who own Paramount), protesting that this was a defiling movie, a disgrace to Christians and believers – even that it depicted Christ as a homosexual. Of course, they had never read the book, since it's against what they believe, so how could they tell? But it was a Catch-22 situation. Then they started telephone campaigns, going directly to the head of Gulf and Western, Martin Davis, so that he would call up Barry Diller and ask him what kind of film he was making. We'd have symposia, with Protestants, Catholics and Jews getting together to discuss God and the whole situation in Hollywood! It was really hysterical.

Every other week, Michael Eisner would call me up and say, 'There's a green light on this picture; it's a "go" picture and Jeff Katzenberg is really behind it.' Two weeks later, Jeff Katzenberg called to say, 'Michael Eisner's fighting for you to make this picture.' I wondered why they were trying to convince me that they wanted to make the film. Wasn't it already decided that it was to be made? So, when we went in to ask for another $2 million, and another ten days, Irwin was told that *The Last Temptation of Christ* had gone from a flashing yellow light to a flashing red, which meant we were now in a stop category. And I thought it was still green! A week later *The Right Stuff*, which Irwin had produced, opened and it took a dive at the box-office: nobody went to see it. Then, my film was cancelled four days before shooting was supposed to begin.

About a month earlier Brian De Palma had done an interview in which he'd said, 'Look at Scorsese, he can't get a film made in Hollywood.' I was offended by that. On the evening of that Thanksgiving morning when Barry Diller told me the film was cancelled, I went to have dinner at Brian's house, and as I walked in he asked me, 'Are you in turnaround already?' What he meant was: had the studio dropped the project? But he'd meant it as a joke. He explained that this was the way at Paramount then, taking you along and then saying they didn't want to make it. The joke was ironic, but I didn't let him know that just that very morning we had been put into turnaround.

By this stage we had the cast, the sets had been built and the costumes made (I discovered in 1987 that the shoes were eventually used in *King David*). So we spent the next four weeks trying to get the project off the ground in Hollywood by every possible means. We would even stop people in the street to try and get the picture made. Every day I had one flight booked to Tel Aviv and one to New York while I stayed in Los Angeles. Aidan Quinn had starved himself to play Christ and Harvey Keitel had dyed his hair red for Judas.

Eventually we brought it back to Paramount at half the cost and on half the shooting schedule, by which time I had another producer, Jon Avnet, who'd produced *Risky Business*. But just two days before Christmas Barry Diller finally said, 'We just don't want to make it. It's not worth the trouble.' He apologized, saying he should have told us this before. At this point, instead of acting out my rage, I went inside, tried to take care of myself and figure out what to do.

The answer was to make a film – any film we could get our hands on – and immediately. I had a good relationship with Katzenberg and Eisner at Paramount and they offered me some scripts straight away. They would look at me and say, '*Beverly Hills Cop*, do you want to do that? It's for Sylvester Stallone.' I asked what it was about and they replied, 'It's a fish out of water.' 'What's a fish out of water?' 'You know, a cop from somewhere else comes to New York.' I replied, 'That's the Don Siegel picture *Coogan's Bluff*.' And they'd say, 'No, no, it's *Beverly Hills Cop*.' We had the same conversation over *Witness*, but I said I couldn't do it – I don't know anything about Amish people and I just couldn't see myself out in Pennsylvania among them. But my agent, Harry Ufland, said this was all that was around.

I got back to New York, where my lawyer at the time, Jay Julien – he plays the lawyer in *The King of Comedy* who's suing everybody – gave me the script of *After Hours*. It was by Joe Minion, who'd written it in his class at Columbia University. The teacher there was Dusan Makavejev, and he'd given it an A! It wasn't really a script, more like a novel. I started reading it and really liked the first two or three pages. I liked the dialogue and almost everything up to the ice-cream truck character.

It was owned by Amy Robinson, who had acted in *Mean Streets*, and Griffin Dunne, a young actor whom I'd only seen in a small part in *An American Werewolf in London*. There he kept showing up in various states of decomposition, so I couldn't really tell very much about his acting – especially as they used a puppet for the last scenes. Amy and Griffin were joined by Robert Colesberry, who'd been my associate producer on *The King of Comedy*, and at that stage they had the backing of Fox Classics for what was going to be a very low budget, $3.5 million. I rewrote the script with them and Joe Minion, then we reinvented the end all over again after we had shot the picture.

Joe Minion's script, originally titled Lies, *then* A Night in SoHo, *followed the misfortunes of Paul, a young computer operator, who accepts an invitation from an attractive woman he's met in a diner, to visit her apartment in the artists' loft district that night. Everything and everyone*

48 Griffin Dunne and Rosanna Arquette in *After Hours* (1985).

he meets seems to be conspiring to prevent him from getting home, or even
staying alive. By taking the independent route – Robinson and Dunne
financed the film with a bank loan predicated upon a studio pick-up –
Scorsese was freed from interference by a major company.

So instead of doing a Hollywood picture I did an independent film, just as
I had done ten years before when I was thirty-two, shooting *Taxi Driver* in
forty days – a very hard shoot too, moving the camera and taking our
chance with tons of rain – and cutting it in about four months. Could I do
it again and make a film in forty days? Of course, this wasn't like the script
of *Taxi Driver*, which was territory I didn't want to revisit. But I geared
myself up to get back into shape.

The producers introduced me to a new cameraman, Michael Ballhaus,
who had done many of Fassbinder's pictures. Michael is a gentleman. He
smiles on the set, he is very pleasant and he's Max Ophuls's nephew.[2] He
also moves quickly. This was a script with one character on the street at
night, a simple production, and with the new high-speed film and lenses
you didn't have to worry too much about lighting. In fact, for some scenes
we had to take the street lights down because it was so bright.

I had laid out all the shots in advance on paper, with little drawings on
the margins of the script. But it worked out at about 500 shots, which was
impossible. The way I had been shooting before this, we managed to do
five set-ups a day and this script required an average of sixteen a day! But
Michael thought he could do it. He had his own crew, he was his own
operator and we worked through the smaller NABET Union in New
York, instead of the IA, because it was an independent film. Usually in the
NABET you have younger people, and they're all film enthusiasts, which
makes it interesting. On the first day of shooting I realized happily that I
had no time to sit down or wait in my trailer. If I was sitting down, there
was something wrong! It was like a rebirth by the end of that film.

When you are on the set the one thing you can be sure of is that you
never have enough time, and that everything which can go wrong will go
wrong. So you have to have a blueprint, and the drawings I do are that
plan. Certain actors are hard to fit into your kind of camera movement
and I often tell them, 'If you find yourself walking backwards and it's hard
to do, please tell me.' I said to Griffin Dunne, 'There are a lot of crazy shots
here. You have to answer the phone with your left hand and talk this way.
Please, if you can't do it, if you feel uncomfortable, just tell me.' He said it
was all fine, but other guys would say, 'No, I can't do it,' and you'd have to
accommodate the situation. Without those little drawings and without

working out that cutting pattern beforehand, anything could happen on the set and I would be dead.

I signed to do the film on the understanding that we would come up with a good ending. The idea was to shoot the picture, put it together and then we'd realize how to go beyond that – I understood why Woody Allen and Brian De Palma often reshoot at least two weeks after the completion of editing. The original ending in the script had Paul going out to buy an ice cream for June down in the basement, and that was it. I felt something was missing there and we needed an ending that had magic. So Minion came up with June in the basement suddenly growing in size while people were banging on the door shouting, 'We'll kill him, we'll go get him.'

We weren't going to use trick photography, you'd just see Paul and then you'd cut so you'd be looking up between her knees on each side of the frame with this little figure between them. She'd say a line like, 'You know what to do now,' and he'd say, 'Well, I've never really had much experience before in returning to the womb.' She would reply, 'It's really all right if you have a waterproof watch on; just take it off if you don't,' and then he'd go inside her. He just disappears off the bottom of the frame – you don't see any *Tin Drum* stuff – and then you cut to him born naked, curled up on the cobblestones in the middle of 57th Street.[3] The camera's looking down on him; he gets up and then runs like hell home.

After Hours wound up being financed by the Geffen Company, and when David Geffen read this ending, he said, 'Marty, come on!' I protested that it was like *2001: A Space Odyssey*, and like this and that, but had to admit that we'd been racking our brains and still didn't know what else to do. Now the rest of the film had situations in it that were possible – in that order, highly improbable – but all possible, and I directed each one realistically so the bottom line was always that it *could* happen. This ending was a surrealistic way of getting out of the problem, but David felt we had to find a natural solution that flowed from the style of the rest of the picture.

After a screening which Michael Powell and my father attended, they both got very angry that I had just ended the film with Paul being driven off by Cheech and Chong. Michael said, 'That's outrageous, you can't do it, we want to know what happens to him.' Then he said something about Paul falling out of the truck and winding up back at work and he mentioned Kafka. I said that I'd never read Kafka and didn't know anything about that. Then Thelma, Amy Robinson and all of us came up with different ideas. I remember showing the film to Terry Gilliam in

London, then to Steven Spielberg in Los Angeles and everybody agreed on one thing – that he should fall out of the truck!

So we had to go back and shoot him falling out of the truck, but there were still different ideas about where he should fall out. Through a process of elimination we found ourselves with him winding up back at work. So we ended up with what Michael had originally suggested. The Geffen Company gave us the money to go ahead and shoot the extra four days. The final cost was $4.5 million, including a quarter of my normal salary. When I subsequently went to Hollywood to promote my next film I found, to my surprise, some people resented that we had made it for so little.

After Hours is to some extent a parody of Hitchcock's style. Over the years his films have become more emotionally meaningful for me. By the time I realized he was moving the camera, it was over and I had felt the effect of the movement emotionally and intellectually. So if you take the scene in *After Hours* when Paul is running with the invitation in his hand – there's a shot of a hand with the ground below – basically this refers back to the moment in *Marnie* where she's holding the gun and going to shoot the horse. When I first saw *Marnie*, that shot remained in my mind and I kept going back to watch the whole two hours just to see it again. I loved the feeling of it, and then I realized it was also Bernard Herrmann's music, the story and the acting – all these came together over the years and the combination was overwhelming.

As soon as I'd finished *After Hours*, in order to test myself further I directed an episode of 'Amazing Stories' for Steven Spielberg called *Mirror, Mirror*. This was a 24-minute television film, with a six-day shoot and hardly any control at all, at least no final cut. On network television there's no such thing as the right of final cut, unless you are Spielberg. After a certain number of films I had got final cut, though it doesn't really mean that much because they do everything to try and change your mind. They call up your mother, saying 'Maybe you could talk to him a little, tell him to cut that scene, will you?' Then they call your wife. Strange stuff. You really have to be Odysseus tied to the boat! Anyway, *Mirror, Mirror* was in the first season of 'Amazing Stories', which turned out to be a major disappointment for the networks.

To do a story about a man having a nervous breakdown in a house, with very little dialogue but a lot of atmosphere, this was testing the water for me. I'd like horror to be taken more seriously. I recently looked again at the Val Lewton films when they came out on video, including *Isle of the Dead*.[4] I remember I saw it by myself when I was about eleven, and I ran

49 The memorable image of Tippi Hedren shooting her horse in *Marnie*
(1964).

out of the theatre before the finish because it scared me to death! I gave Griffin Dunne a tape of it, and he couldn't watch all of it, for the same reason! I also like Mario Bava's films very much: hardly any story, just atmosphere, with all that fog and ladies walking down corridors – a kind of Italian Gothic. I could just put them on loops and have one going in one room in my house, one going on in another, as I have many televisions around. I do that sometimes, put different tapes on and just walk around, creating a whole mood, a whole atmosphere that way. Bava seems to me nineteenth century, whereas David Cronenberg is definitely twentieth century – late twentieth century! He's like something we have no control over: the imminent destruction of ourselves. I sometimes hardly want to see his films when they come out, but then I get there and it's a cathartic experience. As *Mirror, Mirror* was my first excursion into horror, I used the composer Michael Kamen because I'd liked his lush and romantic music for Cronenberg's *The Dead Zone*.

Mirror, Mirror *opens with a clip from the Hammer production* Plague of the Zombies, *by way of tribute to the Gothic strain of British cinema he especially loves.*

When I went along to the cinema as a teenager with groups of friends, if we saw the logo of Hammer Films we knew it would be a very special picture. I'll never forget going to a midnight screening at the New York Paramount of *The Curse of Frankenstein* in 1957, the day before it opened. The audience loved it, and there was a graphic quality to it that was totally uncalled for and was extremely endearing to us at about the age of fifteen. The next year we saw *Dracula*, which we felt really went further. There's nothing like the introduction of Dracula in that picture, in which Christopher Lee just walked down the stairs, sort of bounced down, and said, 'Hello, I'm Dracula.' Having been reared on Bela Lugosi, with whom you knew you were in trouble, Lee seemed like a very sensible, sophisticated gentleman. So that later on, when one of his 'brides' tries to suck Jonathan Harker's blood and Dracula turns up, eyes bloodshot, in an extreme close-up, it was absolutely terrifying. But he was a very likeable Dracula – we enjoyed his company, we could imagine socializing with him. We also liked Peter Cushing a great deal as Van Helsing, because he had such insight, and he was very precise in his movements within the frame.

On one level these films, with their use of colour, were very lurid, and they were as much a breakthrough as William Friedkin's *The Exorcist*. On another, since Christopher Lee seemed someone you could see in the street, it made the subject more immediate and meaningful to us, making clearer their sub-text of psychological horror and sexuality. In *Frankenstein Created Woman*, I was very surprised to find a discussion, as it seemed to me then in the late sixties, on metaphysics, with the Baron separating the soul and putting it into a little chamber. And then they had the audacity to photograph it, showing what I think was a little blue ball to be the 'soul'. It seemed to me they were striving for something more than a splatter film. They set a mood, with absolutely striking photography, and you were drawn right into it. You knew it wasn't fake.

After Hours brought Scorsese the Best Director prize at Cannes and, although its commercial success was modest, his career now seemed revived. On 8 February 1985 he married Barbara De Fina, who had previously worked in low-budget production and would now become his producer. The consistently high reputation he enjoyed in Europe also led to his most important acting part to date: as Goodley, the manager of Birdland, in Bertrand Tavernier's nostalgic tribute to the great jazzmen of the be-bop era, Round Midnight.

My part in *Round Midnight* came out of bringing Bertrand Tavernier together with Irwin Winkler. I was with Irwin in Paris in January 1983, scouting locations for *The Last Temptation of Christ*, and when it came to lunch I called Bertrand because he knows the best places. Bertrand said that Irwin was the best producer in Hollywood and that he'd like to meet him. Irwin thought Bertrand made good films. And out of that lunch came the film, which Bertrand asked me to be in because he said that when I open my mouth, it's New York. I would save him a lot of establishing shots! He told me, 'You have to play the owner of the club because he's just like you, he's a nice guy, but he's ruthless.' I said, 'Gee, thanks.' But I guess humour loses a lot in translation.

Various projects were announced for Scorsese, including Dick Tracy, *with Warren Beatty;* Winter's Tale, *a $15 million fantasy written by Tom Benedek;* Gershwin, *a Paul Schrader script in the stylized mode of his* Mishima; *and* Wise Guy, *a documentary-style book on the Mafia in New York by Nick Pileggi. But these were superseded by an invitation from Paul Newman to direct a sequel to* The Hustler, *the 1961 pool-room classic directed by Robert Rossen which had given Newman his most enduring image of tarnished heroism.*

50 Scorsese appearing in Bertrand Tavernier's *Round Midnight* (1986).
51 Paul Newman as 'Fast' Eddie twenty-five years on in *The Color of Money.*

Paul Newman had liked *Raging Bull* and wrote me a fan letter addressed to 'Michael Scorsese'! (I've had *The Deer Hunter* attributed to me a lot.) Right after shooting *After Hours*, Paul called me when I was in London and asked me if I was interested in doing *The Color of Money*, which was to be a kind of sequel to *The Hustler*, based on Walter Tevis's later novel, taking up the character of 'Fast' Eddie Felson twenty-five years on. I said I was interested.

He had a script he had been working on with a writer for about a year. I felt that this script wasn't right, and if I wasn't involved in the original idea of the script, then it wouldn't be something I could turn up early in the morning for. So we talked in New York, and he said, 'Let's give the writer just one more draft.' We did, but of course there was the same original intent in the script that I had disliked. I didn't feel the character of 'Fast' Eddie was strong enough, or dramatic enough. I felt it had to go in another direction. Then I had an idea of which way to go. I brought in a new scriptwriter, the novelist Richard Price, who wrote *The Wanderers* and *Bloodbrothers*, as my choice to develop the idea.[5]

Richard had written a script for me earlier that year based on the film *Night and the City*, which Bertrand Tavernier insisted I could do a great remake of. But really I don't want to do remakes. However, I liked Richard, and his script had very good street sense and wonderful dialogue. We visited Paul in California, for me to express my idea to Paul and to introduce him to Richard.

Our concept was that 'Fast' Eddie Felson was not the kind of fellow who, after losing out at the end of the first film, just folded up and did nothing for the next twenty-five years. He's a big hustler, and if Bert Gordon was tough and mean, the only way I know that 'Fast' Eddie could survive was if he was tougher, meaner and more corrupt than Bert.[6] It's a way to survive, becoming everything that he hated. And by the time he's realized that, he's too old to change – until he sees the young kid. He takes the kid under his wing and tries to corrupt him, to make him just like Eddie. But instead what happens is that they exchange roles. How that would happen I didn't know, since we didn't have a plot then. At least Eddie would have to play again, whether he liked it or not. It didn't matter whether he won or lost, but he would have to play.

Paul liked the idea. The next day we came up with an outline and started rewriting the script. Richard would write, bring it to me and we'd discuss it. Then we'd take it to Paul and include him in on our script conference, so it became like a rehearsal with him. As I kept telling Richard, 'We're making a three-piece suit for the man. He's the main character and the reason we're involved in this thing. He's got to look a certain way and the words have to come through his vocal cords.'

We had a pretty good experience, and by the end of nine months we decided to make the film. It took that long to decide whether or not we could work together, seeing how far we could push Paul to discover what he would do. Sometimes it didn't compute: he would push us another way and we'd say, 'I don't know what he means.' Then we'd come back with something else and eventually would reach an understanding. It worked this time. However, I've tried this other times with other people and decided not to work with them. I might have a good time with them personally, but if there's something I don't trust about them, then it's likely to turn into *The Exorcist* on the set – heads spinning and tongues flashing.

It was another challenge for me. For *After Hours* I had taken a cut in salary and the whole cost of the film was $4.5 million. On this picture I would have two major stars. True, we didn't know that Tom Cruise was going to be *that* major a star because we cast him before *Top Gun* came out. But Paul Newman gets a lot of money, and Tom would also get a lot of money based on the success of his film *Risky Business*. I'd seen him in the film Mike Chapman directed, *All the Right Moves*, and liked him. Altogether it was a lot of money, big stars and very complicated pool sequences. A lot of money had already been spent on another writer and paying the Walter Tevis estate, and Paul's previous film, *Harry and Son*, had not been a success. At first Fox had the project, but they disliked the script and didn't even want to make it with Paul and Tom, so eventually it was taken on by Katzenberg and Eisner, who were now at Touchstone.[7]

I felt I wanted to see if I could bring it in on budget and on time, and continue shooting quickly. If I could get Ballhaus, I knew I could do it again. So I got Ballhaus, and my wife, Barbara De Fina, along with Paul Newman's lawyer Irving Axelrad, produced it. We watched the pennies, even down to the phone bill! Imagine, you're going into the picture and you have Paul Newman and Tom Cruise. We all get trailers. Paul needs a phone, Tom needs a phone, so why can't I have a phone? I can't because it'll cost too much. OK, I can make calls from the set. So I started making calls from the set, putting my quarter in and using credit charge, and other people would come and throw me off. It became rather embarrassing. So eventually the teamsters asked if I'd like my own mobile phone. But we still paid for our individual phones and to save more money I'd have people call me back!

In a way it was an experiment for me, to see what it would be like to make a movie with someone like Paul Newman, and not to be a director who'd have five years between films. I wanted to continue to make many films regularly. In case we went over budget, Paul and I put up one third of our salaries each to help make the picture. And because of all the proper preparation, instead of fifty days' shooting, we finished in forty-nine; and instead of $14.5 million, we came in at $13 million. That's the stuff sainthood is made of in Hollywood.

A lot of it was due to Paul being the kind of actor who doesn't like to improvise that much on the set, so that everything was rehearsed beforehand. We did it the way he suggested, which was to take two complete weeks and just work out with the actors in a loft. I was really nervous, because it was like the theatre, which I'd never done before (except for that disastrous experience with Liza Minnelli). So when he said, 'What you do is take a tape and mark out an area for a chair; then you tape out an area for a bed,' I could foresee those terrible theatre things when people pretend a door is there, which I hate. I said, 'What if we use a real chair?' 'A chair is good,' he said, to my relief. So we used a chair, then we had a hospital bed brought in, and so on.

Rehearsals are always aggravating. You are afraid that you are going to say ridiculous things, and the actors feel that way too. We worked out improvisations and changes in the script. We eventually got Richard Price in there too and he worked out some of them with us. Then everyone felt pretty much secure in character, but more important, they were secure with each other, and with the fact that it was all right if they made a mistake. We didn't have all the problems solved, however. In particular, we didn't have the ending resolved and we knew that we'd written ourselves into a corner. We knew that you couldn't have one win over the other, you couldn't have the kid leaving, and you couldn't have Newman not playing him.

We were asked to shoot in Toronto, which is a wonderful city, but much too clean. You can see pool tables for miles, but as my wife, Barbara, immediately said, 'They're incredible, but they're snooker tables!' In order to film, we'd have had to take most of them out. So we shot in Chicago, where we had a very easy winter. Paul Newman did all his own pool playing, as did Tom Cruise. Tom knew how to play pool, but he had to learn the specific shots he played in the film, and the technical adviser Michael Segal taught him those. He played all his own shots except one – the slow motion one when he hits a ball which goes over two other balls. He could have done it, but it would have taken a further two days and I didn't want to spend the time. The important idea was to make

52 Tom Cruise in *The Color of Money*.

each shot fresh. I'd planned out all the pool shots well in advance on paper and we were very well prepared on this level.

Most of the film takes place in bars and pool rooms and when you go in these places there is always music playing on a jukebox. Everywhere we went we'd hear rock'n'roll, black music or swing. I wanted to reflect that the way I did in *Mean Streets*. I called Robbie Robertson to help me out with the music. He was making his first solo record, which was also his first album in ten years, and he was anxious to finish it. But he agreed to become involved, and he sent me a cassette with about fifteen different ideas, then six with about twenty musical ideas on each.

What you hear at the beginning of the film was one of these; we just called it 'Riff', and it was basically Robbie moaning and a drum machine, which we transferred to 35 mm film and dropped into the rough-cut. I liked the warmth of it and it's literally off an ⅛″ cassette piped through the stereo. I wanted Gil Evans to write this stuff up, but Robbie said, 'No, it's good this way,' and then Gil agreed – 'Play it raw, man.' So eventually Robbie gave us twenty minutes of music for the picture, mainly that opening piece and what we called 'The Blues Suite', which Gil Evans orchestrated, which ended up as six straight minutes of music for when Eddie goes back to playing in Chalkie's by himself.

Since *The Color of Money* was going to be a commercial movie, in America today you have to, if at all possible, make a tie-in album. However, Robbie's music was controlled by Geffen Records, and Jeff Katzenberg could not come to terms with David Geffen on this sound-track. I could never understand this, they're friends and they have dinner together, but during the day they negotiate fiercely. So we lost the chance to have Peter Gabriel, and we could only use Robbie without his voice – I was even told I would have to clear the moaning!

These days every damn movie in America, and I guess all around the world, is using recorded music like Jerry Lee Lewis, The Ronettes and all those people I grew up with as nostalgic soundtracks. So, to go a different way, I said, 'Why don't we shape the movie first, and then actually get the artists we like?' Touchstone made a deal with MCA, so that Robbie could talk to their artists like Don Henley and Eric Clapton. We told Eric Clapton that he could do an actual guitar solo for about one-and-a-half minutes where there was no dialogue, when Carmen walks down the aisle with all the guys looking at her before Eddie tells her to leave. So when the song begins exactly at the beginning of the scene, it's no accident. I remember I felt Eric's original lyric – 'He's getting ready to use you' – was a little too on the nose, so Robbie and he conferred on the phone and they came up with, 'It's in the way you use it', which is slightly to one side and much better. It felt like heaven because I was able to mix separate tracks as if I was playing the guitar myself!

Robert Palmer did a little song called 'My Baby's in Love with Another Guy', recorded by Little Willie John, who only made about five singles and no albums. His fifth record had not been a hit and this song, which we thought was just great, was the 'B' side. When the company finally found him in Brooklyn, his wife answered the phone and they said, 'This is Disney and we're going to give you $2,000 to use that song in a film.' She screamed, 'It's a miracle!' Then she woke up her husband to tell him.

A lot of my ideas for the pool scenes came from listening to music late at night, like the Phil Collins song 'One More Night'. I'd hear something on television at two in the morning and I'd write on these little Post-its you leave around the house different ideas of how to do these scenes. Over the years I've been very much influenced by music that way.

I was thinking of making *The Color of Money* in black and white, but the studio begged me not to do it and then I realized that I didn't want to make any allusions to *The Hustler*. Michael Ballhaus, myself and Boris Leven – it was his last film; he died the week it opened – designed the first two-thirds of the film in grey, black and white, like the winter in Chicago. Then we went to Atlantic City, where everything gets a little more lively. I guess that from now on what I intend to do is paint with colour. After our campaign against the fading colour problem, Kodak came out with their new stock, which they claim is twenty times more durable and will last 500 years. But I still believe if a film calls for black and white, it should be used.

I do think the endings of *After Hours* and *The Color of Money* maybe have a little more hope in them than my earlier pictures. Once you make a decision at a certain point in your life that you're going to live, when you realize you've got to go on, then that glimmer of hope will show in your work. That's why in *After Hours* it was best not to end with Paul stuck in the truck; the wonderful thing is that he survives. And in *The Color of Money* Eddie's just back where he's supposed to be. It doesn't mean he's winning.

Immediately after the opening of The Color of Money, *Scorsese received another unexpected commission. Rock superstar Michael Jackson asked him to direct a promotional film for his new song, 'Bad'.*

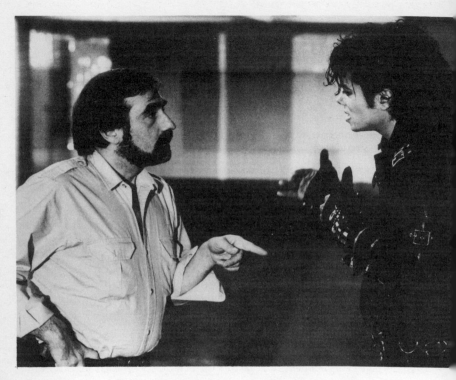

53 Scorsese directs Michael Jackson in *Bad* (1986).

I've always been fascinated by Michael Jackson's performances and especially his dancing. For years I'd been watching the Minnelli musicals; and I had applied the same camera techniques in the musical sequences of *New York, New York* as in the songs done in the studio for *The Last Waltz*. So I was dying to do it again and I realized that Michael's rock video, or whatever you want to call it, would involve dancing and I'd be able to move the camera and have some fun with it. Quincy Jones contacted us and sent me the song 'Bad', which I liked. The offer came at a time when I could do it, and I wondered what kind of thing he'd want. When I met him in California, he said, you come up with the idea, so I brought in Richard Price and we came up with this idea based on a real incident in Harlem.

We put Michael in with black actors in Harlem and we shot the dramatic sequences in black and white, very much in the spirit of Shirley Clarke's *The Cool World*.[8] The whole film is about 16 minutes long, with the dramatic section taking up ten. At the crucial moment, when the music comes in and he becomes a different Jackson in a new costume, we went into colour. But even then it's in the subway, so it's only white tiles and everyone's dressed in black. Then they come to the song 'Bad', they dance and everything is resolved.

But before this resolution, Michael did something he wanted to do and I actually encouraged him to keep going, which he called a 'breakdown' – a live performance after the song is over, in which he lectures these three guys, with a whole chorus behind him like a preacher, saying, 'It's all over, guys.' We shot it with three cameras, and it makes a nice little scene. Michael Jackson was the studio, he was paying for it, and he enjoyed himself and just wanted to keep shooting. It cost $2 million and my wife Barbara produced.

Working with Michael Jackson on *Bad* was the counterbalance to my experience with Paul Newman on *The Color of Money*, just as *The Last Waltz* was the counterpart to *New York, New York*, *Italianamerican* to *Mean Streets*, *American Boy* to *Taxi Driver* and, I suppose, *Mirror, Mirror* to *After Hours*. I still need to do smaller projects, to keep myself moving. And there are still one or two things I'd like to do in documentary, but for talking heads I'd use video now because it's cheaper than film.

Making *Italianamerican* and *American Boy* showed me how to do *Raging Bull*. I just kept one word in mind: 'clarity', get to the issue. It seemed to free me. What I liked to do in documentaries when people were telling stories was, rather than dissolving from one image to another so as to soften the cuts, to jump around until I was free of the form. A lot of that impulse wound up in *Raging Bull*.

I made a 30-second commercial, my first real commercial in a sense, in Italy for my friend Giorgio Armani. We'd been talking about doing one for four or five years, and the timing was right. It's a boy and girl in bed talking in Italian, and they have clothes on. Originally there was a visual with no clothes, but then we realized, of course, that the commercial was for a clothing designer. I shot it in black and white with Nestor Almendros, in a villa with frescos on the wall.⁹ It's beautiful because it reminds me of the Italian films that I was hooked on in the sixties.

In Scorsese's commercial, the girl is teaching the boy her language by pointing to parts of her body and naming them – the hand, the mouth, the nose, the eyes, the eyelashes, the eyebrows. This was, says Scorsese, how he learned Italian himself.

Paul Newman at long last won a Best Actor Academy Award for his second incarnation of 'Fast' Eddie Felson. Scorsese signed a two-year deal with Walt Disney, giving the company's 'adult' production division, Touchstone, first option on all his projects. With his first commercial success since Taxi Driver, *he was back. The Color of Money was a work-out, a testing of his new self-discipline – which, in retrospect, has made him feel that the film was not tough enough. But if it had been tougher, he readily admits, then it would not have been such a commercial venture.*

The industry is now run by businessmen and if I want to continue to make personal films, I have to show them I have some sort of respect for money, and that it will actually show on the screen. People talk about the great old days of the movie moguls, but that was a different time. I think all the great studio film-makers are dead or no longer working. I don't put myself, my friends and other contemporary film-makers in their category, I just see us doing some work. The studios were over when I began in the early seventies: the old system was a whole different period, a closed, naïve world truthful unto itself. Everything now is too open, too international. I once met André De Toth in California and he said to me, 'Harry Cohn was a difficult man, but we made pictures then, young man, we made pictures!'¹⁰ And he was right.

Notes

1 Scorsese recalls that he was first given the book to read by Barbara Hershey after the shooting of *Boxcar Bertha* in 1972.

2 At the age of twenty, in 1955, Ballhaus had observed the shooting of Max Ophuls's last film, *Lola Montes*; and it was his ability to mount complex camera movements rapidly – a feature of Ophuls's style – which immediately impressed Scorsese. Ballhaus shot a total of fourteen films for Fassbinder, before going to America for the first time in 1982, to shoot *Baby, It's You* for John Sayles.

3 In Volker Schlöndorff's film of the Günter Grass novel *The Tin Drum* (1979), the birth of Otto is shown from inside his mother's womb!

4 *Isle of the Dead* was the tenth and penultimate of producer Val Lewton's low-budget RKO horror cycle, directed by Mark Robson in 1945, starring Boris Karloff, and inspired by Arnold Böcklin's eerie Symbolist painting of the same title.

5 *The Wanderers* was filmed by Philip Kaufman, from a script written with his wife, Rose, in 1979. *Bloodbrothers* (1978), set in the New York Italian–American milieu that Scorsese grew up in, had been directed by Robert Mulligan from a script by Walter Newman in the previous year.

6 In Robert Rossen's *The Hustler* (1961), Bert Gordon (played by George C. Scott) is a gambler–promoter who leads 'Fast' Eddie into the big money and then destroys his prize player's new-found love, finally forcing him out of the game.

7 Touchstone is a subsidiary of Disney formed to produce more 'adult' films that could not be made under the usual Disney code of family entertainment only. Their first successes included *Splash* (1984), *Down and Out in Beverly Hills* (1986), and *Three Men and a Baby* (1987).

8 Shirley Clarke's *The Cool World* (1963) continued the novel exploration of New York's black subculture, and its appeal for 'hip' whites, that she had begun in *The Connection* (1960).

9 Cuban-born cinematographer Nestor Almendros studied in Italy, but made his name in the mid sixties in France where he photographed most of the films of Eric Rohmer and François Truffaut. In 1978, he won an Academy Award for *Days of Heaven*.

10 Hungarian-born André De Toth specialized in westerns and vigorous action dramas in the forties and fifties, and directed *House of Wax* in 3-D in 1953. Harry Cohn (1891–1958) was the hated, feared yet respected head of Columbia Pictures, which he had started as a Poverty Row outfit in the early twenties and built up to become a major, highly profitable enterprise by the fifties.

CHAPTER 6

The Last Temptation of Christ

'It is accomplished.' Jesus in *The Last Temptation of Christ*

When he gave three Guardian Lectures in Britain in January 1987, Scorsese spoke with bitter passion about his failure to get The Last Temptation of Christ *under way. He was not going to give up, but there seemed little chance of support in a Hollywood that thought in 'fish out of water' formulae and clearly preferred him to make* The Color of Money *with Newman and Cruise. But within weeks of his leaving Britain, certain that his next film would be the* Wise Guy *adaptation, a new alignment in the power elite of Hollywood itself would bring the opportunity that had so long eluded him.*

Although I'd heard about Kazantzakis's book when I was a student at NYU, it was Barbara Hershey and David Carradine who gave it to me when we'd finished shooting *Boxcar Bertha* in 1972.[1] At that time there was an incredible feeling of spirituality in America, and we thought that making a film of it would help to bring about change. It took me a number of years to read it – I liked it so much I didn't want to finish it! – and I finally reached the end while visiting the set of *The Meadow*, the Taviani Brothers' film, in Florence in 1979.

I found the representation of Christ, stressing the human side of His nature without denying that He is God, the most accessible to me. His divine side doesn't fully comprehend what the human side has to do; how He has to transform Himself and eventually become the sacrifice on the cross – Christ the man only learns about this a little at a time. In the whole first section of the book, He is acting purely on human emotions and human psychology, so He becomes confused and troubled. I thought this neurotic – even psychotic – Jesus was not very different from the shifts of mood and psychology that you find glimpses of in the Gospels. For example, Christ cursing the fig tree, throwing the money-changers out of the Temple and saying, 'I've not come to bring peace, but to bring a sword, set father against son, mother against daughter,' and so on.

I had a sense of this problem in Kazantzakis. There's a wonderful confession scene – in the film it's with Jeroboam – in which Christ says, 'Lucifer's inside me, he's saying I'm not the son of Mary and Joseph, I'm the son of God, I am God.' So He thinks it's the Devil inside Him saying this, and He believes He's the worst sinner in the world. I felt this was something I could relate to: this was a Jesus you could sit down with, have dinner or a drink with. Even in the Gospels, the Pharisees and the Sadducees complain about His eating and drinking, saying He wasn't in the tradition of prophets like John the Baptist, who went out into the desert all the time and fasted, and refrained from hanging out with prostitutes and money-collectors. So for me this was a very human Jesus.

Knowing that Paul Schrader and I have close affinities, I thought it would be interesting to see what a Calvinist approach to the book would be. It's a very long book and I wanted a normal-length film, not a six-hour mini-series, so I thought Paul would be able to strip away all the unnecessary elements. The whole relationship between Mary Magdalene and the Apostles and how they were fighting with each other, all that was fascinating, but couldn't be put in the film. I thought that I would be making it just as George Stevens did *The Greatest Story Ever Told* and Nicholas Ray did *King of Kings* – both at the end of their careers.[2] But when Paul delivered a ninety-page script after four months, I realized that we could tackle it now.

I'd always wanted to make a film of the life of Christ, ever since I first saw Him portrayed on the screen in *The Robe* when I was eleven years old. I was an altar boy, and I was taken by our diocesan priest on a little field trip up to the Roxy. He hated the film for its absurdity, but I'll never forget the magic of walking down the lobby and getting a glimpse of that gigantic CinemaScope screen for the first time.[3] And when I heard the music in stereophonic sound, it became confused in my mind with the Gregorian Chant for the Mass for the Dead, at which I used to serve every Saturday morning at 10.30. I remember once an old Italian man of about ninety years of age had died, and his widow, who was about ninety-three, attacked the coffin and knocked it down in her grief, and we altar boys had to help her. So, with the confusion of these experiences in my mind, the whole film became a holy experience, and the first image of Jesus carrying the cross in the street was very shocking to me.

The first images of Christ that I recall were the plaster statues and crucifixes in St Patrick's Old Cathedral. The strongest impression was of a human being who had been tortured and beaten, then put on the cross, and this was someone you would have loved, who had been a very good person. I remember being taken to a Mass and wondering why my parents had never taken me before. It was so impressive, with different coloured vestments for the different Masses: white and gold, or green and gold. I guess I made the association between going to the cathedral and to the movie theatre at an early age. In fact, as kids we used to joke about Mass being the same show every day.

My First Communion was very important to me, participating in confirmation and making my first confession. At this time I was fascinated by images of the crucifixion and drew endless pictures of it, which I gave to the nuns at school. Regarding ancient religions, such as in Carthage, where they sacrificed 500 five-year-old children, or the blood sacrifices of the Israelites, finally up to the sacrifice of Jesus on the cross, and beyond that the sacrifice of the Mass – there has obviously been a 'civilizing' of religions, I feel, but this primal instinct towards bloodletting is still part of our subconscious. Travis in *Taxi Driver* is an Old Testament figure in that sense: in order to be righteous and correct the only answer was to call down the wrath of God. I remember finding the sequence in which God directs Abraham to sacrifice Isaac in John Huston's film of *The Bible* very beautifully staged.

Paul wrote the first version of the script coming out of the psychological trauma of his mother's death, and it was a very heart-felt piece of work. He felt that the supernatural should exist alongside the natural, so he added Jesus taking His heart out, as well as a literal version of the Last Supper in terms of swallowing the flesh and blood of Jesus. I said, 'Paul, come now,' but he said it was just between us, a Calvinist teasing a Catholic, and in his second draft that scene was taken out and we went back to Kazantzakis.

But this approach still applies to the way the miracles are done in the film. It's as if to say: what was hypnosis, what was a real miracle and what was a kind of curing? When He cures the blind man, Jesus takes herbs in His hand, adds saliva, rubs them together and puts them on his eyes. I did a lot of research and discovered that many healers at the time used saliva as a healing agent, which is why it's in there. And instead of Jesus smiling at these miracles, He's terrified. Each miracle takes Him a step closer to

54 Cinema decorated for the first CinemaScope release, *The Robe*, in 1953.

55 Abraham prepares to sacrifice Isaac in *The Bible . . . in the Beginning* (1966).

something He knows is going to be difficult; and according to Kazantzakis He eventually finds out that it is the cross.

Paul's second draft was made very quickly and we gave it to Irwin Winkler and Bob Chartoff. I believe it went first to United Artists, who turned it down, and then by the time *The King of Comedy* was released at the beginning of 1983, Paramount had signed up to make the film. I had one meeting with Barry Diller, then head of the company, along with Jeff Katzenberg and Michael Eisner, and when I was asked why I wanted to make this film, I replied, 'So I can get to know Jesus better.'

In a way all my life I wanted to do that: first I was going to be a priest, but it didn't work out. The idea of loving and forgiving one's enemies seemed so obvious and Gandhi had shown that it could be put into practice. I felt that maybe the process of making this film would make me feel a little more fulfilled. Their reaction was very sweet, but they didn't want that answer. They asked me how much money I wanted to spend and I explained that the idea wasn't to go the traditional route of the American or Italian epics (though I love them, despite all their flaws and silliness, for the craftsmanship and artistry of design), but to go the other way and make it an intimate character study – which meant less money. And they were ready to go with that.

We began in January to scout locations in Israel, looking at different areas, and then we found villages in Morocco that really looked 2,000 years old, including Oumnast, which we later used in 1987 for filming. So we talked about doing the first two-and-a-half weeks in Morocco and finishing up in Israel, where we received terrific treatment and co-operation from the Mayor of Jerusalem and even from the President. But the fundamentalists, the Moral Majority, had got wind of it all and the letters started pouring in. They went to Gulf and Western, where the head, Charlie Bluhdorn, had recently died and whose place had been taken by Martin Davis. I'm not sure of the politics, but things were different when Barry Diller had worked with Bluhdorn.

By September the film had been cast, the budget was up from $12 million to $16 million, and the shooting schedule increased from ninety to a hundred days. But after a final meeting that month, Irwin Winkler (whose association with Bob Chartoff was ending – this was to be their last film together) felt that he would have to leave the picture. That was a blow that made it difficult for the studio to stand by us, and on Thanksgiving morning Barry Diller told me he didn't want to go with the picture. I don't think his relationship with Gulf and Western was very good, because he soon left for Twentieth Century–Fox, while Katzenberg and Eisner took over Touchstone Pictures. We then tried to cut the budget in half and went round every studio, yet we were still rejected. But the beauty of that year was that none of it was wasted, because we learned how *not* to make the picture.

I began to think the film couldn't be made in Hollywood, by which I mean with major funding from a major company. Salah Hassanein, at that time the East Coast head of the United Artists theatre chain (the biggest in America), called up Frank Mancuso, head of distribution at Paramount, and told him he would not show our film in his theatres. Furthermore, he wouldn't show it on his cable stations – and he had the cable franchise for Home Box Office. So we met Salah, who had been executive producer on George Romero's *Creepshow*, and found that he hadn't read the script, though his family had told him he should read the book and that it was great.

But he said, 'You people only make the films, I have to show them and deal with the public when they rip up the seats and fights break out in the theatre.' Then he said, 'Don't tell me about religious films' – he's Egyptian and half-Protestant – 'in the fifties I had a picture about Martin Luther and the Catholics picketed it. Then people picketed *The Greatest Story Ever Told* too, and with *Messenger of God* there were bombs in the theatre.' So it became clear that to make a film with any guarantee of distribution, it would have to be for a cost so small that it could play in one theatre in America for a while, until people realized that it wasn't offensive.

Throughout 1983 I rewrote Paul's script, as I'd done on *Raging Bull*, with his permission and on the understanding I'd take no credit. I mentioned this to Jay Cocks and he said he'd help me, though he knew he'd get no credit either. Out of three major sessions we produced, I think, six drafts. Some of the best lines for me are those from the book that Paul originally included, such as, 'If I was a fire I'd burn, if I was a woodcutter I'd cut out my heart and lungs'; and towards the end when the angel turns to Christ and says, 'Are you satisfied?' and He replies, 'I feel ashamed when I think about it, all the mistakes I made, all the wrong ways I looked for God.'

A new possibility emerged, to make the film as a French co-production with the help of state funding, since Mitterrand's Minister of Culture Jack Lang had developed a policy of offering support (and asylum in the case of persecuted directors such as Yilmaz Guney and Andrez Wajda) to non-French film-makers of international standing. But even as Scorsese and

The Last Temptation of Christ *began to be mentioned as possible candidates for this aid, so a Catholic equivalent of the American fundamentalist movement started to campaign against the project. The controversy over Godard's* Je Vous Salue, Marie, *which continued throughout 1985 and included papal denunciation, made French religious protesters even more determined to nip other 'blasphemous' films in the bud. The Archbishop of Paris, Cardinal Lustiger, finally delivered a solemn warning to President Mitterrand about the misuse of public funds for a project founded on subverting scripture.*

During 1985 a number of people were trying to get the film made for me including Jack Lang, the French producer Humbert Balsan and Maroun Bagdadi, a Lebanese film-maker. They asked me to go to Cannes in 1986 with *After Hours*, so that they could announce *The Last Temptation of Christ*, saying it could be made for $5 million in Egypt. I didn't go, among other reasons because of my fear of flying. Usually, I'm able to deal with it, but sometimes I just become completely irrational.

A number of new locations were considered for The Last Temptation of Christ. *The original plan to film mainly in Israel had proved too expensive; sets had been built, including villages, and about $5 million of Paramount money had to be written off. Scorsese was particularly sorry to lose such settings as Timna for the raising of Lazarus, and the Roman amphitheatre in Beit Shear for Pilate's scene. It was necessary, in Scorsese's words, to give the film 'a completely new look'. Michael Powell's associate Frixos Constantine even sought money from Moscow with the idea of making the film in Tashkent. When that fell through, meetings were held to see whether Greece was feasible. Then it became apparent that the rights to the novel might fall into other hands.*

It happened by this point we'd been letting our options drop a little because nobody was interested in the book, so together with Harry Ufland, my agent, and John Avnet, the producer Paramount hired after Winkler left, we pooled our money to make sure they were secured.

From the time it was stopped in 1983, up to 1986, Harry was constantly trying to have the film made. In 1986 he tried to set up the film with John Daly's Hemdale company, but that fell through by the end of the year. My next film looked as if it was going to be *Wise Guy*, based on the Nick Pileggi book. But while I was promoting *The Color of Money* in Los Angeles in October, I began talking to Mike Ovitz of CAA,[4] who was

Paul Newman's agent and had largely put that film together behind the scenes. I decided to change representation from Harry Ufland, who was my agent for twenty years, to Mike Ovitz. So I met with Harry in November and we worked out that the official start of my new association with CAA would be 1 January 1987. After the shooting of the Armani commercial in Milan, and the Guardian Lectures in Britain, I returned to New York and suddenly Universal were interested in talking – the one studio in Hollywood that had never courted me before.

Mike had arranged a meeting in Los Angeles with Tom Pollock, the new head of the studio, and Sean Daniel, and it went well. Then we went out to Marlon Brando's island Tetiaroa to talk to him about a project, and we were there for three weeks. There was only one phone on the island and we only made a couple of calls, but Mike was saying to me, 'You know, Marty, these people may make this film, so you'd better come back here.' I didn't realize the power involved here, how he could work deals, reason with people, and give them the feeling they've pretty much come out with what they wanted. When we returned to Los Angeles, we had another meeting and it was clear they were really serious. Tom Pollock had read the script when he was representing Harry Ufland the previous year, and he'd liked the project. Mike and Tom gave the script to Garth Drabinsky of Cineplex Odeon, the biggest theatre chain now in America and Canada, who liked it enough to put up half the money. In a sense, the film had been the laughing stock of cocktail parties in Hollywood until the minute I signed with CAA – then it was made!

In April we went to scout locations in Tunisia and Morocco, and came back through Rome having decided pretty much that Morocco was the place. Then we spent the next few months in negotiations between Universal and Paramount, who had spent $5 million on the project back in 1983. There was some animosity between them at the time over another movie, so we had to wait this out before we went off again to Morocco at the end of August to find the actual locations. Shooting began on 12 October, and as we were backed up against Christmas we had to move very fast.

During the summer of 1987, Jay Cocks and I got back together and produced another two versions of the script, in which we wound up undoing most of the suggestions the original producers and studio had given us. They asked so many questions – like why does He go to the monastery? Why does He pray to God the Father, if He's angry with Him? Nevertheless, they were not to be underestimated because they do have the pulse of the public.

Because of Cineplex Odeon providing half the budget, we knew that if the worst came to the worst we would have at least one theatre for the film to open in. In a sense it's an 'art movie' according to the American definition, in other words not a commercial mainstream movie: it runs two hours and forty-three minutes and it was not made for exploitative reasons. I know from a priest friend that the Kazantzakis book is used in seminaries, not as a substitute for the Gospel, but as a parable that is fresh and alive, which they can discuss and argue about. And this is what I hoped the film would do.

I believe that Jesus is fully divine, but the teaching at Catholic schools placed such an emphasis on the divine side that if Jesus walked into a room, you'd know He was God because He glowed in the dark, instead of being just another person. But if He was like that, we always thought, then when the temptations came to Him, surely it was easy to resist them because He was God. He could reject the temptation of power in the desert; He could reject especially the temptation of sex; and He could undergo the suffering on the cross, because He knew what was going to happen, what death is all about.

Over the years I've drifted away from the Church, I'm no longer a practising Catholic, and I've questioned these things. Kazantzakis took the two natures of Jesus, and Paul Moore, the Episcopal Bishop of New York, explained to me that this was Christologically correct: the debate goes back to the Council of Chalcedon in 451, when they discussed how much of Jesus was divine, and how much human. I found this an interesting idea, that the human nature of Jesus was fighting Him all the way down the line, because it can't conceive of Him being God. I thought this would be great drama and force people to take Jesus seriously – at least to re-evaluate His teachings. Most non-Christians also misunderstand the importance many believers give to images of Jesus. For example, in his wonderful movie *Hannah and Her Sisters*, Woody Allen tries to become a Christian and is confused by seeing in a store window a 3-D picture of Jesus on the cross, winking at him! So through the Kazantzakis novel I wanted to make the life of Jesus immediate and accessible to people who haven't really thought about God in a long time. I certainly didn't think the film would destroy the faith of those who believe strongly.

I interpreted the 'last temptation' in the book very much the same way as the Devil tempting Christ in the desert, taking Him up to the top of a building for Him to throw Himself down. The last temptation is for Christ to get off the cross and live the rest of His life as a normal human being. He marries Mary Magdalene, makes love to her for the purpose of having

56 Willem Dafoe as Jesus in *The Last Temptation of Christ* (1988).

children, and then dies in bed. I imagined it as a series of literal visual tableaux which the Devil shows Christ, so that thirty-six years might go by in a second.

I must say there are times in the film when I return to traditional Catholic imagery, for example, the big rock in the Garden of Gethsemane where Christ prays, which came right out of my childhood. I imagined this picture of Him sweating blood just as I'd seen it at Catholic school. But then there are other times when I enjoy just wallowing in this kind of imagery. The minute I saw Willem Dafoe, I felt very comfortable with his face. When Christ changes after returning from the desert, or at the moment when He takes His heart out – which refers to the Catholic Sacred Heart motif – He becomes the Jesus we are familiar with in the Aryan Christian tradition. Oddly enough, all the guys we considered for the part were blue-eyed!

One reason why we started shooting so late was that I was waiting for Aidan Quinn to make up his mind about playing Jesus. He was in the Seychelles, having a difficult time on *Crusoe*, and since he was about to get married, he felt it was too big an undertaking. He also still had some religious problems with the part. Eric Roberts or Chris Walken were also considered in 1983, but then Willem Dafoe came up and he was a CAA client. I'd only seen him in *To Live and Die in L.A.*, playing the villain, and I'd liked him in that, so I wanted to see if he could play on the other side. Speaking with him, in a room together, he was really very good; then I saw *Platoon* and thought, sure, let's go!

I brought back most of the original cast – Harvey Keitel, Barbara Hershey and others – except Sting, who had been going to play Pilate. He was busy on one of the Amnesty tours and he spoke to me in Morocco, but though we tried to work something out between his dates we couldn't. However, I'd always wanted to work with David Bowie, and he ended up flying to Morocco and doing his scene in one day.

All the religious movies I saw and loved as a kid, such as *The Robe* and *Quo Vadis*, were more about spectacle and epic film-making than religion. Later, I enjoyed Christopher Fry's beautiful writing for John Huston's *The Bible*; and more recently the mini-series *A.D.* which Anthony Burgess wrote. But I wanted the Jesus in my film to be more accessible, more immediate, and to engage the audience. Because I'm an American, I have to think of the American audience first. If, suddenly, the screen opens up and it's Panavision (instead of the 1:1.85 that I used) and there's Miklos Rosza's music with heavenly choirs and clouds in the sky, like in Nicholas Ray's *King of Kings*, and the titles in gold lettering and the people beautifully dressed and speaking perfect Queen's English – then the American audience is going to turn its ears off. They're going to say, 'Great, it's another epic,' and know they don't have to think because it's safe.

I was thinking about New York, Manhattan, 8th Avenue and 48th Street, the block where we shot *Taxi Driver* at night, a very dangerous area where there are drug pushers and pimps and prostitutes – it's my vision of Hell. If you were to go there, those ten blocks from 42nd to 52nd Street on 8th Avenue, and say, 'Blessed are the meek for they shall inherit the Earth,' you'd get robbed, or beaten up, or killed. But if you go there and grab people and say, 'Look, I want to tell you about Jesus; I want to tell you about something He just said,' then it's a confrontation. I tried to do that with the Sermon on the Mount; we had to destroy the beautiful poetry of it, and convert it to suggest, almost, that he's getting the idea for the first time.

And there had to be American voices, New York accents and different ones too: Harry Dean Stanton, as Paul, is sort of Southern Baptist, maybe Appalachian; and Gary Basaraba, who played Andrew, is Canadian. When it came to the outside forces, the Romans, and the world of Satan, they had to have a different accent, but the same language. The only way I could think of doing this was to borrow William Wyler's idea in *Ben Hur*, to make them British.

We took so many risks that there was bound to be something that people were not going to like. The ancient Judaeans and the Romans obviously didn't speak like us, although we took great pains to make the language exactly the way it is in the film. I don't think Jesus came from the House of Herod; He was a carpenter and must have spoken like a carpenter; and Judas especially must have been a street tough – that's my interpretation. I remember talking in Andrew Sarris's class at Columbia University when *The King of Comedy* came out, and he said, 'Now you're off to Jerusalem. What's that going to be like, *Mean Streets* in Jerusalem, huh?' And I felt that when the film came out, if it didn't work, one of the first criticisms would be that it's like everybody hanging round the street corner in Jerusalem, saying, 'What do you want to do tonight?' I figured I'd have to wait a few years to get past that.

Some of the humour would have to be there, but it would need to be more forceful. For example, there's a moment in the book when Christ is in a monastery and He says, 'I just saw a sign, what does it mean?' The monk tells Him to go out and preach. I felt that you couldn't say that nowadays, we would have to find another word for preach, so we'd have to rack our brains, talk to people about it, and find different ways of saying it in straight American. The other way of solving the problem is, of course, just to do the whole thing in Hebrew with subtitles. Then it'll probably be called a masterpiece – the irony being that it would go over much better, because you avoid the issue!

Well, New York audiences understood the humour. When Jesus exasperates Judas because every day He has another plan – first He says pick up the axe, then He says He has to die – and Judas responds, 'I don't understand, we need you alive,' he's expressing all our own exasperation with God. It's a man yelling at God, treating Him as if he were talking to another person on the same level, and it's actually very funny – and I found it worked with a paying audience.

It also happens in a few places that are not exactly intentional. The lion in the desert has a kind of wink when it says, 'Don't you recognize me, I'm your heart,' which is a little bit ironic, because Harvey did this alone with me in a room, and I used it just as it came. There's also street humour, just like in *Mean Streets*, especially in the olive grove when Judas says to Jesus, 'You said we should turn the other cheek, I don't like that.' The audience roared with laughter because – well, who does? It's a genuine question, and it was very hard for Willem to answer.

Kazantzakis wrote in demotic Greek, but the language is very specialized, so that the translation into English is very thick and verbose and too 'poetic'. We wanted a straightforward representation of speech, anti-poetic in a way. Jay Cocks and I wrote the dialogue as if we were speaking together, putting ourselves in the scenes and saying, how would we react? I thought it would be interesting to consider how the Apostles would deal with sleeping round camp fires, eating and living on mats on the ground.

Or take the case of the Sermon on the Mount, which is usually presented as a man standing on a hill, surrounded by 3,000 people. There's that wonderful scene in *The Life of Brian*, when nobody can hear at the back – 'it sounds like "Blessed are the cheesemakers" ' – they say, 'I guess he said, "Blessed are the cheesemakers", how very nice of him!' Well, if you hang out in North Africa long enough, you discover that in these villages where we shot the film, where there's no electricity and only a few donkeys, the number of people to gather would be, at most, twenty-five or thirty. That's why we used a small crowd, so that Jesus could really speak to each person, go inside the crowd and talk to them individually, making them understand this new philosophy and sharing His soul with them. That's the attitude we took, and it's why Willem was able to attack it that way. He had this incredible bravery about dealing with the role on

57 Michael Ballhaus and Scorsese on location for *The Last Temptation of Christ*.

58 *The King of Kings*, directed by Cecil B. De Mille in 1927.

the simplest level; he'd just try anything. It was a therapeutic experience to be able to sit with Willem and look at him as Jesus, to have lunch with him and argue with him, and then create this fantasy.

I found the actual making of the film the most physical experience I've ever had, rather than a spiritual one. But later, looking at what we'd shot and constructing it in the editing room proved to be a very emotional and loving experience. I don't really look at my own pictures when they're finished, but on this one I had to look at screening after screening, and every time I see it I'm moved by the idea of trying to find out how one can live like that. How can one really live with this concept of love? I try, but I don't purport to be able to do it myself.

I never really quite believed the representation of Judas in films based on the Gospels. It was too easy either to make him totally political or to make us believe he betrayed Jesus for thirty pieces of silver. In Philip Yordan's script for King of Kings they went the first way, and even in Kazantzakis he's strongly political, but then he gave Jesus the line, 'God gave me the easier job, to be crucified.' I think everybody who worked on the film, and everybody who's read the book over the years, feels it's the first time you can really believe in this relationship – that Judas did not want to betray him, but had to go through with being God's instrument for the sacrifice of Jesus. I always wondered, if Jesus is so forgiving and preaches love, why is Judas condemned to Hell by Him for committing suicide? While we're not saying our version is the whole truth, it makes you question and maybe understand the concept of loving a little better.

Scorsese came to making The Last Temptation of Christ *after many years of studying films based on the Gospels. The most important for him were those which were released in his youth –* King of Kings *(1961),* The Greatest Story Ever Told *(1965), and* The Gospel According to St Matthew *(1964, but released in the USA two years later). Surprisingly, perhaps, the first version he saw was from a much earlier age of cinema, one which Scorsese confesses he finds hard to appreciate.*

I saw the silent *King of Kings*, the Cecil B. De Mille 1927 version, on re-release when I was fifteen or so in a small theatre in New York. I found it hard to concentrate on silent films having grown up in the sound era, and therefore some of the emotions were lost on me. Although I like De Mille's films, and particularly their design, I just found this one very boring. The first time you see Jesus in the film, when He cures the blind child and you see Him from the child's point of view, De Mille uses, quite effectively, in a naïve way, the special effect of a ray of light. I wondered, if Jesus was really like this, why didn't everybody listen to Him? Why wasn't His ministry more successful at the time and why was He crucified? It seemed to me to deny completely the human nature of Jesus. H. B. Warner wears such heavy make-up, he's obviously much older than he's playing, and I thought Jesus was young – Willem Dafoe was thirty-two when he played it. I remember vividly the Casting Out of Devils, with those images coming out of her body: it made quite an impact on us as kids, mainly, I think, because of the sexuality of it.

Then I saw *Ben Hur*, which again was not so interesting. But the first full story of Christ I can remember which excited me was Nicholas Ray's *King of Kings*, and being a strong Roman Catholic at the time I found it offensive! Jeffrey Hunter was almost like a pin-up, especially in the Garden of Gethsemane. But I liked the beginning of the film, the visual style of it – and at that time I didn't know very much about directors. I found certain scenes very shocking in 70 mm, like Pompey going into the Holy of Holies and cutting through the gauze, and the overhead shot where Herod is dying and he fights with his son. The film is full-blown Hollywood, very emphatic and vulgar: on the positive side, it's almost like doing the Jesus story in the style of story-book illustrations, with each frame a self-contained image.

And using a movie star for Jesus, they aren't able to deal completely with the human side. When Jesus is tempted in the desert, He looks up at the sky and sees, matted in, what looks like Baghdad, which has a kind of charm![5] Jeffrey Hunter doesn't look as though he's been forty days in the desert, he doesn't look as if he's suffering at all and you don't feel it. But the film had this remarkable staging of the Sermon on the Mount, where Jesus was walking around preaching, and people on the edge of the frame would say, 'How do you stand on divorce?' and He'd turn round and say, 'Well, I stand this way.' He'd answer these questions like a modern press conference, and I thought this was an interesting interpretation. What offended me most was the political aspect, having Harry Guardino as Barabbas constantly yelling about freedom while in chains. It was really pounding us over the head with that sort of thing.

Yet over the years the film has a resonance – I think because of the intelligence of Philip Yordan's script, in particular the discussions with Pilate before Jesus is put on trial. And I always thought Nicholas Ray's use of the wide screen was so fascinating. In the last image of the movie, when Jesus goes to the Apostles by the shore and you see His shadow, he went for simple iconography, and it works. Michael Powell did a similar thing

59 The Sermon on the Mount, according to Nicholas Ray's *King of Kings* (1961).
60 Final scene of Ray's *King of Kings*.

with the nuns at table in *Black Narcissus*, and he didn't worry about whether it's naïve or not, either, it's just beautiful.

I saw *The Greatest Story Ever Told* in 70 mm in 1965, and I found a lot of the imagery fascinating; Max Von Sydow was a beautiful Christ, especially the way he held his hands. I remember being very excited about Von Sydow because I'd previously seen him in Bergman's *The Seventh Seal*, which was a very religious film for me. But Stevens's film had an antiseptic quality about it, a hermetically sealed holiness that didn't teach us anything new about Jesus. Of course, there's a whole school of thought which argues that Jesus isn't to be identified with, that He is above sin. But in 1965, with Vietnam, the United States went into a whole different consciousness and the message needed to be made alive and accessible.

Jesus talks about forgiving everyone, but, I thought, what about guys on Death Row, rapists and killers who face the death penalty? If they look at this movie, there's no hope of any spirituality, because they'd feel again He's just someone who glows in the dark. He doesn't understand my suffering. Stevens did have the brilliant idea of using the American southwest, with the Grand Canyon area standing in for Israel, but here is Jesus speaking to thousands, and they all manage to hear Him! What we did in *The Last Temptation of Christ* was to stage these scenes with small groups so that He was heard by all. In Stevens's film there's a self-conscious emphasis on design, dressing the disciples in white, and there's no sense of real people living. I think the pictorial aspect – the pageantry – took over. But although it follows many classic paintings, of all the films about Christ I retained it least in my mind. We didn't even look at it when researching *The Last Temptation of Christ*.

One film that I did find a revelation, and I only saw it in 1981, was Richard Fleischer's *Barabbas*, which was based on a book by a Danish author who won a Nobel Prize.[6] I found it very moving because of Barabbas's struggle to understand why he was spared and what God wanted from him, until he ends up being crucified himself. In the struggle of his character to transcend through spirituality, I found that it's probably one of the best performances Anthony Quinn has ever given. He's hooked up with another slave, played by Vittorio Gassman, who unfortunately is directed like a saint. He tries to get Barabbas to wear a medallion and believe in Jesus, to understand why he was the one who was spared. Then there's a crack-down on Christians in the slave area and the Romans question him, asking if he believes because of the medallion, and he says, 'No, I try to believe, but I can't.' It's a remarkable film about a man trying to find himself.

61 The Sermon on the Mount in George Stevens's *The Greatest Story
Ever Told* (1965).
62 Preaching to small village groups in *The Last Temptation of Christ*.

63 Anthony Quinn in Richard Fleischer's *Barabbas* (1962).
64 Jesus walking, in Pasolini's *Gospel According to St Matthew* (1964).

The biblical film that made the biggest impact on me, when I was at film school, was Pasolini's *The Gospel According to St Matthew*, which in Italy was just called *The Gospel According to Matthew*. Up to that point, I had had an idea to do a film on Jesus, in *cinéma-vérité* style, in the Lower East Side of New York with everyone wearing suits, a modern-day interpretation of the story we know. So I was moved and crushed at the same time by the Pasolini film because in a sense it was what I wanted to do. Jesus was played by a Spanish law student, and it was shot in the south of Italy. In fact, we wanted to go and shoot *The Last Temptation of Christ* there, pretty much in the same areas as Pasolini. But Morocco was better for us; it had the whole Middle Eastern look.

Pasolini's use of faces was marvellous. It reminds me of Renaissance art even though it's in black and white, and I love the music – the Missa Luba and Bach. Just compare his Christ with Jeffrey Hunter. He doesn't act walking, he is walking; it's not self-conscious and yet it's very determined. The simplicity of the film reminds me very much of the early Rossellini pictures, *Rome Open City* and *Paisa*. This European style, in its simplicity, gave me the key to be able to make *The Last Temptation of Christ*. The images have to resonate and be very, very strong.

One problem I have with Pasolini is the editing. It seems like a patchwork at times, because of the seemingly off-the-cuff shooting style. But I like his Christ as a kind of conspirator. It was a revolutionary Jesus. In fact, at the time, people referred to him as a Marxist Christ. The strength of Matthew's language comes out very clearly, and it's purer because it doesn't try to make it a straight story from beginning to end. There are no transitions between scenes, characters come and disappear, then reappear in no dramatic way.

Yet the key to the whole picture is Jesus – how forceful He is and how He carries through. 'Do not think I have come to bring peace on this earth, I have come to bring a sword . . . He who loves his father and mother more than me, is not worthy of me.' This is not the stuff you usually hear on Sunday morning in church! He's a very strong Christ, you're either for Him or against Him, and some of the sermons do give you the sense of being yelled at and beaten down. Also, I love the way Pasolini did the miracles; for example, when Jesus cures the leper, with the Leadbelly steel guitar on the soundtrack. Just a simple cut, and it's so shocking and beautiful: he's looking into the eyes of Christ, who says, 'Go show yourself to the high priest.'

The costumes for Pasolini's film were by Danilo Donati, who I tried to get for my film back in 1983, but he was too busy. He did tell me to go and

65 *The Crucifixion* by Antonello da Messina (1475).

study the Sistine Chapel, though. John Beard, my designer, looked at this film with me a lot. Pasolini had many more extras than me – we had a total in the Temple scene of 135, including five Roman soldiers who kept appearing in different parts of the Temple to make it seem like twenty-five or more! I remember reading how Pasolini had gone to Israel first, thinking to make his film there, but then he realized it was no longer the Israel of antiquity, so he created it in the south of Italy. And it really worked beautifully, the film is so joyous: he was a great poet.

Over the years I've always been fascinated by Christ in art. I remember buying many prints around 1970–2 in Rome, and having them framed and put on the wall in my house in California. One of them was by Da Messina, showing Jesus on a perfectly constructed cross in the centre, and the two thieves crucified on trees. In my research, I realized that if Golgotha was such a killing ground, there would be maybe 2,000 or 3,000 skulls of zealots up on that hill, as Pilate says in the movie. I thought it must have been a real charnel house, and that there would be some trees like a no man's land from the First World War.

When I was about eleven years old, I went to the Metropolitan Museum of Art with some friends, and in one of the rooms I saw in a glass case a fourteenth-century German wooden carving of the three crosses, and the figures on them were naked. And at the time we all said, of course, that must have been how it was. After the film was first cancelled around 1983, I subscribed to the *Biblical Archeology Review*, and a lot of our art direction came from that magazine, and clippings I've kept over the years. One whole issue dealt with the only archaeological evidence of a crucifixion, a young Jew in his twenties in about AD 100. Sure enough, he was crucified naked, sitting sideways with his legs bent, and we followed this exactly in the film, even down to the blocks of wood on the wrists.

The shot of Christ carrying the cross in slow motion came from Boris Leven, who showed me a painting by Bosch in which the surrounding faces gave no sense of three dimensions. It took all morning to do that shot, at 120 frames per second. To keep the people around him, some of them laughing or pointing at him, we had to tie them together with ropes, so they could only move one step at a time. We took Christ's wounds from the Shroud of Turin, where the crown of thorns was not a crown but a skull-cap, and the scourging completely covered his back. If we didn't show the blood, it seemed to me to weaken the extent of his sacrifice, and diminish what it meant for him to die on the cross.

In the De Mille *King of Kings*, the high priests in the Temple wore round their necks the twelve stones of Israel, only they looked almost machine-made, something that you could take apart in sections like a child's toy. Each stone represents one of the Tribes of Israel. So I went through the Atlas Mountains with John Beard, Laura Fattori, the production manager, and Barbara, my wife and producer, and we bought these differently coloured rocks from young boys, and broke them up. Then I designed something for the high priest to wear with the rocks tied together with leather, so that it had a much more primitive, hand-made quality.

The visual style of the film came out of the way I normally work, planning most of it beforehand in New York. There are some overhead shots and I used a lot of moving camera: sometimes it swirls round Christ's head and moves up, though on this film I couldn't afford a crane, much as I was tempted to use one. I wanted to express the energy that Jesus had, that I wanted Willem to have, so we adopted a very fluid and almost nervous way of moving the camera. Because He was unsure of Himself, the camera would be hiding and creeping around Him, caught between following Him and, at the same time, trying to pull back far enough so that you could see the landscape. We had a jib arm which only goes up twelve or eighteen feet, but it was enough for the scale of our story; for example, when Jesus and Judas are sleeping in the olive grove and we start in high, the camera moves in and we cut to His face.

For the music, I came up with a lot of ideas from listening to a great deal of Moroccan music by a group called Nass El Ghiwane, who I saw in a film called *Trances* (advertised as *Moroccan Rock'n'Roll*), shown on cable television back in 1982.[7] It's not really rock'n'roll at all, but a famous group in Morocco, their equivalent of Bob Dylan, in a way. The lyrics are beautiful poetry and they could apply to any religion any time. It was just the same as when I was living in California and driving everywhere listening to rock'n'roll on the radio, I'd find myself fantasizing about scenes in movies, and scenes in movies I was going to make, how I would cover them with the camera. People would hate to drive with me because I'd always miss the turning off the freeway!

In *The Last Temptation of Christ* the rhythms of this Moroccan music gave me the feeling for designing the shots, and that's why I'm so glad that Peter Gabriel was able to do the soundtrack. Peter took many of the rhythms from Turkey, Greece, Armenia, North Africa and Senegal, mixing them together to make the music as primal as possible. I began listening to Peter's music back in 1982–3, and I especially liked 'Rhythm of the Heat' with its drums, and then 'I Go Swimming', where the lyrics start quite ordinarily before taking off to reach a spiritual level, especially in the live version. I first met him the week before the picture was cancelled

Sc 68   p. 92

Jesus Carries his cross.

① Med Shot to MCU — Jesus Carries Cross
   from Bosch Painting   SLOW MOTION

NOTE: → 48, 96, 120

   Long Lens - 600 or 400 mm.

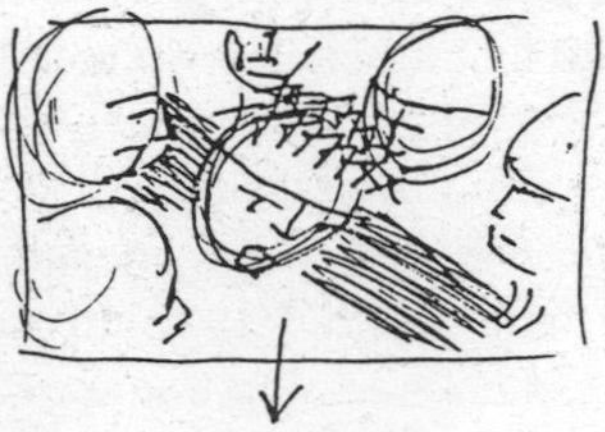

All Faces around him Squeezed into frame
like painting.

He falls — Soldier picks him up by Rope
around neck.

⊗ This Maybe Only Shot Needed for
   Sequence.

   But, see next sheet for others —

66 Page from Martin Scorsese's shooting script for *The Last Temptation
of Christ*.

67 *The Ghent Christ Carrying the Cross* by Hieronymus Bosch (early
sixteenth century).

in 1983, in a café one morning; Robbie Robertson got us together. I said I'd be interested in having him do the music because, for me, the rhythms he uses reflect the primitive, and his vocals reflect the sublime – it's as if the spirit and the flesh are together right there.

We stayed in touch over the years: he sent me a tape from Senegal, and I told him that was the direction we wanted to go. He visited the set on the last day of shooting in Morocco, and we talked more closely. Of course, he had to do it as a labour of love because there was hardly any money in it. Normally, he says, it takes two years to do forty minutes of music, and this was two hours and forty minutes, which he did in three months! He used drummers from Egypt and vocals from Pakistan, and an Indian viola player, Shankar, who fused the violin with the viola in imitation of the human voice, so that you would swear it was someone singing. It was really a great job, and I hope Peter is recognized for it.

In the search for locations, an uncharted village near Marrakesh called Oumnast was discovered that served for Nazareth and Magdala. Ancient Jerusalem was originally conceived as a set, but at Mekenes the Moulay– Ismael Stables came to be used as the interior of the Temple, the Passover baths and the palace of Pontius Pilate. The final scenes of the film, in the 35-minute 'last temptation' sequence, were shot in the Atlas Mountains and around the Roman ruins of Volubilis. In the end, only one third of the shots planned for locations in Israel had to be altered for filming in Morocco.

In the desert, you often get a sense of being in a trance, of time standing still; it's a special kind of existence which I tried to convey with camera movement and music – for instance when the men are waiting in the antechamber for Mary Magdalene; in the olive grove when Jesus wakes up and performs, the apple tree appears before Him; or when the camera goes through the trees in the Garden of Gethsemane and He asks God to take the cup from His lips. When the camels appear almost as an apparition in the market-place, I wanted a sense of what it was like to be there at midday. I'll never forget André Gregory getting off the plane from New York to play John the Baptist, being taken while jet-lagged to the set in the desert at night, and he saw faraway a little flame and a bunch of tiny figures trying to make sense of God and man. And he said, looking at these ants and this flame representing the Archangel, it seemed so ridiculous – with him suddenly having to be John the Baptist too – it was one of the most surrealistic experiences of his life!

I liked the flame that came up in slow motion; that way the angel at the end could just turn into it. For the temptations in the desert, I thought of a man awake and fasting for ten days and ten nights. Then a snake goes by. How would He perceive it? No doubt the snake would speak to Him. But we wouldn't see the mouth move, it's really an inner voice. And a lion walks by and doesn't kill Him because He's so static. All this could have been done without anything, just voices and sound-effects, but I wanted to take the risk and keep the supernatural on the same level as the natural.

I wrote the scene of the raising of Lazarus myself even before Jay Cocks began working on the script. The minute Christ raises Lazarus, He knows that He is God. And with Lazarus's hand clasping His, pulling Him into the tomb, it gave a sense of death pulling Him in, an image of the struggle between life and death. Death which He will – despite being God – have to suffer as man.

In the book and Paul Schrader's original script, the angel at the end was a little Arab boy, but I felt that brought connotations and we'd have difficulties. People would get upset and it would get in the way of what the film's really about. So then we decided it should be an old man – we had Lew Ayres cast in 1983 – but that concept didn't seem right. So we went with a little girl, even though we couldn't get away from Pasolini's use of a young girl as an angel, whose face is so extraordinary, like Botticelli. When Christ looks up on the cross, He sees the sun breaking through the clouds, and that's the last shot I took in Morocco. Granted it's clichéd, shot with the angel appearing, but after all, it's a scam, it's the Devil. Of course a little girl has appeared as the Devil before, in Mario Bava's *Kill, Baby, Kill*, and again in Fellini's *Toby Dammit*, where she plays with the ball, but our young girl is older, she's thirteen. When the Devil became a male voice, I used Leo Marks, the man who wrote *Peeping Tom*, with my voice behind him.

One problem I have with the book is the relationship between Jesus and Mary Magdalene. If there had to be sexual temptation, it could be another woman; for it to be Mary seemed kind of obvious. And the fact that she became a whore specifically because He rejected her is almost as bad as the Hitchcock movie *I Confess*, where Montgomery Clift becomes a priest basically because he was jilted by Anne Baxter. As the young priest whom I adored when I was young said, that doesn't happen, because you have to have a vocation otherwise you'd only last a week in the seminary! *I Confess* is an interesting movie nevertheless, but I found a similar difficulty with Kazantzakis.

Many people have said that the book is more Kazantzakis than Jesus.

68 Anne Baxter and Montgomery Clift in Hitchcock's *I Confess* (1953).

I've only been able to read a little of his other work; I'm not a very well-read person, because I grew up in a house without books, and basically everything I learned was visual. But I've read about many aspects of Kazantzakis's life; I met his widow Helen and talked about him, and I find it fascinating how he followed different routes to find God or his spirituality, going up to Mount Athos and staying in a monastery, and finally writing these books in the last ten years of his life. But he lived in Greece, went through the Second World War, then went to Russia, while I'm just in Manhattan, New York – they're very different worlds.

I go more towards *Mean Streets* where you try to find yourself, because I'm dealing with this urban existence. I'm not like Thoreau, I don't go to Walden. When I think about it, I say, 'Well, maybe that's the thing to do, that's the way you should be.' But maybe prayer is really dealing with what you have in the home, dealing with your family, and how you raise your children, how you relate to your wife. Maybe that's what prayer really is in the modern world. However, I still find these remarkable men who go on spiritual quests very romantic.

Notes

1 Two other novels by the controversial Greek author, Nikos Kazantzakis (1883–1957), were previously adapted for the screen: *Christ Recrucified* (filmed by Jules Dassin as *He Who Must Die* in 1957) and *Zorba the Greek* (Michael Cacoyannis in 1964).

2 Stevens took five years to make *The Greatest Story Ever Told*, released in 1965. It was his penultimate film. Ray's *King of Kings* (1961) had earlier proved to be his penultimate commercial production.

3 *The Robe* premiered in September 1953 at the Roxy as the first demonstration of Twentieth Century–Fox's new widescreen CinemaScope process and was a great box-office success.

4 The Creative Artists Agency is now one of the most influential agents in Hollywood. It has become common practice for agents to 'package' movies for the studios with their own clients.

5 A matte shot involves blocking out part of an image and combining it with another, typically when a 'magic' effect is required.

6 The novel *Barabbas* was written by Pär Lagerkvist; the English screenplay was credited to Christopher Fry and Nigel Balchin. The film was released in 1961.

7 Ahmed El Maanouni's *Trances* is a fascinating documentary about this Moroccan band, who combine stadium appeal (they are seen playing in Carthage) with an awareness of the ritual roots of North African music.

CHAPTER 7

New York Stories – GoodFellas
– Cape Fear

'John Ford made Westerns. We make street movies. Let's do that.'

Martin Scorsese to Joe Pesci

In January 1988, before the storm of controversy broke around The Last Temptation of Christ, *Scorsese directed a promotional video for his old friend Robbie Robertson's first solo album since leaving The Band. After 'Somewhere Down the Crazy River', the pair planned another concert film, provisionally titled* Robbie Robertson and Friends, *which would have involved Peter Gabriel and U2. The unavailability of these 'friends' led to a more ambitious feature project, described by Robertson in* Rolling Stone *as 'a combination of* The Red Shoes *and* All That Jazz, *only dealing with music instead of dance'. Nothing came of this either, and Scorsese turned next to a project first proposed to him two years earlier,* New York Stories.

Towards the end of 1986, Woody Allen called me to ask if I would be interested in doing an episode film with him and Steven Spielberg. We met in a screening room and talked about it, though by this stage he didn't know what studio he was going to get to back it. The inspiration was those Italian episode films like *Boccaccio '70*, and he felt we could just make our own films, and the next time we would have to meet would be when it opened! Each episode would be a certain length, and it would be a 'New York story' (though we didn't have such a title then). I had a couple of ideas, so did Steven, but he backed out a few months later and Francis Coppola came in.

At the beginning of 1987, I asked Richard Price to write my story. About the same time, Jeff Katzenberg asked me to go to see *Me and My Girl* and that night said, 'Well, how's it going?' I told him that I might be doing this short with Woody Allen. And he became very interested, because Touchstone had been negotiating to get Woody Allen to work for them. Next thing I know it's a Touchstone film.

Richard wrote a 40-minute piece for me about the end of a relationship between an artist (though it could have been a writer or even a film-maker) and his assistant, who's also an artist. He would be around fifty, and the young woman would be in her early twenties, and their relationship would come full circle. It's based on this idea that I've wanted to do for years, though different aspects have shown up in my work, drawn from Dostoevsky's *The Gambler*. In 1973, Paul Schrader wrote me a synopsis for a screenplay, but it never got further than that. Now eventually I think someone is going to make it, although there was a version called *The Great Sinner* with Ava Gardner and Gregory Peck.

I was fascinated by this idea of a woman telling her lover to go and prove his love by insulting a respectable old noblewoman.[1] In 1972 the book was reissued in a new translation with the diaries of Dostoevsky's mistress, Polina Suslova. She was an admirer in her early twenties, while he was forty-two and his career was just about to take off with *Notes from Underground* and *Crime and Punishment*. The diaries reveal the real woman behind the character in the book, and I wanted to make a film about this relationship. She's an aspiring writer and he's in love with her. They are planning to go to Italy together and she's waiting for him in Paris. Then she sends a letter saying that the trip is off and not to bother coming to see her.

But he arrives, says he's ready to go to Italy, and she replies, 'Didn't you get my letter?' He says, 'What letter?' She says, 'I tell you I'm not going, I'm not in love with you any more.' He's crushed. She goes on to tell him it's because of another man, and he's even more crushed, but then she says it's worse than that! He asks what that could be, and she says, 'This man doesn't love me.'

His response is to tell her that there's no sense in them breaking up and not going to Italy together, that he can help her to get over the situation. He even suggests their relationship can be platonic, that she doesn't have to sleep with him, but he asks her not to give him up. Eventually what happens in the diaries is that he helps her to write letters to this other man. Finally they do go to Italy and he finds every excuse to get into her room: 'Oh, let me close that window for you' – things like that. He's also fascinated by her feet, and that was something we had some marvellous fun with in our contemporary version!

Our story is based on the diaries and it's lighter in tone than *The*

Gambler. Richard felt that making him a writer was so static, maybe he should be a painter, maybe both should be painters. So he put this character in SoHo as a famous painter, and she's his assistant. He goes to pick her up at the airport, and she says, 'Oh, you showed up,' and he asks her what's wrong. She says, 'Didn't you get my message? I left it on the answering machine.' He replies, 'No, I don't listen to that.'

So it goes on, and then she reveals she's in love with a performance artist in New York, a young guy who doesn't even know she exists. She had an affair with him and then, you know, it's not the guy's fault, he just doesn't care for her or need her, it didn't work out for him. This performance artist is a guy who's like a comic, he does monologues and various acts of subversive behaviour. My friend Jay Cocks reckons that the only people more loathsome than performance artists are mimes! I don't know whether I agree entirely with that, but it's pretty much the attitude of this painter.

The painter's played by Nick Nolte as this sort of big bear with a beard, always growling and drinking a lot. And he tries to persuade his assistant not to move out of the loft where she's living with him, that they're adults, they don't have to sleep together any more. He's a big man, he's been married, he knows these stories, and he'll help her through this period. So what you have is the beginning of the end of a relationship over a few days. At the beginning of the piece, he's about to have a big show, but he can't paint. The minute she comes back, he's able to work.

What interested me was the pain of this situation, how much of it is needed for his kind of work, and how much he creates himself. He asks her why she should leave when she's working for one of the most important living painters, she has a room rent-free, she has a salary, and 'life lessons' that are beyond price. That's why I called it *Life Lessons*. He's a mature artist, an institution, he wears Armani tuxedos even though he's covered in paint all the time. But she's an artist herself, though not fully developed, and she's benefiting from his magic, though she's nowhere near his status. It's an aspect we touched upon in *New York, New York*, in the relationship between Francine and Jimmy, and it's one of those themes I've always wanted to make a film about.

I really had to force myself to make this film, because it was a hard schedule, returning in September 1988 from the Venice Festival and London to two weeks' pre-production and then shooting it in four weeks. Then I shot another commercial for Armani in Milan before beginning the editing. An agency in France presented the idea to me, and I thought I could play around it. But when I was there, I still had one foot in the plane because I wasn't sure I really could do it.

69 Rosanna Arquette and Nick Nolte in the *Life Lessons* section of *New York Stories* (1989).

It starts with the Armani man, with his hair slicked back – a look that reminds me of Visconti films – who's lying dressed in the bedroom of his apartment. Suddenly this very upset woman comes in, who doesn't know he's there. She finds a photo of him with another woman, perhaps his wife or girlfriend, and throws it down in anger. There are a lot of shots of him peering through a door, with the camera slowly moving in on his eyes, then he takes his coat and leaves, knocking over a bottle of perfume. She's going through his closet looking for some souvenir, and when she runs into the bedroom it's empty. All that's left is the perfume, and she kneels down and puts it to her face and that's it – just the essence of the man. Michael Ballhaus shot it and we had a lot of fun.

Later, in 1990, I made a documentary about Armani, called *Made in Milan*, which gave me a good excuse to go back to Italy and work there for a while. I have always had a very strong fascination with clothes, and in my movies you usually find that the costume of a character is the character – the tie a man wears can tell you more about him than his dialogue. To a certain extent I think the Armani 'look' comes from film and, since we've become good friends, I wanted to understand what goes into the style and texture of his clothes. This film is about a man with style working in a city that hides its elegance.

Following the release of New York Stories, *Scorsese began shooting the previously postponed adaptation of* Wise Guy *for Irwin Winkler and Warner Brothers, with a screenplay he had co-written with the book's author, Nick Pileggi. Since the title had already been used for a TV series and for Brian De Palma's 1986 comedy* Wise Guys, *the film became* GoodFellas. *The story is the life, as told to Pileggi, of a Mafia 'foot soldier' turned FBI informer called Henry Hill, who was born into a mixed Irish–Italian New York family and started running errands for the local Mafia while still a kid.*

I read a review while I was in Chicago shooting *The Color of Money* which said, 'this is really the way it must be'. So I got the book in galleys and really enjoyed it because of the free-flowing easy style and the wonderful arrogance of it. This was something I knew from my own experience. I grew up on the East Side, which was a very closed community of Sicilians and Neapolitans, and it took me years to work out what was happening among the organized crime characters. But I was aware of these older men and the power that they had without lifting a finger. As you walked by, the body language would change, you could just feel the flow of power coming from these people, and as a child you looked up to this without understanding it.

I knew it would make a fascinating film if we just could keep the same sense of a way of life that Nick had in the book – what Henry Hill had given him – and still have an audience care about these characters as human beings: to be as close to the truth as possible in a fiction film, without whitewashing the characters or creating a phoney sympathy for them. And if you happen to feel something for the character Joe Pesci plays after all he does in the film when he's eliminated, then that's interesting to me. It raises a moral question, like a kid getting older and realizing what these people have done, but still having those first feelings for them as people. Throughout the picture I was always telling people, 'There's no sense in making another gangster picture, unless it is as close as possible to a certain kind of reality, to the spirit of a documentary.'

Nick and I decided separately which sections of the book we liked and began putting them together like building blocks. I persuaded him that there was no need to follow traditional narrative structure and then we started to have real fun with it. You take the tradition of the American gangster film and deal with it episode by episode, but start in the middle and move backwards and forwards. Every time Nick brought me a new draft of the scenes we liked best, I would compress it and then certain things just fell away until a very clear line emerged. I discovered that scenes could be compacted, so that you could have a wedding, then go directly to the result of the marriage – the mother arguing because they were living in her house. It was a constant accumulation of these details, and I realized that if the scenes were kept short, the impact after about an hour and a half would be terrific. Then, of course, there were some scenes which would take longer, because the exuberance, the exhilaration of the lifestyle carries you along, until they start to have problems and it stops – and you have to deal with that.

The real trick, of course, was the voice-over. I showed Nick the opening of *Jules et Jim* to explain what I was aiming for. So he understood when I started pulling lines out from here and there and mixing voice-over and using stills – really all the basic tricks of the New Wave from around 1961. What I loved about those Truffaut and Godard techniques from the early sixties was that the narrative was not that important. You could stop the picture and say: 'Listen, this is what we're going to do right now – oh, by the way, that guy got killed – and we'll see you later.' Ernie Kovacs did the same kind of thing on TV in the early fifties.[2] He would stop and talk to the camera, doing crazy, surreal things. I learned a lot from watching

70 Martin Scorsese on the set of *GoodFellas* (1990) with Robert De Niro.

MICHAEL POWELL PRODUCTIONS

PLEASE REPLY TO:

November 14, 1988

Dear Marty

Re: the script of Wise Guys

It is one of the best constructed scripts that I have ever read.
At the same time it is not academic, it is not a script just on paper.
It is very much alive.

The first question I would ask you, is what is the tone of
the director? It is a take-it-or-leave-it tone? It is a dispassionate
tone? Is it meant to be the wiseguy's thoughts – or meditations –
or memories? And, in the final hiding place, is he resigned to his
completely anonymous existence, or does he expect that they will catch
up with him some day?

I think that the narration is brilliantly handled on the page,
and the tone of the narration will be equally important. How have
you managed to sustain the action and narration side by side for the
whole length of the script? It's a masterpiece. I can only compare
it with the script of The African Queen, or Billy Wilder's Double
Indemnity.

Yes, it is a little long, and the pause, or the length, seems
to come about the 100 minute mark. By the way, the women, when they
arrive, are very good, but I would love to see one of the women in
the early part of the film as a young girl, or even a little girl.
I mean a new character – either his sister, or a ten-year old girl.
Some of the best scripting is in the first twenty pages. How are
you going to handle the youngster?   There are not many actors who
can play from ten years old to thirty years old.

Dear Marty, it is a stunning script, and will make a wonderful
film, and a priceless social document.

Michael Powell

71 Letter from Michael Powell to Martin Scorsese about the script of
GoodFellas (working title: *Wise Guys*).

him destroy what you were used to thinking was the form of the television comedy show.

Everything was pretty much storyboarded, if not as drawings then in notes. These days I don't actually draw each picture, but I knew exactly how I wanted the camera to move. I wanted a very fluid style, as usual, but I also wanted it to be as if I had been doing an Al and David Maysles cinéma-vérité documentary on these guys for twenty-five years with the ability to walk in and out of rooms with cameras.[3] There had to be even more movement than I normally have and a frenetic quality of getting as much over to the audience as possible, almost overwhelming them with images and information, so that you could see the film a couple of times and still get more out of it. There's such a lot of detail in every frame because the lifestyle is so rich – and I have a love-hate attitude to that lifestyle.

The use of freeze-frames was partly influenced by *Jules et Jim*, but also by the way they're used in documentaries. I wanted images that would stop because a point was being reached in his life; like 'everyone has to take a beating sometime' – freeze – then go back to the whipping. This isn't to make the usual point that his father beat him, therefore he was bad; it's to say, 'Look, I can take a beating.' The next thing is the explosion and a freeze-frame, with Henry frozen against it and the hellish image of a person in flames. And he says, 'They did it out of respect.' It's very important where the freeze-frames come in that opening sequence, because I wanted to re-create the sort of things that make an imprint, that have an impact on you as a child. Later on, when Henry is walking with Jimmy, he realizes that Morrie, who he likes, is going to get whacked. But when Jimmy says, 'You think Morrie talks to his wife?' Henry says, 'No, no,' then the frame freezes and we hear what he's really thinking, 'He's going to get killed, what can I do?' Then the shot unfreezes and it's just two guys walking down the street. It's a dramatic and unexpected way of dealing with how these people behave.

A virtuoso sequence in the film shows in one continuous steadycam shot how Henry uses his growing power to impress his future wife, Karen, by entering the Copacabana nightclub through the kitchens. When they reach the crowded restaurant floor, a table and chairs are magically produced to seat them directly in front of the stage.

There was a practical problem: we simply couldn't get permission to go in the short way, so we had to go round the back. But I like doing that kind of thing. I'm torn between admiring things done in one shot, like Max

Ophuls and Renoir or Mizoguchi on the one hand, and the cutting of Eisenstein or Hitchcock on the other, which I probably love even more. But here there was a reason to do it all in one shot. Henry's whole life is ahead of him. He's the young American ready to take over the world and he's met a girl he likes. Because he works with these guys and he's smart and something of an outsider so he can make a lot of money for them, he gets his reward. His reward is not having to wait in line at the bakery or worry about getting a parking ticket – and getting into the Copa that way, having the table fly over the heads of the other patrons and being seated right in front of the singer, who would have been Frank Sinatra or Bobby Darren at that time. So it had to be done in one sweeping shot, because it's his seduction of her and it's also the lifestyle seducing him.

We get an insider's look into the actual workings of a family involved in organized crime, even a small family like Henry's family. It's a rare and interesting opportunity to show how a woman, who's not from that group – she's Jewish and from another area – is attracted and stays. She gets sucked into Henry's world because it's so insular and hermetically sealed that they only deal with each other. I was fascinated by the moment when Karen says, 'Hide that cross', before he meets her parents; and the next thing you know is they're getting married in a Jewish ceremony *and* he's wearing a Star of David and a cross. The point is, it doesn't make any difference to him. I guess it's 'materialism versus a spiritual life' once again, which interests me.

Henry was only a minor organized crime figure, a 'foot soldier', and he could never be a 'made man'. Even Jimmy Conway, being Irish–American, could never be a confirmed member of that world, although he was very successful as a gangster. He had a genius for working out plans like the JFK airport heist, and really enjoyed stealing. According to the FBI, he was also a very successful hit-man and killed a lot of people – 'allegedly', as they say in America. I think this is especially interesting for Americans, because in a way it's the American dream gone completely mad and twisted.

But you can't go around killing and robbing without getting caught in the end. Jimmy got caught because of a technicality which Henry Hill revealed to the police. They couldn't prove he'd killed anybody, but he was arrested on other charges and is still in prison. He had a good, long run in the world of crime, but he was not a mafioso. They had a code that they wouldn't talk about each other. I met the policeman who arrested Burke (Conway); he had taken him up handcuffed in an aircraft over JFK airport, and Mr Burke looked out and said, 'To think, once that was all mine!'[4] Then the policeman implied that it would go easier for him if he

72 Ray Liotta and Lorraine Bracco enjoy the best table in the Copacabana in *GoodFellas*.

73 Robert De Niro and Ray Liotta confront each other in *GoodFellas*.

would co-operate with the police. But Burke said, 'Don't even finish your sentence.' The policeman said, 'I understand.' It was the same with Paul Cicero (Paul Vario): he didn't say a word and died in jail. But Henry Hill was not like that, he was an outsider, and he talked.

Joe Pesci comes from that world and he's always said there's a lifecycle for a wiseguy: maybe eight or nine years before the revolving door starts and they go in and out of jail. At first it's so fast that it almost explodes, but once they start to go in and out of jail it goes on for maybe twenty years and jail becomes part of the lifestyle.

Pesci, memorable as Jake La Motta's brother and manager in Raging Bull, *plays Tommy de Vito, who grew up with Henry Hill and started as a minor gangster at the same time. Unlike Henry, he is fully Italian–American and so able to become a 'made man'. But the lure of this prize is used to trap and kill Tommy in a chilling scene of mob 'justice' when his uncontrollable psychopathic violence threatens to bring unwanted attention to the mob's business affairs. Henry and Jimmy learn of the execution in a phone call as they wait to celebrate his big day.*

The fact that Tommy gets killed that way is very important. Neither Henry nor Jimmy could have done anything about it, because it was among Italians. It was my father on the phone telling Jimmy, 'He's gone.' Bob De Niro asked my father not to tell him directly what had happened, but to talk around it. I suggested my father should say he had done 'everything he could'. In fact, the mob had been shielding him for years, but he was out of control, causing a lot of trouble and angering everyone. Finally they decided he had gone too far.

Even Jimmy and Henry are not part of the big organization, though Jimmy was a *professore* type, in charge of the young kids. I especially liked the way Bob held down the emotion after he comes out of the phone booth. He's just standing there with his hands on his hips. Henry doesn't even know yet. The body language is great between the two of them. It puts them all in their place, and it's the beginning of the real end.

I liked the book's detail very much. So the film is more about tangents, things off the point rather than the point itself, because I find that's more interesting. In a sense it was an experiment to see what would happen, building up to Henry's last day as a wiseguy, when he's under pressure from all sides. This was the hardest part to do. I wanted to create for the audience – people who have never been under the influence of anything like cocaine or amphetamines – the state of anxiety and the way the mind

74 Joe Pesci as the troublesome Tommy taking a man out in *GoodFellas*.

races when on drugs. So when Henry takes a hit of coke, the camera comes flying into his eyes and he doesn't know where he is for a split second. It's impossible for Henry to recognize what's important and what's not. He's selling drugs against Paulie's orders – not because Cicero takes a moral stand against drugs, but because he doesn't want to be involved with anyone who could send him to prison, which is exactly what happens. There's a helicopter chasing him, which could be the FBI – we don't know and neither does he – and the correct stirring of his tomato sauce seems just as important. After a while on drugs and under these pressures, you become functionally insane and that's your downfall.

Suddenly everything stops and there's a gun held to his head. Then for the rest of the movie, the last twenty minutes, I pulled back and put it all together again. What I found interesting about Henry in the book was that he was upset but not sorry for the things he had done. At the end, he regrets that he's no longer a wiseguy, but there's no hypocrisy about being sorry for his life, it's just, 'Gee, no more fun.' Now you can take that any way you want. I think the audience should get angry at him and I would hope they do – and maybe with the system which allows this. Maybe it was the affluence of the late fifties and sixties which led to the disillusion and corruption of the seventies, and Henry's journey reflects that.

Even the music becomes decadent. When Stacks gets killed and Henry comes running into the bar, Jimmy and Tommy tell him to drink up and not worry. What you hear on the soundtrack at this moment is an incredible version of 'Unchained Melody' by Vito and the Salutations. It's degenerated from the pure Drifters of Clyde McFadden singing 'Bells of St Mary's' to the Italian doo-wop of Vito and the Salutations – which actually I like, because I'm a part of the seventies and eighties! – decadent or not.

The eclectic compilation soundtrack of GoodFellas *ranges from fifties Italian–American pop to the classic rock'n'roll of the sixties and ends with punk as Henry pays the final price for his amoral career. The careful choice of music reflected Scorsese's encyclopaedic knowledge of popular music and plays an important structural role in the film as well as charting its chronology.*

A lot of music is used in movies today just to establish a time and a place and I think this is lazy. Ever since *Who's That Knocking* and *Mean Streets*, I wanted to take advantage of the emotional impact of the music. Some of it even comes from the forties. The point is that a lot of places had juke boxes which were still carrying Benny Goodman and old Italian stuff when the Beatles came in. On *GoodFellas* the only rule was to use music which could only have been heard at that time. If a scene took place in 1973, I could use any music that was current or older. For example, I wanted to use one Rolling Stones song at the end – 'She Was Hot' – for that last day in 1979, but it came out a year later, so I had to use something else. Some people said it was impossible that gangsters would have been listening to 'Sunshine of Your Love' by Cream in 1967, but I pointed out that the song was on American radio in the Top 40, so they heard it anyway, whether they liked it or not! I used that song for the scene when Jimmy is at the bar looking around and deciding that he has to get rid of all these people, and the camera moves into his face very slowly. We tried ten songs and the most interesting turned out to be 'Sunshine': we found his eyes were just perfect with that shot at high speed, and it gave a real sense of danger and sexuality.

A lot of non-dialogue scenes were shot to playback, so for example we had 'Layla' on the set while shooting the discovery of the dead bodies in the car and the meat-truck. Then sometimes we put the lyrics of songs between lines of dialogue so that they commented on the action; for example, when the baby is put in the pram for the drug smuggling, you hear the Rolling Stones' 'Monkey Man', and the first lyric is 'I'm a flea-bit peanut monkey and all my friends are junkies'. There's also part of 'Memo to Turner' from *Performance*, where you hear the beginning of that incredible Ry Cooder slide guitar coming in when Henry puts the guns in the trunk. The music was mainly chosen for the rhythm and emotion of each scene.

At $25 million, GoodFellas *was Scorsese's most expensive film, although still only a medium budget by prevailing Hollywood standards. It was also the first film he was obliged by a studio to preview.*

There's a danger these days of underestimating the audience, or being afraid of them. But I believe the audience is always ahead of you and at least a certain segment will go with the picture. We previewed *GoodFellas* twice in California and as a result we shifted a few things and tightened the last two reels. A lot of the preview audiences were agitated by the last day sequence, but I argued that they *should* be agitated; and it's interesting that one of their favourite scenes was a very long sequence I'd developed with the actors. It's where Joe Pesci is telling a story and Ray is responding to him – the 'what's so funny about me' scene. This was all improvised; I kept adding set-ups to let the whole moment play out. I feel

75 Scorsese's Post-It notes about possible songs for *GoodFellas*. 'Layla', 'Atlantis', 'Ain't That a Kick in the Head', 'Monkey Man' and 'Life Is but a Dream' all feature on the final soundtrack.

that if what the actors are doing is truthful and enjoyable, the audience will accept longer scenes and a slower rhythm.

Immediately after shooting on GoodFellas *had finished Scorsese flew to Japan to fulfil a long-standing commitment to play a cameo role in Akira Kurosawa's* Dreams. *The two directors had met in 1980, when Kurosawa attended the New York Film Festival for the presentation of Kagemusha, and Scorsese was using every opportunity to publicize his call for more durable colour film stock from Eastman Kodak, to preserve film-makers' work for the future.*

One master to whom colour really means a great deal is Kurosawa, so I got five minutes to talk to him. Knowing I only had a few minutes, I guess I must have been quite intense in explaining why I needed his name on the petition. He was very polite, but after five minutes that was it – I had to leave the room. A few months later he sent a telegram saying we could use his name. Later, when he wrote to me about playing Van Gogh he said, 'I want the same kind of enthusiasm and intensity that you had when you were explaining why I should put my name on that petition.'

This was really a challenge, because I wouldn't normally act that way. In *Guilty by Suspicion*, directed by my friend and former producer Irwin Winkler, they asked me to play a director. Well, that was easy, although I had to shave my beard, because directors in Hollywood in the fifties didn't have beards! Then I had to go on the set, wait in the trailer, go back to the set, wait while they played around and did different angles. It was torture to try acting, but it was also doing my friends a favour: 'Let's have Marty come in and do a scene.' I did a similar kind of thing for another friend, Bertrand Tavernier, in *Round Midnight*. But for Kurosawa it was a serious role.

I studied it while I was working on *GoodFellas*, trying to memorize it during the delays while I waited in my trailer. But we went a few weeks over schedule on *GoodFellas*, and the only scene Kurosawa had left to do was mine, so we were causing him problems with *his* schedule. So I left the last few second unit things to my assistant director Joe Reidy and left immediately for Japan. I memorized the scene, spent three hours being made up twice, and after a couple of rehearsals it was very easily shot in four takes with two cameras.

After the première of Dreams *at Cannes in May 1990, Scorsese stayed on in Europe to make* Made in Milan. *Later that year, he returned to Italy to meet his parents, and received the honorary citizenship of the town of*

76 Scorsese as Van Gogh encountering Akira Terao as an aspiring painter in the 'Crows' episode of Akira Kurosawa's *Dreams* (1990).

*Ciminna, near Palermo in Sicily, where his maternal grandmother had
lived before leaving for America.*

It was the first time my father had visited his home town, where his mother
was born; and I found out the real spelling of our name: it was originally
'Scozzeze'. Some time ago I had felt I was really Italian and planned to
spend more time there. Then later I realized that I'm really, truly American
and that it's not easy for me to understand the social and political
conditions in modern Italy.

*When Universal backed The Last Temptation of Christ, there was an
understanding that Scorsese would go on to make more commercial films
for them. One of the properties still owned by the studio was the thriller
Cape Fear, based on a novel by John D. Macdonald, directed by J. Lee
Thompson and released in 1962. Wesley Strick had already written a
script for Steven Spielberg, which Scorsese read but didn't want to do.
However, De Niro was keen to re-create the part of the vengeful ex-con
Max Cady, originally played by Robert Mitchum, and eventually persuaded Scorsese that they could both learn something from revisiting a
traditional Hollywood genre and accepting its discipline.*

*The story follows Cady's escalating campaign of terror against the
Bowden family as revenge for his imprisonment. In Scorsese's version,
Sam Bowden has become Cady's former defender instead of a witness
who testified against him; and the family is far from united, with tension
between Sam, his wife, Leigh, and their teenage daughter, Danielle.*

It's like a fairytale that can be told over and over again, with a moral
dilemma which roused my interest in the piece, if I could work with the
right people. Apart from De Niro and the writer Wesley Strick, there was
the casting of Nick Nolte and Jessica Lange. These were all people who
had confidence in each other and who felt we could do something special
within the limits of the genre.

We talked to Robert Redford about the role of Sam because he
represented a wholesomeness which it would be interesting to have De
Niro play against. But ultimately we didn't need that kind of symbolism in
the casting. I didn't think of Nick Nolte at first because I had just worked
with him on *Life Lessons*, in which he was fat, had a beard and was
drinking brandy as the character. So I didn't see him as a possible lawyer.
Then when *GoodFellas* was shown at the Museum of Modern Art, Nick
showed up in a blazer and tie, thinner and wearing glasses, with his hair

parted. I nudged Bob and said, 'Look, that's our lawyer.' It's funny, sometimes you know people for years, but they still have to appear looking like the character before you change the image you have of them from their previous work.

Spielberg was originally going to direct the film and the script I first read was written for him. It was more black and white than I could accept. For instance, the family was happy, sitting round the piano singing – the kind of thing Steve could do genuinely quite well because he believes in it. And the scene in the theatre between De Niro and Juliette Lewis (who played Danielle), which I eventually played as a seduction, was originally written as a scary scene. Max was chasing the girl through the basement and classrooms of the school, and finally she was hanging on to a shade on a windowsill which was breaking. She didn't fall into his arms, but was saved by someone else. This was based on the scene in the original film where it's the janitor and not Mitchum who's coming after her.

It would have been a real *tour de force* Spielberg chase, but although I like seeing that kind of film-making, I would be bored trying to do it. So we started work on that scene in the theatre and built the film out from it. For me this is still the most upsetting scene. We were playing on the idea of evil being attractive and dangerous. Max uses logic and emotion and psychology very much in the way Satan speaks in the Bible. I know a couple of women friends who said that they had similar experiences of being attracted at first to a dangerous character. He destroys what little respect and trust Danielle had left for her father.

The other level is that the weakness in the family is almost begging for someone to come in and disrupt it even further. It colours their judgement and they make mistakes. You even begin to think that maybe Max *is* telling the truth. Because of their malaise, their disappointment with their lives, they are more susceptible to what he's saying: and to some extent, Max has actually been created by Sam, because Sam made a moral mistake. But what interests me is that anyone with a feeling of compassion would have been tempted to do the same thing, to let Max serve fourteen years in jail. The change from Sam as the witness who testified against Max to the Public Defender who held back information because of his moral outrage was a script element that was in place before I became involved, but I liked it.

De Niro was already committed to the project before he persuaded Scorsese to join it and, as in earlier films, he embarked on an intensive physical programme in preparation for the role of the demonic Max Cady.

77 Robert Mitchum as the menacing Max Cady in J. Lee Thompson's
version of *Cape Fear* (1962).

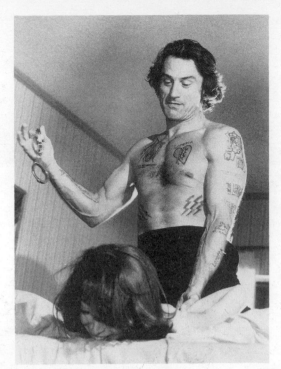

78 Evil as attractive and dangerous: Robert De Niro as Max Cady in Scorsese's *Cape Fear* (1991).

79 The body as lethal weapon. Robert De Niro displays his tattoos in *Cape Fear*.

De Niro started work several months in advance with his trainer, Dan Harvey, building up his character by building up his body. When we were rehearsing and shooting, he would wake up around three in the morning and work out for three or four hours, before coming to work. All the scenes where his body is shown at its best were done at the very end of the film when he had developed as much muscle tissue as possible. I felt he should look like a lethal weapon, his body itself should be a weapon – we kept adding tattoos to this effect. The lightning bolts on his rib cage, which I thought were really good, were his idea.

He also did a lot of research from tapes. Alan Greenberg knows a lot about regional accents and music, and he interviewed rapists and killers in prison. De Niro studied those tapes and then we worked on the script with Wesley just ahead of shooting, trying to get a little more in here and there. We've known each other for a long time now, so there's a kind of shorthand between us.

The image of Stalin seen near the beginning of the film evokes the Man of Steel, which is what Max wants to be. His philosophy is Nietzsche's 'superman' in its most negative form. He also identifies with Alexander the Great and with the martyred saint of South America who was impaled on spears, because he sees himself as a victim.[5] So there are these conflicting ideas chasing around his psyche which make him believe that he's an instrument of God carrying out his revenge.

The way I saw Max, which may not be how Bob or Wesley saw him, was that he becomes the collective guilt of the family. So when Bob had the idea that he wanted to be under the car, an entity which is almost unstoppable, like *The Terminator*, it fitted perfectly with my idea that they would never get rid of this guilt however far they ran, until they confronted it. What I tried to do is make Max's transition as emotionally and psychologically real to the apocalyptic ending, and the scene under the car is the key to this, and it should be audacious. Immediately before it, the movie begins anew when we cut to the sign that says 'Cape Fear'.

Scorsese took the opportunity on Cape Fear *to shoot for the first time in CinemaScope and to work with a director of photography he had long admired, the English cinematographer and director Freddie Francis.*[6]

I enjoyed working out all the suspense shots with Freddie, where the camera is tracking around the outside of the house and moving down a hall so that you're expecting a character to break in at any second. I also like the camera going through the trees to discover the supposedly safe

80 An instinct for suspense and horror: a shot from Freddie Francis's *Torture Garden* (1968).

81 Apocalypse and redemption for the family in *Cape Fear*.

houseboat. One of the reasons I wanted to work with Freddie was his instinct and deep knowledge from the suspense and horror films he worked on. I could speak to him in shorthand about a certain style and shots that are used in this genre, because this was something I wanted to learn about.

I would say to Freddie, 'This shot's not working,' and he would always add something to it to help make it work. For example, Nick Nolte's face during the attempted rape of his wife where you see him watching through the venetian blind. I originally drew the shot full-face, but when we lined it up I realized it was going to look ridiculous and probably get a laugh. Then Freddie said, 'With the combination of water on the window and the venetian blind and lightning, we'll start on his single eye and then zoom out.' I realized it would make it look strange, almost like a fish watching. That kind of collaboration is a lot of fun.

Then there was the challenge of making the traditional movieland storm to end all storms. I had never done a sequence like that before and Freddie and I worked closely on planning it. There were over two hundred drawings and we actually built a sound stage in Florida to do it. It took six or seven weeks to shoot and that proved quite an education. But it was important, because the characters' journey has to culminate in violence in order for them to come out redeemed. Even Max is redeemed in a way, he's done his job by helping them. We certainly didn't set out to make a religious film, but maybe it turned out that way, which must have been my influence on the script and actors. In fact, it took me time to understand what the blood on Nick Nolte's hands meant; he has his hands full of blood, with the guilt and a sense of a horrible deed he has committed, and then it's washed away. There is some sort of forgiveness and redemption.

One of the things that made me want to make the movie was seeing a news programme on television one night about a normal couple who had to actually kill a serial killer because he was going to kill them. They were an average husband and wife, and they talked about the process of having to save themselves by killing this man, which went on for hours. Hitchcock made it clear in *Torn Curtain*, in the scene where Paul Newman and the woman who doesn't speak English try to kill the Russian spy, that it isn't easy to kill a person. But what struck me about this couple was how long it took. They were downstairs and they hit him a few times, then they shot him, and he came back up and it went on for hours. As they were describing it, their faces were drained of colour, and it was absolutely shocking.

I realized we were taking risks in *Cape Fear* with this ending, but still

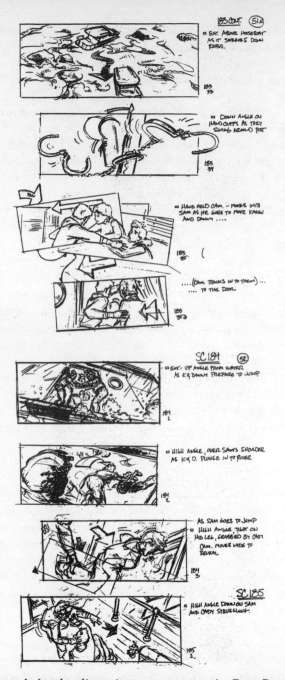

82 Storyboards for the climactic storm sequence in *Cape Fear*, drawn by a professional illustrator and based entirely on Scorsese's script notes and sketches.

83 The difficulty of killing somebody: Paul Newman struggles with a
Russian spy in Hitchcock's *Torn Curtain* (1966).

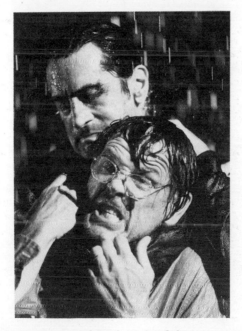

84 Robert De Niro and Nick Nolte fight it out in *Cape Fear*.

the truth of what a couple might go through emotionally and psychologically is there, far-fetched as it is – being set on fire, coming back seven times, etc. I just knew the characters had to suffer and it was very important they came through on the other side. Maybe the experience will tear them apart – I don't necessarily think the family is going to be together because they've saved each other – but at least they'll never be the same again.

I think it's best if you see my version and the original *Cape Fear* as well, maybe a week apart. There are many threads running between the films, with Gregory Peck and Robert Mitchum and Martin Balsam, Bernard Herrmann's music (reworked by Elmer Bernstein) and Saul and Elaine Bass doing the titles.[7] They didn't do the original titles, but the style of their work was extraordinary and we wanted the audience to be very aware of the lineage of this type of film. The sadness for me is that I can't make films in the old style, the studio system style, because I'm a product of a different world and society. And even if I regret the passing of the golden age of Hollywood and the studios, I have to remember it's a trade-off; what we lost in the past, we gain in freedom in the present. Ultimately, I doubt very much if I could make a true 'B' film or 'genre' film.

Notes

1 In *The Gambler*, Polina takes the narrator Alexis at his word when he swears he would do anything to prove his love, including kill himself. On a whim, she orders him to insult a pompous German baroness, thus embarrassing the General, who is the head of their Russian party staying at 'Roulettenburg'. The germ of this survives in *Life Lessons* when Paulette tells Lionel to go up to two cops in a patrol car and kiss one. When he returns from this hazardous mission, she has disappeared. The translation of *The Gambler* with Suslova's diary is by Victor Terras, edited by Edward Wasiolek, University of Chicago Press, 1972.

2 Ernie Kovacs (1919–62) was a highly original American television comedian of the fifties whose premature death cut short his promising film career.

3 Albert (b. 1926) and David (1932–87) Maysles were pioneers of 'direct cinema' documentary in the USA, filming and recording unobtrusively to enter the lives of their subjects with as little disruption as possible, as in *Salesman* (1969) and *Grey Gardens* (1975).

4 The Jimmy Conway character, played by De Niro, is based on James 'Jimmy the Gent' Burke. Similarly, Paul Vario in the film is based on Paul Cicero.

5 San Felipe de Jesus became the first Mexican martyr and saint in 1597 after he had been impaled and crucified twenty years earlier in Nagasaki, Japan, along with twenty-five other Christian missionaries.

6 Freddie Francis (b. 1917) unusually has combined careers as a distinguished cinematographer and a director specializing in the staple British horror genre. After winning an Oscar for the cinematography of *Sons of Lovers* (1960), he worked on such classics as *Saturday Night and Sunday Morning* and *The Innocents*, and later *The Elephant Man* (1980) and *The French Lieutenant's Woman* (1981). As a director, his films range from *Paranoia* (1963), *The Evil of Frankenstein* (1964) and *Torture Garden* (1967) to *Legend of the Werewolf* (1974) and *The Doctor and the Devils* (1985).

7 Saul Bass (b. 1920), a graphic designer by profession, started to create movie title sequences in the mid fifties and over the next decade became a Hollywood institution, working for Billy Wilder, Otto Preminger and especially Hitchcock. He returned to film credits design in the late eighties, in partnership with his wife, Elaine, and they have worked on *GoodFellas, Cape Fear, The Age of Innocence* and *Casino*.

CHAPTER 8

The Age of Innocence – A Personal Journey

'Say I'm old-fashioned. That should be enough.' Newland Archer in
The Age of Innocence.

*In April 1991, Universal Pictures announced that Martin Scorsese had
signed a six-year deal with the studio, with the intention of directing one
picture a year for them and producing up to twelve others in that period.
Since co-producing* The Grifters *the previous year, Scorsese had become
more involved in potential producing activities, and the first such title for
Universal was to be* Mad Dog and Glory, *directed by John McNaughton
and starring Robert De Niro. Scorsese Productions now moved office in
New York and became Cappa Productions, named after his mother's
maiden name. However, alongside his commitment to Universal, Scorsese
already had certain projects placed with other studios.*

If Cape Fear *was a project which was brought to Scorsese and was made
relatively quickly, then his next film would be the fruit of considerable
thought and personal investment. The novel* The Age of Innocence *was
published in 1920, and with it Edith Wharton (1862–1937) became the
first woman to be awarded the Pulitzer Prize. In 1902 her close friend
Henry James had urged her to 'Do New York', and in this novel she
painted an intimate portrait of the enclosed world of 1870s upper-class
New York which she had grown up in – the world of the great American
families such as the Roosevelts, the Astors and the Vanderbilts. It was a
society based on carefully organized idleness, in which manners and
conventions were all, and to defy them was to be thoroughly excluded.
Wharton's story is one of frustrated passion: Newland Archer, enduring a
protracted engagement to May Welland, falls in love with his betrothed's
cousin Ellen Olenska, who has arrived in New York fleeing a disastrous
marriage to a philandering Polish count. Given Scorsese's previous*

excursions into the world of impossible relationships, as well as his
intense curiosity about social and tribal codes as previously displayed in
the Italian–American criminal sector, it was perhaps not so surprising that
he should be fascinated by what is arguably Wharton's greatest novel.

Jay Cocks gave me a copy of Edith Wharton's *The Age of Innocence* in
1980. I first met Jay in 1968, and we became friends rather quickly. For a
period he was the movie critic for *Time* magazine, when he could not
review any of my movies. As he liked them all, it was too bad! The real
relationship developed over the fact that I'd go with him to see movie
screenings of practically every movie that came out, and we'd have all
kinds of arguments and discussions. We tested each other over the years,
and discovered that we liked the same sorts of movies. He would show me
Georges Franju's *Judex*, and I'd show him *A Matter of Life and Death*. So
we developed a language together, and trusted each other in our work and
taste. Before I even started making feature films, our dream was to make
movies in all sorts of genres – a western, or a revisionist gangster picture;
and I said that some day I'd like to do a romantic piece. When Jay gave me
this book, he said, 'You want to do a romantic piece, a costume piece;
well, this is the one, because this is you.' He didn't mean that any of the
characters were me, rather basically the idea of it.

He tried to sell me on it, telling me a little about the story, but I wasn't
interested. I was finishing up *Raging Bull*, and was about to go into *The
King of Comedy*, and the moods of those films were eating into my
lifestyle, which was not conducive to thinking about this novel. I
eventually read the book in 1987; by then a number of things in my life
had calmed down and I was able to be a little more reflective. I was on the
Guardian lecture tour in Britain, and maybe the atmosphere of being there
helped, as well as the fact that films like *Room with a View* were being
rather well received at the time. I was very taken by the story of the love
between Newland Archer and Ellen Olenska, and the most interesting
part of it for me was that they couldn't consummate their relationship. So
throughout the film, there would be a kind of emotional and erotic
tension. I became fascinated by the way that they tried to communicate
with each other, and I thought this would be a challenge to try to do.

What also was very interesting to me was how Edith Wharton wove a
tapestry of detail throughout the book, so that you're almost reading an
anthropological study at the same time as the story. You wonder at times
why she's discussing certain types of flowers, certain types of rum and
punch, different courses of food at dinners. But as the book progresses,

85 Michelle Pfeiffer and Daniel Day-Lewis play out an impossible relationship in *The Age of Innocence* (1993).

you realize it's all these elements which are keeping Newland Archer in his place in society. So I suddenly became very enamoured with the book, and told Jay that we should try to write a script of it. Twentieth Century-Fox picked up the rights, and for two years Jay would come over once or twice a week and we'd talk about structure and how I wanted to make it different from the usual, theatre-bound film versions of novels. Then in January 1989, just as I was about to go into *GoodFellas*, we took about three weeks to write a script.

The first draft of the script was completed in February 1989. Filming, however, would not begin until 26 March 1992, by which time Twentieth Century-Fox had dropped the project at the eleventh hour, and Columbia Pictures had stepped in. The cast included two leading American actresses – Michelle Pfeiffer as Ellen Olenska, and Winona Ryder as May Welland – with the majority of other roles filled by British actors, including Daniel Day-Lewis as Newland Archer. By adjusting accents on both sides, this would allow for a close approximation to the speech of the period. As production designer, Scorsese chose Dante Ferretti, whom he had first met on the set of Fellini's City of Women, *and together they worked on the colour schemes of the homes and the elaborate presentation of the social occasions to be depicted. Eighteen months of research into the period had been undertaken by Robin Standefer, creating twenty-five large reference books. An etiquette consultant, Lily Lodge, whose grandmother had been a close friend of Wharton, was to be on call during filming at all times. Scorsese was determined that the texture of the film be faithful both to Wharton and to history.*

My feeling was, the book is very, very good, so why change it? We dropped maybe two characters, that's about it. I couldn't say, well, this is a wonderful story for today's audience. I really have no idea what a good story for today's audience is. I just hoped that if it was honest enough and emotionally compelling, there might be some people out there who it would address. Sometimes people call these kinds of movies costume dramas or costume period pieces. Well, some people might consider *GoodFellas* a period piece! Actually, in Los Angeles they do, because taking place in the seventies, there are seventies cars, seventies clothes, all of which build up the budget. I would prefer to say that *The Age of Innocence* is a romantic film.

I think I became enamoured of this type of film from the British costume films I saw in the early days of American television. Also, my father would take me to theatres to see different kinds of movies, usually westerns, which were often the bottom half of a double-bill. On the top half would be some wonderful films, like *Sunset Boulevard* or *The Bad and the Beautiful*. One time, when I was about ten years old I think, it was *The Heiress*.

The film has very strong images, with solid camera positions – William Wyler positioning! I remember David Lean talking about the 'solid' images that Wyler could put up on the screen. I think what he meant by that was that there is no other real angle for the scene; *that* is the angle, the camera's *here* and this scene cannot be interpreted in any other way, with no cuts. And these images have a confidence that makes you feel as though you're in the hands of a real master. They know where the camera should be. That's why I sometimes get annoyed with the over-use of long lenses, where people just pick up things to sort out later in the cutting. In any event, I remember a scene where Ralph Richardson, the wealthy doctor who lives in a town house in Washington Square, has his daughter, Olivia de Havilland, sit down in the drawing room, and tells her that the young man who wants to marry her, played by Montgomery Clift, can't really be serious about her. Because Richardson points out she's not very pretty, in fact she's really quite plain, and not very clever, so he has to be marrying her for her inheritance. In fact, he's always resented her because when she was born her mother died, and of course she couldn't take the place of her mother.

Coming myself from a tenement area in downtown Manhattan, looking at this very beautiful place these people are living in, I was amazed by the civility of the communication between the two of them, because the message of it was so brutal for a child to hear from a father. Certainly that came across to a ten-year-old. I never forgot that image, as well as the final resolution of the film, with Montgomery Clift pounding on the door, and one of those incredible William Wyler staircase shots as Olivia de Havilland, her heart now completely made of stone, comes towards the camera with a lamp. I'd never seen anything quite like that, especially as these were people who lived in such nice surroundings, wore beautiful clothes, and seemed to be so tasteful and polite. So I think the emotional impact of that film always stayed with me.

In preparation for *The Age of Innocence*, we screened *The Heiress* and also *The Magnificent Ambersons*, which is beautiful and moving, but I'm not a great devotee of it. For some reason, I sense the destruction of it – maybe if I could ever see the complete version, I would be overwhelmed.[1] But I don't really understand the people, it's not a society I can easily relate to. More important for me was looking again at certain Visconti pictures.

86 Brutality in a civilized society: Ralph Richardson, Miriam Hopkins
and Olivia de Havilland in Wyler's *The Heiress* (1949).

I think the first Visconti film I saw was *Rocco and His Brothers*, and of course it has related to other pictures I have made – the emotional power of it went into *Raging Bull*. I think it was *The Leopard* that I saw next, in the cut version dubbed into English, but it didn't really matter. Being about Sicily where my family comes from, I was quite taken with the picture. The fact is, of course, that these are Sicilian aristocrats, and I come from peasant stock, but still the look of Sicily, the *palazzos*, the change in time, the Risorgimento, all of that made an impact. At first when I saw the film, I thought the ball sequence was way too long, but I liked the attention to detail in the piece. Then I got to see *Senso*, and again I liked the elegance of the film, and also the opera; not just the performance of *Il Trovatore* which opens the piece, but the opera of the people in the picture. I like how Visconti tends to go melodramatically over the top with them, and then brings them down. *Senso* is really a very gutsy movie; maybe a flawed one, but it has always been one of my very favourites.

In Edith Wharton's novel there is an opera, a performance of Gounod's *Faust*. Apparently, *Faust* was performed every year, and everyone went to see not the opera but each other, and that's why in the film we wind up past the singers on the opera audience at the end. Choosing the scene involving the picking of flowers, and her singing that he loves me, he loves me not, has a great deal to do with the rest of the picture. When I read the novel, I thought this was a wonderful piece to begin the film. After the opera, we go to the ball, so that for the first twenty minutes of the film you have a complete presentation of the way these people lived, with all the rules and the possibilities of embarrassment and the politeness – but politeness covering the cynicism and gossip of the time.

I wanted to see how we could bring a sensibility like mine to the visual interpretation of the film, and how it would be different from Wyler or Visconti. *The Leopard* dealt with Sicilian aristocrats living in palaces; for these people in New York, the houses were smaller, the ballrooms were smaller. Mrs Astor's ballroom could fit only 400 people; that's where the phrase 'The New York 400' came from. If you were invited to the ball, you were one of the 400. In this case the biggest room would be the Beauforts' ballroom. And the Beauforts are a new class, a rather decadent one. The established upper class had a great deal of money but the buildings they lived in had to be brownstones, nothing very elaborate, as it was quite vulgar to show their wealth. I was interested in expressing through the camera the emotions of Archer, Ellen and May, taking chances with certain camera moves and revelations. All these camera moves were written into the script beforehand, and we thought about them very carefully.

87 The ballroom sequence in Visconti's *The Leopard* (1963).

88 The social ritual of the opera in *The Age of Innocence*.

89 The annual performance of Gounod's *Faust* in *The Age of Innocence*.

(#3)
FAUST
che cosa dici si som-
messo?

MARGHERITA
El m'amal
El non m'ama no el
m'ama no, el non m'
ama no el m'ama

Che cosa dici
Timing:
13 seconds
At the final "ei m'ama"
she drops the flowers
and rises flushed. Faust
quickly kneels.

el m'ama

SHOT #3
che cosa dici-el m'ama
Proscenium shot

See diagram #2

(#4)
COVER
FAUST
Si credi a questo
fior il dell'amor egli
ti dice al cor quel che
il cor tuo brama, ei
t'ama non sal tu com'
e felice amar? amarl
portar in cor
un ardor ognoi ferventel
inebbriarsi ancor d'amor
(#5)   eternamentel

Si credi a questo
Timing:
52 seconds
Faust picks up the flower
to say "si credi a
questo fior". He rises
downstage to sing his love
song

eternamentel

SHOT #4
Si credi a questo fior-
fervente
Cover Faust-
sideways tracking left to
right and moving in and out
on Faust.

SHOT #5
eternamente
Side view high angle move
in to XCU on Faust

MARGHERITA E FAUST
Sempre amarl   Sempre sempre!

Sempre amar
Timing:
30 seconds
Margherita is behind
Faust and joins him in
singing this

See diagram #2

(#5A)

(#6)
COVER
For Dialogue in wellard Box
FAUST
Notte d'amor,
tutta splendor,
begli astri d'oro,
O celeste volutta,
udirsi dir t'amo,
t'amo, t'adoro

Notte d'amor
Timing:
2 minutes
Margherita puts her head
on Fausts' breast, & he
sings "Notte d'amor".
Margherita answers him,
still leaning on him. At
the first "parla ancora"
she turns to look directly
at him. Margherita takes
his hand and leads him right
and slightly back. By "Ahl Si
t'adoro" they are in position
downstage, center right.

SHOT #6
Notte d'amor-t'amo
t'adoro
Cover high angle boom
down onto Faust close up.

SHOT #7
Ti voglio amar-morir
2 shot, left to right to
close up on Margherita

(#7)
COVER
MARGHERITA
Ti voglio amar
idolatrarl parla
ancora lo tua saro
si t'adoro per te
voglio morirl parla
parla ancora ahl si
t'adoro per te voglio
morir, per te voglio
morir.

morir

SHOT #8
Shot for repetition of morir

90 Scorsese's directing notes for the opera sequence in *The Age of
Innocence*.

Although *The Age of Innocence* may look lavish, the editing, the angles, the dissolves and the length of the images were all worked out way in advance to give the impression of extravagance. In fact, the budget was only $32–34 million, and some of the most complicated things, like the beginning of the ball sequence, only took three-quarters of a day.

Though I'm moved by *The Heiress*, it is based on a play, and the three acts are what makes it satisfying. The conflicts are played out in traditional dramaturgy: characters talk in a room and confront each other, all in dialogue. I wanted to get away from this three act approach. Over the past ten years in Hollywood, you find studio executives saying things like, 'The script is good but we need a new act two', or 'act three just isn't there'. Finally I said to a bunch of students, 'Why are we using the term "acts" when the damn thing is a movie?' Now I like theatre, but theatre is theatre and movies are movies; they should be separate. We should talk about sequences – there are usually five or six sequences in a film, which are broken up into sections and scenes. I screened a few films for Elia Kazan in 1993, including *East of Eden* and *Wild River* – neither of which he had seen since he had made them! We discussed them afterwards and I found that he too had been trying to get away from conventional theatrical dramaturgy. With *The Age of Innocence*, I wanted to find a way of making something literary – and Americans are cowed by the tyranny of that word – and also filmic.

Above all, I wanted on film to give people the impression that I had when I finished reading the book, to have some of the literary experience along with the visual experience of the picture. So we decided to use a voice-over narration from the book, in which the narrator seems to be standing apart and observing events. But Edith Wharton writes the book from the point of view of Newland Archer, so that you don't realize what the other people are doing until later on when he realizes it. That was such a surprise to me, and satisfying, because poor Archer is trying to do so many things, and yet he underestimates a lot of people. In the final dinner scene, rather than playing it out in normal dramaturgy, with Newland at the head of the table talking to Ellen and everyone smiling, I decided to use mainly voice-over, literally from the book. The gracefulness of the prose has a kind of scathing, ironic violence to it. The shot begins high looking over the table, and you hear, 'It was, as Mrs Archer said to Mrs Welland, a great event for a young couple to give their first dinner.' She describes everybody at the table, Roman punch, gilt-edged cards etc., and then the camera comes up on Newland's face for the words, 'at her farewell dinner for the Countess Olenska'. Then I'd imagined the camera would rise up, and you'd have the table, and that would be enough. When we had the camera set up there and I realized we had the footmen in the shot too, all around the room like guards, I said, 'This is wonderful – the armed camp!'

From the way people are behaving so politely at this dinner party, as if nothing has happened, it suddenly dawns on Newland that they know about his feelings for Elena. In the following scene, the camera's panning around each of these people, and then we pick up on May, she smiles, gets up, comes towards the camera and disappears out of frame. The camera then moves over to Mrs van der Luyden, and she calls over Ellen Olenska. Ellen gets up, goes to speak to Mrs van der Luyden and Larry Lefferts and his wife Gertrude. They're talking about the Martha Washington Ball they give every year for the blind, and Sillerton Jackson then walks over to Larry Lefferts, and as he does someone crosses the frame and blacks it out. At the moment of the most important line of narration, May is revealed smiling at Newland, and he realizes his wife believes he's Ellen's lover. It's a very chilling moment for him. I had a real problem picking up on May at the end, because the room we were shooting in was too small, and I didn't know how to get back to her.

We started laying out the shot on Friday night, so it had to be done first thing on Monday morning. On the weekend I was thinking about it, and Jay Cocks came over on Sunday when we would regularly run old 16 mm prints. I'd finally got hold of a print of *Pink String and Sealing Wax*, Robert Hamer's first feature as director, I'd never seen it before. So we put it up on the screen, just sat there and watched it, and somehow in the way he visually interpreted the picture – and I guess there's a similarity in that it's also a costume drama – it cleared my mind and made me realize through the easy elegance of the camera moves how to reveal May at the end of the shot. It wasn't any particular shot, but just through the experience of watching that film on 16 mm, I was able to think freely about it.

An important camera move for me was when, at the opera, Larry Lefferts lifts his opera glasses and looks across the audience and ends up finding Ellen Olenska for the first time. Normally in a film, you'd just have the camera panning and then put a binocular masking over it for his point of view. I felt that wasn't unique enough and also that it didn't duplicate what you would see if you were actually looking through opera glasses and panning over an audience. I wanted to give it more of an edge, so that it would be more important when the camera finally stops and you see Ellen slipping into the box. We devised a way of doing it through a kind of stop-action photography where we just took one frame at a time and then panned. But Michael Ballhaus thought that would be too fast, so I suggested I could print each frame three times. Then in the editing it was still too choppy for me, so finally we decided to dissolve between each set of three frames. I settled on that effect because I saw how you began to notice people, with the glitter of their jewellery, and then this incredible woman appears in a blue dress, and the blue is very different from what everyone else is wearing.

Where possible, The Age of Innocence *was filmed on authentic period locations. The Academy of Music in Philadelphia stood in for the opera house, the National Arts Club in Gramercy Park, New York City, became the Beaufort mansion, and the New York town of Troy, with its three-storey brownstones, proved ideal for almost all the city exteriors. Three period sets were built: Archer's library, the Beauforts' ballroom, and the main hall of the Metropolitan Museum.*

In the Merchant-Ivory films, where they make use of English settings, one wide shot says it all, and you really get a sense of who these people are. I remember speaking to a British journalist while we were editing *The Age of Innocence*, and he said something like, 'In England, we think these films are easy.' Well, it's not that easy to make this kind of film in America, especially since we no longer have the studios that have all the props and sets. In fact, we were able to find most of our interiors in Manhattan, Brooklyn and the Bronx, but the neighbourhoods that used to surround them are completely gone. It's tragic. In the Merchant-Ivory films and even in Polanski's *Tess*, you are taken out of today and put very securely in a world that looks more civilized, at least if you had enough money, and where it took you a day to travel from one town to another.

I'm a history buff. I read a lot of history, mainly the ancient world, but also the eighteenth and nineteenth centuries. I'm interested in the way these people lived, the physical details as well as the codes of their society. Sometimes from my townhouse (built in the 1860s) late at night, at one o'clock in the morning, I can hear a horse and carriage go by. And that's the sound of the nineteenth century. Maybe we're yearning for a quieter time, even one without the advantages we have today in terms of medicine, of picking up the telephone and speaking to anybody anywhere in the world, or crossing the Atlantic on Concorde. I think we've lost something.

It was in Rossellini's *The Rise of Louis XIV* that I discovered that the more detail you know, the better you know the people. Other films do that too, but Rossellini did it in a bolder way. I was really interested in the way he tied up the entire story in the dramatic climax of the film, which is the presentation of the meal. In *The Age of Innocence*, we have eight meals, and they are all different in order to make different dramatic points. The food was important as a sign of what the people are. It couldn't be there just to be eaten, it had to be presented in a certain way. It was just one more detail which is a sort of rock holding Newland Archer down. As you became older and older in that society, it became harder and harder to break away. Apparently they really ate a great deal, with many different courses. So in the scene with Mr Letterblair, it was exactly as written in the book – a dinner for two people, comprising five courses.

Jay Cocks showed the film to an audience of Wharton specialists who included R. W. B. Lewis, who wrote the Pulitzer Prize-winning biography. And he told me their reaction was extraordinary, because every time a dinner service was shown, or when Mrs Mingott selected the silver plate, they laughed. They knew what the presentation of that particular piece meant. So when the van der Luydens create a dinner for Countess Olenska, they are making a statement and daring people to go against them. I tried to convey the importance of their status by the attention I gave to the dinner itself; the fact they use Roman Punch in the middle is almost like having a triple high mass for a funeral rather than a low mass. They are saying, 'Not only will we defend you, but we are going to do so on the highest level. If anyone has a problem with that, they are going to have to answer to us.' I remember in *The Razor's Edge*, when Gene Tierney throws a plate at Herbert Marshall, he says, 'My goodness, the Crown Derby!' Here it's: 'We're going to have to show the Crown Derby, aren't we?' And Jay said this audience of Wharton specialists loved these scenes in *The Age of Innocence*.

Such occasions were the most official way these characters could sign someone on and make them credible in that society. For instance, when Ellen Olenska arrives late at the party given for her, it's not important to her. The next day Newland Archer says, 'All New York laid itself out for you last night.' She answers, 'It was so kind. Such a nice party.' The audience has to understand, this wasn't just a party, lady! Newland is in effect saying, 'I'm getting married to your family, and we have agreed to take on the disgrace of your separation from your husband and we are going to do it with a stiff upper lip. So you really should know what we are doing for you by putting on a party.' In a way it's at that point the picture proper begins, because up to then it's setting the scene.

In actual fact, the details give you the impression of what Newland has to cut through in order to break away from that society. You keep adding and adding the imagery of detail and explain what these details mean, then there is nothing casual about anything, and you begin to realize how difficult it is for him to make a move. He's been bred that way; if he came in from the outside, it wouldn't mean anything. Very often, I just like the look of the ritualistic use of objects.

The paintings in the film reflect the characters of the people who own them and who are displaying them in their homes. Edith Wharton talked about certain paintings in her book, especially the Beauforts', who were lavish and tinged with decadence in their tastes; whereas Newland Archer's mother had more bucolic paintings, featuring farms and cows. Mrs Mingott, being a little more eccentric, had lots of paintings of dogs. I had the idea of putting the painting of the Louvre there, so that you dissolve into the painting within the painting. When I said, 'We'll go up the paintings along the wall up the stairs', my production designer Dante Ferretti suggested, 'Why don't we have a trip up the Hudson River?' So we followed these paintings by Thomas Cole and the Hudson River Valley School, ending on the scene of Native Americans killing a woman.

My researcher Robin Standefer found out who the families in the novel were actually based on, and from there we were able to find out what paintings those people had in their houses at that time. Through the New York Historical Society and other places, we were able to track down those paintings. I chose maybe about 150 for use in the film. Of course, we had to make replicas, and since it was going to cost too much money, I had to cut down the numbers further.

When Newland visits Elena's house for the first time, the book calls for him to look at paintings he has never really seen before. We had to let a modern audience know that there was something very different about this woman from the paintings she had on her walls. My researcher found the school of Italian painters, pre-Impressionist, called the Macchiaioli School. One featured a woman with a parasol but no face, which would certainly be shocking to the audience. Another was a seascape painted on a very long plank of wood, which enabled us to enjoy a joke about wide screen cinema at the same time!

I was interested in the use of colour like brushstrokes throughout the film, and how the characters expressed themselves by sending each other flowers. While there was a great deal of sensuality in their lives, they didn't appear to be overtly sensual, so it seemed the flowers were expressive of their emotions. It just didn't seem right to fade to black, it had to be

91 The rituals of old New York: a visit to the Van der Luydens in *The Age of Innocence*.

something rich in colour and texture, so I used fades to red and yellow. Sometimes the colours were darker images. When the voice-over says, 'The refusals were more than a simple snubbing. They were an eradication', Ellen looks towards the camera and it goes a rust colour, rather than a bright colour like red. When May gets the yellow flowers, we burst into yellow, but then we couldn't go from yellow to another colour, so we went to white in the aviary. We spent a lot of time working out exactly how long the bursts of colour should be on the screen. In *Black Narcissus* there was a fade to orange when Kathleen Byron faints, and in *Rear Window* there was a similar effect when the flashbulbs go off.

A lot of the dissolves were scripted, but I also stumbled upon the idea of shortening many shots, like a brush coming through and swishing by, painting bits and pieces of colour. For example, in the conservatory scene at the ball, when Newland says he wants to kiss May, it was all shot as one take and it took ages before I had them sit down. So I dissolved, he kisses her, and when they start to move, I dissolved again and they're sitting down. There was a similar problem with the dinner scene in France during the honeymoon montage. There's a high angle of the table, the camera booms down, and then there's a dissolve as the camera goes over the table and the food, and then it tilts up to see Newland and Riviere talking. Originally it was all one shot, and as I was doing it I thought, 'This is impossible, how many more tracks are we going to stand in this picture?' So I decided to pull the middle out of the shot, and to me it's one of the best dissolves in the film because it reminds me of an Impressionist painting.

When The Age of Innocence *was announced, there was inevitably some surprise that Scorsese should have moved into such different territory. Yet many critics noted that the film had an emotional thrust which pointed to a deep identification with its characters.*

Although this film deals with New York aristocracy and a period of New York history that has been neglected, and although it deals with codes and ritual, and with love that's not unrequited but unconsummated – which pretty much covers all the themes I usually deal with – when I read the book, I didn't say, 'Oh good, all those themes are here.' I was just hit by the impact of the scene near the end where Newland tries finally to tell his wife May he'd like to leave – and by her response. I loved the way I was led by Wharton down the path of Newland's point of view, in which he underestimates all the women, and how he winds up being checkmated by them, and how his wife becomes the strongest of them all. I find that admirable. Even though I may not agree with May totally, I like the growth of her character from a young girl to a person who takes control. You see how important her role is in the second opera house scene, which is the first time May has worn her wedding dress since the wedding. We see her seated between her mother and Mrs Van der Luyden – they have passed on the responsibility for continuing their lifestyle to her. And that means never giving an indication that she knows anything.

I played the film like the book, so that you never really know when May knows about Newland and Ellen. If you go back and look at the picture and study it, you'll see that when May is at Mrs Mingott's right after the ball and her mother is helping her with her coat, she glances over at Ellen. That's possibly the first time. Then, when they're walking in the aviary, and he says, 'I sent some roses to your cousin Ellen, too. Was that right?', she says, 'Very right. She didn't mention it at lunch today, though. She said she'd gotten wonderful orchids from Mr Beaufort and a whole hamper of carnations from Cousin Henry van der Luyden.' That's quite cruel. Later in the scene, she says, 'Did I tell you I showed Ellen the ring you chose? She thinks it's the most beautiful setting she ever saw. She said there was nothing like it in the rue de la Paix.' She never gives an indication that she knows anything, because that's the way May would have done it. I had the feeling that she was pretty aware of it.

In the book, the first indication of him *thinking* that May knows is when she says in the hallway at night, 'And you must be sure to go and see Ellen.' Newland wants to think that nobody knows, and I was interested in putting you in his mindset throughout the film. One of my favourite scenes is just after Mrs Mingott has had a stroke, and Newland says he'll collect Ellen at the railroad station. When they walk out, May says, 'But how can you meet Ellen and bring her back here if you have to go to Washington this afternoon?', and he replies, 'I'm not going. The case is off. Postponed.' Newland doesn't give anything away, even when May persists in asking him about it, and says, 'Then it's not postponed?' and he has to reply, 'No. But my going is.' I even had to tone down her glance. She just glances to the right as she walks off. Winona asked, 'Could I just give a second look?', and I said, 'No, no, don't. She wouldn't give a second look.' Because he already knows she's on to something.

By the end of the film, when she gets up and says to Newland that she's afraid the doctors won't let her go, you know he's finished. I figured out that as she gets up from the chair, we should do it in three cuts, three separate close-ups, because I thought he'd never forget that moment for the rest of his life. He'd play it back many times. When she gets up, I

92 'The strongest of them all': Winona Ryder as May in *The Age of Innocence*.

thought we should play it back like a memory. It's a medium shot, then a shot of her coming into the frame, and then a third one, so that she almost grows in stature. We shot it very quickly, three takes each, one at 24 frames, one at 36 and one at 48. There was something about the way her dress moved, like a flower opening or something growing, that meant at 24 frames it was too quick, but at 48 it might be better – not too slow, but a little overcranking. The beginning of the scene is the only time that you see them in a wide, theatrical, almost proscenium frame. He's sitting all the way in the left of the frame, and she comes in on the right. It's as if they're on stage, and now the final act is going to be played out. This was the key scene that made me want to make this picture.

What's very significant to me is that when you fall in love, you can't see what other people see. You become as passionate and obsessive as Newland, who can't see what's going on around him. And I was also fascinated by the sense of loss in the love story. A situation where just a touch of the hand would suffice, not necessarily for the consummation of the relationship, but at least to keep him alive, and to keep each other alive for a few months. Just a knowing glance at the theatre or a dinner party would keep his heart alive. It seems to be a theme I like a lot, and it's in movies like *Who's That Knocking at My Door?* or *Taxi Driver*, where Travis Bickle becomes obsessed with Betsy. I can identify with those feelings of wanting to take and not taking, of wanting to proceed with something and not proceeding, for many different reasons – shyness, a certain kind of propriety, or deciding that it wasn't such a great idea. I had a late adolescence in a way, I would say even up to the point when I started making *The Age of Innocence*. It has made me think, at the age of fifty, what if I'd been a different type of person, one who could have handled such things easily? Would my life have been very different?

I found the way this dilemma plays out in *The Age of Innocence* so wonderful, but then Wharton goes beyond that and makes a case for a life that's not exactly well spent, but a life that happens to him. Newland has his children, then he finds out that his wife knew all along about his love for Ellen and even told his son about it. Essentially, he is what they call in America a 'stand-up guy' – a man of principle who would not abandon his wife and children. When he really wanted something, he gave it up because of his child. That's very interesting to me. I don't know if I or a lot of other people could do the same, but I know that even today there are many who would. It's about making a decision in life and sticking to it, making do with what you have. And then, of course, during the conclusion you realize that a generation has gone by. The children don't react in the same way; the First World War is looming ahead and they can't understand why everybody was angry. I don't say it's a happy ending, but it's a realistic and beautiful one.

Premièred at the Venice Film Festival on 31 August 1993, The Age of Innocence *had been Scorsese's most extended production schedule to date. One reason for the delay had been the long illness of Scorsese's father, who died on 23 August, and to whom the film is dedicated.*

Because there's so much coverage now of the entertainment business in America, with all the new channels having to talk about what's going on, I found that they'd suddenly painted this picture of me as someone who's obsessed with detail – as if that trait is a negative one! – that I sometimes take six months to cut a film, and in this case it was nine or ten months, so that I must be mad! But the situation these days is that the studios have a release date, and they have trailers showing while the film is still being shot. Very often that's the case with adventure films, which they consider more commerce than art. But I still think you have to know how to edit these kinds of films, that the best part of adventure films is in the action, and the action is inherent in the editing, and if we agree that, as Kubrick pointed out, editing is the most original element in the film-making process, why short-change that? In fact, I did try to finish *The Age of Innocence* by December 1992, but I really couldn't, and then it took another seven or eight months because the studio said, 'We can't release it in the spring, and we certainly can't release it in the summer, so it must be September.' In a funny way, it would have been better if they'd said, 'OK, Marty, it opens in June, so finish it!' Then I would have worked fast. But in fact we took our time, and though no scenes were cut or dropped, we worked on improving the rhythm and pacing. And in the meantime, I was also writing other scripts.

Those scripts included a number of projects that Scorsese had been developing: Mine, *a musical biography of George Gershwin, with the first script by Paul Schrader put aside and a new one written by John Guare;* Silence, *from the novel by Shusaku Endo, about a Portuguese priest in seventeenth-century Japan;* The Gangs of New York *(originally announced in 1987), based on Herbert Asbury's study of turn of the century urban underworld, and co-written with Jay Cocks; and* The Neighbourhood, *a collaboration with Nicholas Pileggi about three generations of an Italian family in America. This last, a highly personal project, was begun during Scorsese's work with Pileggi on* GoodFellas.

It's really the story of my family, starting with my mother and father on Elizabeth Street in New York, with flashbacks to my grandparents in Sicily and how they came over to America. Then it follows the courtship of my parents, and continues right up to the war and the early sixties. Basically the story of immigration and how Sicilian ethnicity is retained until about the third generation. So it's a story about Italians, then Italian–Americans and finally American–Italians. We finally finished it about three weeks before my father died. We might do it as a mini-series, because it's about two hundred pages, but I'm not intending to shoot it for a while yet.

In 1993 Scorsese undertook to make a documentary on American cinema as part of a series initiated by the British Film Institute and Channel 4 Television. The aim was to celebrate the centenary of cinema in 1995 by asking leading film-makers to give their view on the films produced in their own country. Originally planned to be an hour each, Scorsese's contribution grew to nearly four hours, encompassing a wide range of films which he saw as representing a personal expression – primarily that of the director – within the studio system of Hollywood. Produced by Florence Dauman and co-written with Michael Henry Wilson, the project involved editing together a vast number of film extracts, a process made simpler for his editor Thelma Schoonmaker by the new non-linear video editing equipment (in this case, Lightworks) based on computer memory. The film, entitled A Century of Cinema: A Personal Journey with Martin Scorsese through American Movies, *was completed during a very busy time for Scorsese and premièred at the Cannes Film Festival in May 1995.*

I wanted to make it clear to everybody through the title of the documentary that this was *one* personal journey. There are many others I could take, but at that moment I wanted to deal with this particular one. I wanted to direct it towards an audience of younger film-makers and film students who might not be aware of certain kinds of pictures or trends in American movies that interest me a great deal. I was trying to resurrect certain names, such as Budd Boetticher or André De Toth. Also silent films like Frank Borzage's *Seventh Heaven*, as well as show my own discoveries. I only really began to appreciate silent films very recently, when I saw them in restored prints on the big screen at the right speed; it's a whole world that's been opened to me. Of course, there are many people I wasn't able to cover, but then, when I was asked by *Film Comment* magazine to come up with ten guilty pleasures, I came up with a hundred!

It's like a journey through a little museum – I say we'll stop at this display and then at another display, and maybe we'll pass up two other displays as we don't have time right now. It was hard because we'd look at clips and say, let the whole clip play, but you have to keep things moving to make the points you want to make. I didn't have the luxury of Kevin Brownlow's thirteen-hour series 'Hollywood' on the silent cinema, which is really quintessential. I plan to make another film like this, as well as one on Italian cinema, again presenting these films to young people in this country who have never heard of most of these directors.

I began the journey with the first film I remember seeing by title, *Duel in the Sun*. That led me to King Vidor and his relationship with his producer, David O. Selznick. There you're dealing with the whole issue of personal expression within the studio system. Vidor made a very personal film, *The Crowd*, but then he followed it with *The Champ*, and so he had struck a bargain. But others took a different approach. Within the system there were many people who said what they wanted to say, but almost disguised it within the form, using the genres of the period.

I think I would have liked to have been one of those directors working at Warner Brothers, as they made the kind of pictures – the gangster films, the musicals, the westerns – that I would have liked to have done. But it's just some sort of dream, nothing to do with the reality of today. My movies certainly spring from a very passionate love for the old cinema of America, and I don't know how to compare what I'm making with the old ones. People say, oh, but I love your films, and I reply, 'Well, I've seen a lot more pictures than you!' So I know what I'm compared against.

For me, there's got to be a way that I can experiment and just keep working. Not every picture you make is necessarily going to come totally from the heart. I'm trying to make films in the mainstream, in the system – and yet stay true to the way I see things. My definition of a 'director' is one who could flourish in the old studio system, who could do a really professional job on whatever script he was given. I prefer to be the film-maker, as being a director is a really hard job, to find the energy to feel for material that doesn't originate from you. I would include, in terms of what I mean by originating from me, material that I read, like Edith Wharton's book. But every now and then I'd like to continue making a picture like *Cape Fear*, to keep working on the technical aspects of my craft, and try to combine style from the old days with my own interests and obsessions.

Notes

1 Orson Welles's *The Magnificent Ambersons* (1942) originally ran over two hours, but was cut by RKO (with a new ending directed by Robert Wise) and released at 88 minutes. The original material has never been recovered.

CHAPTER 9

Casino

'I think I learn more in a movie or in a story when I see what a person does wrong and what happens to them because of that. Antagonists are more interesting.'
Martin Scorsese in the production notes for *Casino*

Following The Age of Innocence, *the trade press talked of Scorsese possibly directing* Oceans of Storm, *an astronaut love story to star and be produced by Warren Beatty. But a more likely project appeared to be* Clockers, *with a screenplay by Richard Price based on his own novel. However, Spike Lee finally became the director on* Clockers, *and Scorsese agreed with Universal Pictures to make* Casino. Casino *was another project based on a factual book by Nicholas Pileggi, this time about the Mafia involvement in Las Vegas in the seventies. Pileggi began researching the subject while* GoodFellas *was being completed, intending to finish his book before filming began. In the event, Scorsese and Pileggi began work on creating a script from the subject before the book was completed, writing together over an intensive five-month period at the end of 1994.*

Casino *is based on the true story of Frank 'Lefty' Rosenthal, employed by the Mob to take control from the Teamsters of casinos in Las Vegas, beginning with the Stardust in 1971. His muscle man, who fronted as a restaurateur, was Tony Spilotro, a childhood friend from Chicago who had no qualms about murdering those who stepped out of line. Lefty's problems began when he fell in love with Geri McGee, a beautiful 'chip hustler' and sometime prostitute and topless dancer. He proposed to her, pointing out that at the age of thirty-one her 'professional' future was uncertain, while promising to put $1 million aside for her. However, their marriage was to break down over her alcoholism and adultery with a former pimp, and his becoming absorbed by the casino scene. The decisive moment came when she began an affair with Tony, bringing the personal into business with deadly results.*

In the film script, these characters were fictionalized: Lefty became Sam 'Ace' Rothstein, played by Robert De Niro; Geri became Ginger, played by Sharon Stone; and Tony became Nicky Santoro, played by Joe Pesci. James Woods was cast as Ginger's lover, stand-up comic Don Rickles as Rothstein's sidekick; other actual Vegas stars featured included Alan King, Steve Allen and Jayne Meadows. The Las Vegas of the seventies was an 'adult' playground, what Scorsese described in Vanity Fair *as 'Vegas at the end of its heyday. It was almost like the end of the Wild West, the end of the frontier towns of the 1880s.' In Pileggi's view, the characters in* Casino *are 'genetically incapable of doing anything straight'. He sees the film as the third part of a Scorsese gangster trilogy, following* Mean Streets *and* GoodFellas, *with the men portrayed by De Niro and Pesci playing the highest stakes and dealing in big-time corruption in* Casino.

The first newspaper article Nick Pileggi showed me was about the police covering a domestic fight on a lawn in Las Vegas one Sunday morning. And in that article, this incredible ten-year adventure that all these people were having slowly began to unravel, culminating in a husband and wife arguing on their lawn, with her smashing his car, the police arriving, and the FBI taking pictures. As you work back to the beginning, you find this incredible story with so many tangents and each is just one more nail in the coffin. It could be the underboss of Kansas City, Anthony Piscano, constantly complaining that he always had to spend his own money on trips to Las Vegas and never got reimbursed. Or it could be that unrelated homicide that made the police put a bug in the produce market that Piscano kept in Kansas City. Even they've forgotten about it, but it picks up all his complaining and alerts FBI men around the country to all these names. They're surprised to hear the names of the Vegas casinos being mentioned in a Kansas City produce market. What's the connection?

Then, quite separately, a court decrees that Phillip Green's former business partner, Amanda Scott, should have her share of the money as a partner of the president of the Tangiers Hotel. But instead of settling with her, the mob shoot her, which also really happened. This then brings police attention to their front man, the president, although he was in no way involved in the decision to kill her, and he begins to realize what's going on, although there's nothing much he can do about it. And then you have Ace Rothstein and Ginger and Nicky Santoro, all very volatile characters. I just thought it would be a terrific story.

Pretty much everything is based on real characters. Piscano is Carl DeLuna, who kept all those records. Mr Nance, who brings the money from the casino to Kansas City, is based on a man named Carl Thomas, who was recently killed in a car crash. Mr Green, the Tangiers president, Rothstein, Ginger, Nicky Santoro and his brother – these characters are all based on real people. But, of course, we reshaped. Characters are combined and some things that happened in Chicago are placed in Vegas. We had some legal problems about being specific, which meant saying 'back home' instead of Chicago, and having to say 'adapted from a true story' instead of 'this film is based on a true story'.

What interested me about Las Vegas was the idea of excess, no limits. People become successful there like in no other city. Recently there's been a spread of new casinos all around America, which reflects desperation, when people think that with one throw of the die their whole life will be changed.

It's also the Old Testament story: gaining paradise and losing it, through pride and through greed. That was the idea: Sam is given paradise on earth. In fact, he's there to keep everybody happy and keep everything in order, and to make as much money as possible so they can take more on the skim. But the problem is that he has to give way at times to certain people and certain pressures, which he won't do because of who he is. When people warn him about Ginger, he says, 'I know all the stories about her, but I don't care; I'm Ace Rothstein and I can change her.' But he couldn't change her. And he couldn't control the muscle – Nicky – because if you try to control someone like that you'll be dead.

The real Frank Rosenthal's Las Vegas career ended when his car was blown up in 1982. However, he survived this murder attempt to tell Nick Pileggi his life story.

When his car was blown up it was pretty obvious who gave the order. But as Nicky says at one point in the film, so long as they're earning with the prick, *they'll* never OK anything – the gods, that is – meaning they'll never authorize killing him. But Nicky likes to be prepared, so he orders two holes to be dug in the desert. That's the way they talk. This is the actual dialogue from a witness protection programme source.

In the very first script we started with that scene of them fighting on the lawn. Then we realized that it's too detailed and didn't create enough dramatic satisfaction at the end of the picture. So Nick and I figured we would start with the car exploding, and him going up into the air. You see him in slow motion, flying over the flames – like a soul about to take a dive into hell.

I show it three times in different ways. The third time, we see it the real way, as Rosenthal remembers it. He told me he saw the flames coming out of the air-conditioning unit first, and he didn't know what it could be. Then he looked down and saw his arm on fire and thought of his kids. The door wasn't properly locked, so he rolled out and was grabbed by two secret service men who just happened to be casing the joint because of Ronald Reagan's visit the following week. They pulled him aside and it was only when the car went up that he realized it was intentional. That's why I showed all the details. Once you realize you could have been killed, then you never forget those moments.

Sam Rothstein is so successful that he soon becomes a pillar of Las Vegas society and is given a presentation by the country club.

He says when he accepts that plaque, 'Anywhere else I'd be arrested for what I'm doing. Here they're giving me awards.' This is the only place he can use his gambling expertise in a legitimate way, and so become a part of the American WASP community. But as Nicky tells him in the desert, 'I'm what's real out here. Not your country clubs and your TV show. I'm what's real: the dirt, the gutter, and the blood. That's what it's all about.'
    They really did have to go out into the middle of the desert to talk. And Nicky had to change cars six times. I always imagined that Nicky must be so angry, and getting angrier each time he changes car until he gets out of the last one, and before Sam can say a word he lashes right into him. But in this case I'm on Nicky's side. The rest *is* artifice, and if you buy into it, it's hypocrisy. Know where it's coming from and know what the reality is. Don't think you're better than me, or than the people you grew up with.

One scene in Casino *attracted immediate controversy as an index of the film's supposed violence. Nicky is sent by the Chicago boss Remo to find out who committed an 'unauthorized' raid on a bar and when he finds the culprit, he tortures him by putting his head in a vice.*

The incident actually occurred in Chicago in the sixties. There was an argument among the young turks which ended with guns, and two brothers and a waitress were killed. It caused such outrage that the bosses wanted the men who were with the culprit, and they finally got them and killed them all. After two days and nights the guy didn't talk, they were desperate and so Joe Pesci's character put his head in a vice. Remember, this is a true story. But for our scene based on this, Joe found the human way of playing the scene – 'Please don't make me do this.' He's a soldier who has to carry out orders, and he has to get that name otherwise *his* head is in the vice. After two days and nights of questioning they didn't know what else to do.

Very often the people I portray can't help but be in that way of life. They're bad and they're doing bad things. And we condemn those aspects of them. But they're also human beings. I find that often the people passing moral judgement on them may ultimately be worse. I know there were people who felt I was morally irresponsible to make a film like *Good-Fellas*. Well, I'll make more of them if I can. Remember what happens at the end of *Casino*, where you see Nicky and his brother beaten and buried. That's all based on fact – I saw the pictures of the real bodies when they dug up the grave. Now, we shot it in a certain way, very straight. And I happen to like those people. Nicky *is* horrible. He's a terrible man. But there's something that happens for me watching them get beaten with the bats and then put into the hole. Ultimately it's a tragedy. It's the frailty of being human. I want to push audiences' emotional empathy with certain types of characters who are normally considered villains.

When I was growing up I was around many of these men, and most of them were very nice. They treated me and my family well, and they were attractive. I knew they were tough, and some were tougher than others. But it's a matter of the hypocrisy that those who condemn others often turn out to be twice as corrupt. I know it sounds like a cliché, but that's because it's real.

It's an interesting dilemma for Sam and Nicky. They both buy into a situation and both overstep the line so badly that they destroy everything for everybody. And eventually a whole new city comes rising out of the ashes of what they've destroyed. Who knows the reality of Las Vegas now, where you've gone from a Nicky Santoro to a Michael Milken or a Donald Trump? Who knows where the money's going? But I'm sure it's got to be worth it, somehow, for those entrepreneurs to come in with the money. You'll probably see a film in fifteen years exposing what they're doing now.

What we show in this film is the end of the old way and how it ended. They got too full of pride, they wanted more. If you're gambling you always want more, like the Japanese character in the film, Ichikawa, who bets less money than he normally would when he's tricked into coming back. But for him he hasn't won ten thousand, he's lost ninety thousand, because normally he would have bet a hundred thousand. We always had problems with where this episode was going to be placed in the structure.

But I knew it was very important to keep the move into Bob's face at the end of it, when he says, 'In the end we get it all.' They do, they really do.

What we show is a bunch of cheats watching cheats watching cheats. Sam Rothstein and those guys knew how to cheat, with handicapping and basketball games. They make it seem so natural that you can't tell whether the game is fixed. Sam notices Ginger for the first time when she's cheating the guy she's been with all evening. Before they had the video eye in the sky, they hired men with binoculars who had been cheats to go up on the catwalks, trying to find other cheats. I just thought it was really wonderful, with nobody trusting anybody.

This was twenty years ago, before the old mob lost their control. At that time every casino was 'owned' by some mob from a different part of the country. The Tangiers is fictional, but there were four – the Stardust, the Fremont, the Frontier and the Marina, where the Rothstein/Rosenthal character worked. So we just made them one giant hotel and combined all the elements. Where else could a great handicapper become the most important man in the city, with total control? We tried to show how far his control ran, even over the kitchen and the food. Insisting on an equal number of blueberries in each muffin may seem funny, but it's important because if the muffins and the steaks are good, the people who are playing there will go and tell others. It's not just paranoia and obsessive behaviour, there's a reason: to make the Tangiers the best place on the Strip.

While Rothstein's fanatical attention to detail makes the Tangiers prosper, it also destroys his relationship with Ginger.

I think there's something in Ace's character that ultimately destroys everything, although they may have had a chance if it wasn't for that city and what they were doing in it. Ginger tells him exactly how things are in the scene where he proposes. When you reach the age of forty and find someone, you want to try to make it work in a reasonable way. But I think he's responsible for the emotional alienation. She goes to the restaurant with a woman friend and gets a good table by saying, 'I'm Mrs Rothstein', and the other woman says, 'Well you might as well get something out of it.' It's the way he treats her. He won't let her go. If he lets her go, he believes he'll just never see her again. He'll hear from her through a lawyer, but he'll never see her again.

Their daughter Amy is unfortunately just a pawn to be used. By the last third of the film, Ginger is definitely disturbed, she's no longer in her right mind. Whether it's from drugs or drink doesn't matter, she's completely gone. It doesn't excuse anything she does, but it does heighten the horror of what's going on, like tying up the child – which really happened when the real couple's child was younger (they had two children). This is not something you'd invent, any more than you would her reaction to Sam in the restaurant when she says, 'Oh, for God's sake, the babysitter wasn't there, and it was only for a little while, I was going to come right back.'

De Niro was very generous in helping Sharon Stone throughout the film. It's a scary role, a tough one, like when she takes cocaine in front of the child: that was her choice. She also worked a lot with the clothes, like the David Bowie-type gold lamé outfit she wears for the last third of the picture. It's a little baggy in places, because she tried to make herself look as bad as she could.

Costume, as always in Scorsese's films, plays a key part in revealing character, and in the re-creation of the glitzy Vegas of the seventies there were unusual opportunities for excess. Casino was also shot entirely on location in Las Vegas.

Rita Ryack and John Dunn did the costumes. We had fifty-two changes for Bob, which was a lot, but in reality the person he's based on had even more amazing clothes. The mustard-yellow suit, the dark navy blue silk shirt with the navy blue tie and crimson jacket – we chose all the colours very carefully. Our ritual in the morning, once we had narrowed down the choice of which outfit, was to choose which shirt, then which tie, then which jewellery. If you look closely, the watch-faces usually match the clothes – even the watch he wears when he turns the ignition on. I wanted a close-up of him turning on the ignition, so we see it through the camera, and think, oh yes – the wristwatch. We set the angle in order to show the watch as well as possible, for the short amount of time it's on. And if you look at the film again, or on laser disc, you can see a lot of detail in the frames. Nicky had about twenty or twenty-five changes and Ginger had about forty, I think.

We shot during working hours in a real casino. Barbara De Fina figured out that the costs of doing it this way would probably have been the same as building one. And you wouldn't have the electricity, the life of the casino around you, which is what we got. We would fill the foreground with extras dressed in seventies costumes, and the background would sort of fall off. Sometimes we shot at four in the morning. I really love the scene when Joe comes in with Frank Vincent and they're playing blackjack, even though he's banned from the place, and he's abusing the dealers. That was four o'clock in the morning, and you hear someone yelling in the background because he's winning at craps. The dealer went through the whole scene with Joe, who was improvising, throwing cards back at him and saying the worst possible things. Halfway through the scene, the dealer leaned over to me, and said, 'You know, the real guy was much tougher with me – he really was uncontrollable.' This happened a number of times during the shoot. It was comforting to know we were on the right track.

The casino we used, the Riviera, was built in the late seventies. That was the centrepiece. Then we were trying to find houses that were built in the late fifties or early sixties, which are very rare. There was one house which we finally got, and I laid all my shots there, rehearsed, and then about two weeks later we lost it. Then we had to find another house, and finally it all worked out for the best, because that was the best one. It was an era of glitz – a word I heard for the first time in the seventies – and I think you can tell what Dante Feretti, the production designer, brings to a film when you just look at the bedroom. Especially in the wide shots, in the scene where she's taken too many pills and she's crying, and he's trying to help her, for example. There's something about the way the bed is elevated; it looks like an imperial bed, a king's or a queen's bed. There's something about the wallpaper, everything, the dishes on the walls, that says a great deal about a character. Dante made it regal, not just in bad taste, but the quality is good, and that moiré silk headboard is a backdrop for a battleground, like a silk battleground.

You could make ten films about each of those characters, all different, and I don't know if I did justice to any of them. I just wanted to get as much in as possible, plus I wanted to get all of Vegas in there as well. And also the whole climate of the time, the seventies – it was pretty ambitious for Nick and me to do.

Casino is Scorsese's longest film to date, even longer than GoodFellas, *at 177 mins. Making sense of a convoluted storyline and so many characters posed many problems for Scorsese and his editor, Thelma Schoonmaker.*

The structure of the film changed a lot as we worked on the editing. And that's where Thelma came in very strongly, because she was able to watch the footage come in and take charge of elements that were in the middle, like the documentary aspects. Thelma and I used to edit documentaries twenty-five years ago, so she's very good at that. It is the most harrowing kind of editing you can do because you're never sure of the structure and you're not following a dramatic thread. There's no plot in this film: there's story, but no plot. So what you're following is the beginnings of Ace coming to Vegas, then the beginnings of Nicky in Vegas, and the beginning of Nicky and his wife in Vegas with their child. Then Ace is succeeding in Vegas, and what's Nicky doing? He's sandbagging guys. Ace's rise culminates in Nicky being banned. Then that takes us to Nicky's rise, which is his montage of robbery: 'I'm staying here, you're not getting rid of me.' He creates his alternative empire. Then you start to bring the two tracks together. But up to the point at which Nicky builds his own empire there was a lot of reshuffling of scenes and rewriting of voice-over. Finally, we put all the exposition at the beginning. At first we had split it up throughout the film, but it seemed too little too late, although on the page it looked all right. So in the end we took the explanation of the skim and moved it up front.

There's something interesting about voice-over: it lets you in on the secret thoughts of the characters, it's like secret observations by an omniscient viewer. And for me it has the wonderful comforting tone of someone telling you a story. And then much of the time it has a kind of irony. Suppose you see two people saying goodnight and the voice-over says, 'They had a wonderful time that evening, but that was the last time before so-and-so died.' You're still seeing the person, but the voice-over is telling you they died a week later, and it takes on a resonance, and for me a depth and a sadness, when used at moments like that. The voice-over in this particular film is also open to tirades by Nicky. If you listen to him complaining – about the bosses back home, how he's the one out here, the one in the trenches – then you begin to understand his point of view. Why should I have to work for somebody? Why don't I go into business for myself? You can see the kind of person he is from these tirades in voice-over.

The music for Casino *uses the same general approach as* GoodFellas, *but the range is even broader, starting with Bach's* St Matthew Passion *over the scene of Ace being blown up and the 'inferno' credits sequence by Saul and Elaine Bass, which is heard again at the end when the 'old' Las Vegas is shown being dynamited to make way for the new 'family' resort hotels.*

I guess for me the Bach is essential to the sense of something grand that's been lost. Whether we agree with the morality of it is another matter – I'm not asking you to agree with the morality – but there was the sense of an empire being lost, and it needed music worthy of that. It needed music which would be provocative. The destruction of that city has to have the grandeur of Lucifer being expelled from heaven for being too proud. Those are all pretty obvious biblical references. But the viewer of the film should be moved by the music. Even though you may not like the people and what they did, they're still human beings and it's a tragedy as far as I'm concerned.

For me, every piece of music used has its own associations. There's Brenda Lee singing 'Hurt', the Velvetones doing 'Glory of Love' and 'The House of the Rising Sun', which we kept for the end – altogether over fifty-five pieces. Then there's the breakdown of style in 'Satisfaction', from the Stones to Devo. I was very lucky to be able to choose from over forty years of music and in most cases to be able to get it into the film. Certain songs and pieces of music, when you play them against the picture, change everything. So it's very, very delicate. In *GoodFellas* the sound is more Phil Spector, while in this picture it's more the Stones, especially 'Can't You Hear Me Knocking?', which is a key song in the film.

We also tried to keep the music in period, as in *GoodFellas*. When Ace and Nicky need to talk after the argument in the desert, they get into a car in the garage to have a private conversation. What would happen? They'd sit in the car and keep the radio on. And what's playing is 'Go Your Own Way' by Fleetwood Mac, which is a key song of the mid to late seventies. No matter what the mood of the conversation, that music is playing. So we were able to use music at that point to take you further into the time. The sounds change from the beginning of the film from Louis Prima to Fleetwood Mac. You see, it's not so much the Bach that begins the film as the Louis Prima that cuts it off, creating a strong shock effect. I knew Louis Prima had to be in there, but for the splendour of the destruction of this sin city it has to be Bach. Because the old Vegas is being replaced by something that looks seductive, kiddie-friendly, but it's there to work on the very core of America, the family. Not just the gamblers and the hustlers and the relatively few gangsters who were around, but now it's Ma and Pa Kettle. While the kids watch the Pirate ride, we'll take your money.

There is a lot of movie music in the film too, like the theme from *Picnic* over Mr Nance sashaying into the casino count room – the implication being that it was so easy you could waltz in and waltz right out with the money. The theme from *Picnic* was such a beautiful piece of music that it was played on jukeboxes and was in the Top 40 all the time, so you would always hear it, and you still do in Vegas. The other one was 'A Walk on the Wild Side' by Elmer Bernstein, Jimmy Smith version. That has a nervous energy that's good, especially in that sequence where we use it, the killing of Amanda Scott. Again, it was a very famous piece of music that was taken out of context from the film it was written for, and became a part of life in America at the time.

Along with these, it seemed interesting to try the music by Delerue from Godard's *Contempt*, which I love for its sadness. And it's so hard in the end credits to follow the Bach with anything, so we tried *Contempt* to wipe the slate clean. And then after that the only possible thing is one of the greatest songs ever written, Hoagy Carmichael's 'Stardust' – the only piece that could sum up the emotions and thoughts about what you've seen.

After Casino, *Scorsese began production on a film based on the early life of Tibet's exiled spiritual leader the Dalai Lama, provisionally entitled* Kundun.

The film is written by Melissa Mathieson, and it's a very straightforward story of the finding of the Dalai Lama as a young child in the Amdo province of Tibet. It takes you through the maturing of the boy until he is a young man of eighteen, when he has to make a decision which he knows would affect – literally – the life or death of his own country. What interested me was the story of a man, or a boy, who lives in a society which is totally based on the spirit and which finally crashes into the twentieth century and finds itself face-to-face with a society which is materialistic. Mao finally leans over at one point during the Dalai Lama's visit to Beijing and says to him: 'You do know that religion is poison, don't you?' At this point the Dalai Lama realizes that they're all finished, and the only way to save Tibet is for him to leave, and take it with him. What interests me is how a man of non-violence deals with these people – that's ultimately the story. I don't know if we'll be able to pull it all together. But it's the story of a nation that was in such a remote area, closed in by the Himalayas, that its people could not go out, so they went inside. We're thinking about shooting it in northern India. And after that, I hope to make *Gershwin*, a musical.

I'm confident that cinema has a future. I say that because there are these kids who make films cheaply, in fact there seems to be no end of young people who want to say something with a camera. And the spectacle of seeing movies on a big screen is also something I still love, along with a lot of other people. I know a group of people in LA who all went to see the rerelease of *The Wild Bunch* at the Cinerama Dome. And when William

Holden said, 'If they move, kill 'em', the audience burst into applause. Even when people rent videos, they invite friends over and watch them together. I remember three or four years ago going with Spielberg, Raffaele Donato and my agent to see *The Abyss* in Westwood on a Saturday afternoon – the four of us, sitting in the third row. We just wanted to see it with big sound and a big image – give it the best shot.

With widescreen films of the mid-fifties you were literally inside the film. I remember seeing King Vidor's *War and Peace* at the Capitol Theater in VistaVision, *High Society*, *The Court Jester* – all first run. Even a movie which is mediocre, like *Away All Boats*, was quite extraordinary to see in Technicolor and VistaVision. The closest thing to this impact today is Imax. You know you're in for an experience: it's not just a movie, it's a communal experience that I think will always be there.

93 Robert De Niro as Ace Rothstein in *Casino*.

The Last Temptation of Christ – the Controversy

The controversy that raged around *The Last Temptation of Christ* began with the first attempts to make the film with Paramount in 1983. But the concerted campaign to stop the film took wing again five years later, when it was being produced jointly by Universal Pictures and Cineplex Odeon. Fundamentalists were armed with two early versions of the script by Paul Schrader – obtained, Scorsese suspects, from actors who had access to copies for auditions in 1983. This screenplay was of course some way removed from the final version by Scorsese and Jay Cocks, and notorious lines such as Jesus saying to Mary Magdalene, 'God sleeps between your legs', had been taken out at an early stage. But the fundamentalists objected to the portrayal of Jesus as a weak and indecisive man, and in particular to the scene in the 'last temptation' dream sequence, in which Jesus makes love to Mary while being watched by an angel.

In January 1988, Universal, wary of the problems encountered by Paramount, had appointed Tim Penland, born-again Christian and head of a marketing company specializing in fundamentalist interests, to be a consultant on the film. But in June he resigned, complaining that Universal had reneged on their promise to screen an early cut of the film to fundamentalists by this time. Universal countered that Scorsese was simply behind schedule, and that they themselves expected to see the film in July.

By mid July, Christian groups had decided to go to the top, and attacked Lew Wasserman, the chairman of MCA (Universal's parent company), for discrediting the Jewish faith by supporting the film. On 15

July, evangelist Bill Bright offered to reimburse the cost of the film if the studio would hand it over for destruction. Although both Scorsese and Schrader, with Universal's support, had preferred to remain silent up to this point, Scorsese now released a statement:

> My film was made with deep religious feeling. I have been working on this film for fifteen years; it is more than just another film project for me. I believe it is a religious film about suffering and the struggle to find God. It was made with conviction and love and so I believe it is an affirmation of faith, not a denial. Further, I feel strongly that people everywhere will be able to identify with the human side of Jesus as well as his divine side.

Universal issued a supportive statement, to the effect that 'Universal Pictures and Cineplex Odeon Films stand behind the principle of freedom of expression and hope that the American public will give the film and the film-maker a fair chance.'

On 16 July, nearly 200 members of the Fundamentalist Baptist Tabernacle of Los Angeles, led by Reverend R. L. Hymers, picketed Universal Studios, carrying banners saying, 'Universal Are Like Judas Iscariot', 'The Greatest Story Ever Distorted', and 'Wasserman Endangers Israel', as well as staging a mock crucifixion. Protests were also made outside Wasserman's Beverly Hills home, and in the sky a plane circled trailing a banner saying, 'Wasserman fans Jewish hatred with Last Temptation.' On a wider scale, the American Family Association (who had engineered much of the campaign against the film in 1983) were contacting some 170,000 pastors throughout the USA in their bid to stop the film being released.

At this stage, the planned release date was 23 September. Although considered for the opening night film of the New York Film Festival, it was now hoped that it would play somewhere else in the programme. Inevitably, comparisons were drawn with the showing in the 1985 festival of Jean-Luc Godard's *Je Vous Salue, Marie* (*Hail, Mary*), which had been the occasion of disruptive protests. Indeed, the antagonism towards Godard's film among hardline Catholics in France was one of the contributory factors in the collapse of a possible French production of *The Last Temptation of Christ*.

On 12 July, the same day as an early cut of Scorsese's film was shown to invited religious leaders in New York, on the West Coast Penland held a press conference with four Californian fundamentalists, attacking the film and rejecting any need actually to see it for themselves. Among the film's sympathetic viewers was Reverend William Forc of the National Council of Churches, who said on television that *The Last Temptation of Christ* was 'just an idea which should be debated openly'. But while the Episcopal Bishop of New York, Paul Moore, said after the screening that he saw 'nothing blasphemous about it', his counterpart in Los Angeles, Archbishop Roger M. Mahony, said that from what he understood about the film he would probably rate it as 'morally offensive' and recommend it be avoided.

On 25 July, Scorsese finally appeared on national television to say he would not make any changes to *The Last Temptation of Christ*, and stressed that it was a work of fiction, not a version of the Gospels. But two days later, on a discussion programme about the film, Mother Angelica, head of The Eternal Word TV Network, described it as 'the most satanic movie ever made' and declared that it 'will destroy Christianity'. In response to this Jack Valenti, president of the MPAA (the US movie ratings board), wondered how a single film could wreck someone's faith.

The controversy spread to Europe when Guglielmo Biraghi, director of the Venice Film Festival, said he would screen *The Last Temptation of Christ* out of competition, describing it as 'a very Catholic film'. Franco Zeffirelli, whose new film, *Young Toscanini*, was also to be shown in the festival, joined the campaign of many Catholics to bar the film, and was quoted as making anti-Semitic remarks, which he later denied in a full-page letter printed in *Variety*. In Britain, seasoned campaigner Mary Whitehouse expressed her concern to the British Board of Film Classification, threatening to invoke the law of blasphemy if necessary (she had previously brought a successful prosecution against *Gay News* in 1977 for publishing a poem that gave a homosexual interpretation to the crucifixion). Cardinal Basil Hume, on the advice of others, announced that the Catholic community should not see the film, because parts of it would shock and outrage believers.

Then Universal made the sudden decision to release the film on 12 August. Tom Pollock, chairman of MCA's motion picture group, issued a statement that 'the best thing that can be done for *The Last Temptation of Christ* is to make it available to the American people and allow them to draw their own conclusions based on fact, not fallacy.' Universal and Cineplex Odeon said they would both 'support Martin Scorsese's right to express his personal, artistic and religious visions, and the right of individuals to decide what they will see and think'. In response to this, the Reverend R. L. Hymers repeated that Universal should expect violent forms of protest if the film were to be released with the much talked-about sex scene. Further cries of damnation came from evangelists Bill Bright, Jerry Fallwell and Donald Wildman, who even called for a boycott on voting for the Democrats on the grounds that the party had connections with MCA! The US Catholic Conference further declared that its 40 million followers should not see the film. On 11 August, some 25,000 protesters marched before Universal Studios in a last vain hope of stopping the film.

With this deluge of free publicity, *The Last Temptation of Christ* opened on nine screens in the USA on 12 August, accompanied by strong words of support from film-makers (Clint Eastwood – 'Freedom of expression is the American way') and a pledge of solidarity from the Directors' Guild of America. In New York, *The Last Temptation of Christ* was shown at the Cineplex Odeon Ziegfeld Theater (1,141 seats), with extra security and 100 policemen in attendance. Nearly 1,000 protesters assembled outside, the area was closed to traffic, and members of the audience had their bags searched after threats were issued to slash or spray-paint screens. Similar scenes of protest, accompanied by sell-out houses, occurred in Los Angeles, San Francisco, Washington, Chicago, Seattle and Toronto. In three days, the film had taken $400,000. But four major circuits in the USA, amounting to some 2,000 screens, were promising not to show it. On 26 August, a screen was slashed and a print of the film stolen from the Cineplex Odeon Theater in Salt Lake City, and 1,000 people turned out in Atlanta to protest at its opening.

With the film finally released, Scorsese spoke out more in its defence, explaining how the Schrader script had been substantially altered. He emphasized again how the 'last temptation is not for Christ to have sex, but to get married, make love to his wife and have children like an ordinary man'. He also said that he had shown his film to his mother before its release, and 'she thought it was fine'.

In London, the British Board of Film Classification granted *The Last Temptation of Christ* an '18' certificate (adults only), quoting legal opinion that no British jury would find the film blasphemous. Mary Whitehouse, evidently aggrieved by this decision, said she would campaign for local councils to ban the film. In Venice, a local judge viewed the film before its screening on 7 September could go ahead, an event still strongly opposed by the Christian Democrat faction. Two days later it opened in London, with minor protests outside cinemas, and a ban on the poster by London Transport. Scorsese gave a press conference in which he made the following statements:

When I read Kazantzakis's book, I didn't have the feeling that it would be deeply offensive to anyone, especially because I knew my own intent. But by 1987 I was well aware that there would be controversy on its release. One of the reasons it was made so cheaply in the end was the risk that we might not be able to release it. Among the boys who I knew when I was in the seminary, one is now the head of an order in Chicago called the Congregation of the Blessed Sacrament, and happens to be a great fan of Kazantzakis's book. And I know that the book is used in seminaries as a parable to make the Gospel story fresh and alive, a subject to argue about and discuss. This is how I hoped the film would be received. I must say it's the only one of my films that I like to watch.

My feeling is that if you were to take yourself to the point where there are no churches, just you alone with God, that's the plane on which I wanted to make the film. To get down to what the message of Jesus really is. Not just a plastic model on a car dashboard, but someone who gave us the most important message for us to survive as a species on Earth. In *Mean Streets*, the main character, Charlie, tries to live a Christian life; he goes to church, does confession, listens to all the philosophy within the edifice of the church. But outside in the street, life is ruled by the gun. So how does one live a good Christian life in a world of this kind? All these themes have been churning inside me for years, and have finally reached a special combination in *The Last Temptation of Christ*.

When I was a child, I remember the church had on display lists of films, in categories A, B and C. C meant it was condemned by the Legion of Decency – if you walked into a theatre showing that film and had a heart attack, you're in Hell! If you went to see a Max Ophuls film, you were finished. When I was about eighteen or nineteen, I saw *The Seventh Seal*, which was a wonderful religious experience for me. But when I wanted to see it again, it was playing with *Smiles of a Summer Night* – a condemned film! So I went immediately to confession, and said to my parish priest, a sweet man who's now dead, that because I was studying film at New York University I had to see *Smiles of a Summer Night*. I explained that I hadn't really understood the sexual aspects anyway. He replied that I could see the film for my work, but that they had to keep these things from the masses. I think there is that double standard, but I wouldn't want a twelve-year-old going to see *The Last Temptation of Christ* and thinking it was an accurate life of Jesus.

A black minister wrote a letter to the New York *Daily News*, saying he loved the film, was going to use it as a study guide in discussion groups, and that he felt most of the people talking about the film had not seen it. He said they adhered very much to the word of the Gospel, but not to the spirit. Certainly in the middle part of America a lot of people have hard lives; there's drink, drugs, prostitution, wife-beating and murder. Then some guy comes on television, and through him this sinner, so to speak, embraces Jesus. I think that's a pretty good thing if someone then decides to give life a value. And I think they have a great fear of anything that threatens their idea of Jesus, because deep down they feel very frightened they might revert to their original behaviour. So I would say to them, if they really feel they might be offended, stay away, but please allow others to see the film. Some fundamentalist ministers felt they had done themselves a disservice in the end by raising the box-office of the picture, because people who wouldn't normally go to see my films went to see this one. They polled audiences coming out of the theatre, and in the first week 85–90 per cent of them liked the film and said they would tell their friends to go and see it.

Outside the USA and Britain, The Last Temptation of Christ did not always find such an apparently reasonable response. On 28 September, the film opened in Paris to violent demonstrations – there was a riot in the foyer of the UGC Odéon, Molotov cocktails where thrown, and thirteen policemen were injured. Tear gas was sprayed at another cinema. Similar incidents occurred in Avignon, Besançon and Marseilles. On 22 October, fire gutted the Cinéma St Michel, injuring thirteen people. This violence was condemned publicly by Jack Lang, Minister of Culture, and the Archbishop of Paris, Cardinal Lustiger, but it effectively meant distribution of the film in France was rapidly curtailed.

The Last Temptation of Christ was banned in Israel – the country that had once welcomed Scorsese to use its landscapes as locations for the film – because of its being 'offensive to Christians'. The film opened in Greece (where the Orthodox Church had placed Kazantzakis's novel on its index of forbidden books in 1955), but was banned a month later. The opening in Brazil met with more violence. On the other hand, in West Germany the film was given an 'especially outstanding' category by the classification board, and it was passed in Ireland for over-eighteens, provided that no one be admitted after the film had begun, so as not to miss the opening statement that it was based on a work of fiction, and not the Gospels.

By the end of October, Universal had grossed about $8 million in the USA, and felt they were likely to make a modest profit on the film.

However, fundamentalists proceeded to proclaim their victory over Scorsese and his backers, though a move to boycott sales of MCA's video release of *E.T.* clearly foundered completely. In May 1989, MCA announced a low-key video release of *The Last Temptation of Christ*, which provoked further threats of retaliation. Since then, the film has been relatively accessible on video both in the USA and Britain.

Filmography

As director

1963

What's a Nice Girl Like You Doing in a Place Like This?

A writer named Algernon (but called Harry by his friends) buys a picture of a boat on a lake, and his obsession with it renders normal life impossible. He attempts to function again by consulting an analyst and becoming married, but eventually succumbs to his strange anxiety by disappearing into the picture.

Producer: New York University Department of Television, Motion Picture and Radio Presentations, Summer Motion Picture Workshop
Screenplay: Martin Scorsese
Still Photography (black and white): Frank Truglio
Editor: Robert Hunsicker
Music: Richard H. Coll
Cast: Zeph Michaelis (*Harry*), Mimi Stark (*wife*), Sarah Braveman (*analyst*), Fred Sica (*friend*), Robert Uricola (*singer*)
9 mins

1964

It's Not Just You, Murray!

Murray is a small-time criminal whose material comforts derive from his old association with boyhood friend Joe. Murray was sent to jail while Joe eluded the police, and then in hospital married his nurse. Oblivious to the fact that Joe is still exploiting him and clearly having an affair with his wife, Murray continues to extol his friend's virtues.

Producer: New York University Department of Television, Motion Picture and Radio Presentations
Screenplay: Martin Scorsese, Mardik Martin
Cinematography (black and white): Richard H. Coll
Editor: Eli F. Bleich

Music: Richard H. Coll
Production designers: Lancelot Braithwaite, Victor Magnotta
Cast: Ira Rubin (*Murray*), Andrea Martin (*wife*), San De Fazio (*Joe*), Robert Uricola (*singer*), Catherine Scorsese (*mother*), Victor Magnotta, Richard Sweeton, Mardik Martin, John Bivona, Bernard Weisberger
15 mins

1967
The Big Shave
To the sound of Bunny Berigan peforming 'I Can't Get Started', a young man enters a bathroom and proceeds to shave until great quantities of blood flow from round his face and neck.

Producer: Martin Scorsese
Screenplay: Martin Scorsese
Cinematography (colour): Ares Demertzis
Editor: Martin Scorsese
Song: 'I Can't Get Started with You' (Bunny Berrigan)
Art director: Ken Gaulin
Special effects: Eli Bleich
Cast: Peter Bernuth (*young man*)
6 mins

1969
Who's That Knocking at My Door?
(First version, 1965, *Bring on the Dancing Girls*; second version, 1967, *I Call First*; also released in 1970 under title *J.R.*)
J.R., a young man accustomed to the indolent lifestyle of his friends in Little Italy, meets a young, educated woman on the Staten Island Ferry. Their growing relationship is stopped short by his guilt over sleeping with women who are not 'broads', and her well-intentioned revelation that she was raped by a former boyfriend.

Producers: Joseph Weill, Betzi Manoogian, Haig Manoogian
Screenplay: Martin Scorsese
Cinematography (black and white): Michael Wadleigh, Richard H. Coll
Editor: Thelma Schoonmaker
Songs: 'Jenny Take a Ride' (Mitch Ryder and the Detroit Wheels); 'The Closer You Are' (The Channels); 'I've Had It' (The Bellnotes); 'El Watusi' (Ray Baretto); 'Don't Ask Me' (The Dubs); 'Shotgun' (Jr Walker and the All Stars); 'The End' (The Doors); 'Ain't That Just Like Me' (The Searchers); 'Who's That Knocking at My Door' (The Genies); 'The Plea' (The Chantells)
Art director: Victor Magnotta
Cast: Harvey Keitel (*J.R.*), Zina Bethune (*girl*), Lennard Kuras (*Joey*), Michael Scala (*Sally GaGa*), Anne Colette (*young girl in dream*), Harry Northup (*Harry, the rapist*), Robert Uricola (*young man at party with gun*), Bill Minkin (*Iggy/radio announcer*), Wendy Russell (*GaGa's girlfriend*), Phil Carlson (*guide on the mountain*), Susan Wood (*Susan*), Marissa Joffrey (*Rosie*), Catherine Scorsese (*J.R.'s mother*), Tsuai Yu-Lan, Saskia Holleman, Anne Marieka (*dream girls*), Victor Magnotta, Paul de Bionde (*boys in street fight*), Martin Scorsese (*gangster*)
90 mins

1970

Street Scenes 1970

A documentary showing student demonstrations held in May against the American invasion of Cambodia, beginning in Wall Street and culminating in a march on Washington.

Producer: New York Cinetracts Collective
Production supervisor and post-production director: Martin Scorsese
Cinematography (black and white/colour): Don Lenzer, Harry Bolles, Danny Schneider, Peter Rea, Bob Pitts, Bill Etra, Tiger Graham, Fred Hadley, Ed Summer, Nat Trapp
Editors: Peter Rea, Maggie Koven, Angela Kirby, Larry Tisdall, Gerry Pallor, Thelma Schoonmaker
Cast: William Kunstler, Dave Dellinger, Alan W. Carter, David Z. Robinson, Harvey Keitel, Verna Bloom, Jay Cocks, Martin Scorsese
75 mins

1972

Boxcar Bertha

In Arkansas in the early thirties, young Bertha Thompson takes to the road following the death of her father and becomes an associate of union man 'Big' Bill Shelley and professional gambler Rake Brown. Becoming successful robbers of the railroad, the trio are pursued by two ruthless policemen, the McIvers. When Shelley is captured and Brown killed, Bertha falls into prostitution, to be reunited with Shelley just before he is crucified on a boxcar.

Production company: American International Pictures
Producer: Roger Corman
Screenplay: Joyce H. Corrington and John William Corrington, based on *Sister of the Road* by Bertha Thompson as told to Ben L. Reitman
Cinematography (colour): John Stephens
Editors: Buzz Feitshans and Martin Scorsese
Music: Gib Guilbeau and Thad Maxwell
Visual consultant: David Nichols
Cast: Barbara Hershey (*Bertha*), David Carradine (*Bill Shelley*), Barry Primus (*Rake Brown*), Bernie Casey (*Von Morton*), John Carradine (*H. Buckram Sartoris*), David R. Osterhout and Victor Argo (*the McIvers*), Grahame Pratt (*Emeric Pressburger*), 'Chicken' Holleman (*Michael Powell*), Marianne Dole (*Mrs Mailer*), Harry Northup (*Harvey Hall*), Doyle Hall (*dice player*), Joe Reynolds (*Joe*), Martin Scorsese and Gayne Rescher (*clients in brothel*)
88 mins

1973

Mean Streets

The lives of a group of young men in the violent world of New York's Little Italy come into conflict. Tony tries to run a 'clean' bar; Michael wants to be a tough business dealer; the reckless Johnny Boy plunges himself further into debt; and Charlie wants to be respected in the neighbourhood and run a restaurant. Haunted by his religious sense of the evil around him, Charlie's determination to keep Johnny Boy out of trouble, and his

secret affair with Johnny Boy's cousin Teresa, lead all three of them into a bloody
shooting incident when Johnny Boy's debt to Michael cannot be paid.

Production company: Warner Brothers
Producer: Jonathan T. Taplin
Executive producer: E. Lee Perry
Screenplay: Martin Scorsese, Mardik Martin
Cinematography (colour): Kent Wakeford
Editor: Sid Levin
Songs: 'Jumping Jack Flash', 'Tell Me' (The Rolling Stones); 'I Love You So' (The
Chantells); 'Addio Sogni Di Gloria', 'Canta Per' Me' (Giuseppe De Stefano);
'Marruzella', 'Scapricciatiello' (Renato Carosone); 'Please Mr Postman' (The
Marvelettes); 'Hideaway', 'I Looked Away' (Eric Clapton); 'Desiree' (The Charts);
'Rubber Biscuit' (The Chips); 'Pledging My Love' (Johnny Ace); 'Ritmo Sabroso' (Ray
Baretto); 'You' (The Acquatones); 'Ship of Love' (The Nutmegs), 'Florence' (The
Paragons); 'Malafemina' (Jimmy Roselli); 'Those Oldies But Goodies' (Little Caesar and
The Romans); 'I Met Him on a Sunday' (The Shirelles); 'Be My Baby' (The Ronettes);
'Mickey's Monkey' (The Miracles)
Visual consultant: David Nichols
Cast: Harvey Keitel (*Charlie*), Robert De Niro (*Johnny Boy*), David Proval (*Tony*), Amy
Robinson (*Teresa*), Richard Romanus (*Michael*), Cesare Danova (*Giovanni*), George
Memmoli (*Joey Catucci*), Victor Argo (*Mario*), Lenny Scaletta (*Jimmy*), Murray Moston
(*Oscar*), David Carradine (*drunk*), Robert Carradine (*assassin*), Jeannie Bell (*Diane*), Lois
Walden (*Jewish girl at bar*), D'Mitch Davis (*black cop*), Dino Seragusa (*old man*), Julie
Andelman (*girl at party*), Peter Fain (*George*), Harry Northup (*soldier*), Robert Wilder
(*Benton*), Jaime Alba (*first young boy*), Ken Konstantin (*second young boy*), Nicki 'Ack'
Aquilino (*man on docks*), Catherine Scorsese (*woman on landing*), Ken Sinclair (*Sammy*),
B. Mitchell Reed (*disc jockey*), Martin Scorsese (*Shorty, Michael's hired killer*), Barbara
Weintraub (*Heather Weintraub*), Ron Satloff (*Carl*), Anna Uricola (*neighbour at
window*)
110 mins

1974

Alice Doesn't Live Here Anymore

Alice Hyatt, who dreamed of becoming a singer as a child, decides to pursue this career
when her husband is suddenly killed. Going on the road from New Mexico to Arizona
with her impish eleven-year-old son, Tom, she has a tough time singing in bars, has to
escape a violent lover, and ends up as a waitress in a café. There Alice meets divorced
farmer David Barrie, and begins an uneasy romance that leads to her agreeing to try
domesticity once again.

Production company: Warner Brothers
Producers: David Susskind, Audrey Maas
Associate producer: Sandra Weintraub
Screenplay: Robert Getchell
Cinematography (colour): Kent Wakeford
Editor: Marcia Lucas
Music: Richard LaSalle
Songs: 'All the Way from Memphis' (Mott the Hoople); 'Roll Away the Stone' (Leon
Russell); 'Daniel' (Elton John); 'Jeepster' (T. Rex); 'Cuddle Up a Little Closer, Lovey

Mine' (Betty Grable); 'You'll Never Know' (Alice Faye); 'I'm So Lonesome I Could Cry' (Kris Kristofferson); 'Where or When', 'When Your Lover Has Gone', 'Gone With the Wind', 'I've Got a Crush on You' (Ellen Burstyn)
Production designer: Toby Rafelson
Cast: Ellen Burstyn (*Alice Hyatt*), Kris Kristofferson (*David*), Alfred Lutter (*Tommy*), Diane Ladd (*Flo*), Billy Green Bush (*Donald*), Vic Tayback (*Mel*), Jodie Foster (*Audrey*), Harvey Keitel (*Ben*), Lelia Goldoni (*Bea*), Lane Bradbury (*Rita*), Valerie Curtin (*Vera*), Harry Northup (*bartender*), Murray Moston (*Jacobs*), Mia Bendixsen (*Alice at age eight*), Ola Moore (*old woman*), Dean Casper (*Chicken*), Henry M. Kendrick (*shop assistant*), Martin Brinton (*Lenny*), Mardik Martin (*customer in club*), Martin Scorsese and Larry Cohen (*patrons at the diner*)
112 mins

Italianamerican

In their apartment on Elizabeth Street, Charles and Catherine Scorsese reminisce with their son about their Sicilian parents and their own lives. All the time Mrs Scorsese explains how she makes her own spaghetti sauce.

Production company: National Communications Foundation
Producers: Saul Rubin, Elaine Attias
Treatment: Martin Scorsese, Mardik Martin, Larry Cohen
Cinematography (colour): Alex Hirschfield
Editor: Bertram Lovitt
Cast: Charles Scorsese, Catherine Scorsese, Martin Scorsese
45 mins

1975

Taxi Driver

A Vietnam veteran, lonely Travis Bickle, takes up driving a taxi in New York in search of an escape from his sleeplessness and disgust with the corruption he finds around him. After failing to begin a romance with the beautiful Betsy, who is working on the election campaign of presidential candidate Charles Palantine, Bickle's pent-up rage leads him to buy a set of guns. While training himself to use them, he meets a teenage prostitute, Iris, and becomes determined to rescue her from her sordid profession. Foiled in his attempt to assassinate Palantine, he goes to Iris's room and kills the men who 'own' her. Failing to commit suicide after this ritual act, Bickle becomes a hero in the press, and returns to driving a taxi.

Production company: Columbia Pictures
Producers: Michael Phillips, Julia Phillips
Screenplay: Paul Schrader
Cinematography (colour): Michael Chapman
Editors: Marcia Lucas, Tom Rolf, Melvin Shapiro
Music: Bernard Herrmann
Songs: 'Late for the Sky' (Jackson Browne); 'Hold Me Close' (George (Oobie) McKern)
Visual consultant: David Nichols
Cast: Robert De Niro (*Travis Bickle*), Jodie Foster (*Iris*), Cybill Shepherd (*Betsy*), Harvey Keitel (*Sport/Matthew*), Steven Prince (*Andy, the gun salesman*), Albert Brooks (*Tom*), Peter Boyle (*Wizard*), Leonard Harris (*Charles Palantine*), Diahnne Abbott (*woman at concession stand*), Frank Adu (*angry black man*), Richard Higgs (*Secret Service agent*),

Gino Ardito (*policeman at rally*), Garth Avery (*Iris's companion*), Copper Cunningham (*prostitute in cab*), Harry Fischler (*cab dispatcher*), Harry Cohn (*cabbie in Bellmore*), Brenda Dickson (*woman on soap opera*), Nat Grant (*stick-up man*), Robert Martoff (*mafioso*), Beau Kayser (*Man on soap opera*), Victor Magnotta (*Secret Service photographer*), Norman Matlock (*Charlie T.*), Murray Moston (*caretaker at Iris's apartment*), Harry Northup (*soldier*), Bill Minkin (*Tom's assistant*), Gene Palma (*street drummer*), Peter Savage (*the john*), Robert Shields (*Palantine aide*), Robin Utt (*campaign worker*), Joe Spinell (*personnel officer*), Maria Turner (*angry prostitute on street*), Carey Poe (*campaign worker*), Ralph Singleton (*television interviewer*), Martin Scorsese (*man watching silhouette*)
113 mins

1977
New York, New York

Determined to find a girl on V-J day, 1945, in New York, saxophonist Jimmy Doyle relentlessly pursues singer Francine Evans, who persistently rejects him. But at an audition the following day they are hired as a double act, and go on tour together in Frankie Harte's band. They marry, Jimmy takes over the band and makes it a success, but Francine becomes pregnant and returns to New York. While Francine develops into a popular ballad singer, Jimmy moves towards playing modern jazz in Harlem. With the birth of their baby, Jimmy walks out on Francine and they pursue individual careers. A brief reconciliation backstage is not, however, followed up.

Production company: United Artists
Producers: Irwin Winkler, Robert Chartoff
Screenplay: Earl Mac Rauch, Mardik Martin
Cinematography (colour): Laszlo Kovacs
Editors: Irving Lerner, Marcia Lucas
Original Songs (by John Kander, Fred Ebb): 'Theme from New York, New York', 'There Goes the Ball Game', 'But the World Goes Round', 'Happy Endings' (Liza Minnelli)
Other Songs: 'You Brought a New Kind of Love to Me', 'Once in a While', 'You Are My Lucky Star', 'The Man I Love', 'Taking a Chance on Love' (Liza Minnelli); 'Blue Moon' (Mary Kay Place); 'Honeysuckle Rose' (Diahnne Abbott)
Music: 'Opus One'; 'Song of India'; 'I'm Gettin' Sentimental Over You'; 'Don't Blame Me'; 'It's a Wonderful World'; 'For All We Know'; 'South America Take It Away'; 'Just You, Just Me'; 'Do Nothing Till You Hear From Me'; 'Don't Get Around Much Anymore'; 'Hold me Tight'; 'Bugle Call Rag'; 'Avalon'; 'Night in Tunisia'; 'Wonderful Girl'; 'Billets Doux' (Hot Club of France Quintet)
Musical supervisor: Ralph Burns
Saxophone solos: Georgie Auld
Production designer: Boris Leven
Cast: Robert De Niro (*Jimmy Doyle*), Liza Minnelli (*Francine Evans*), Lionel Stander (*Tony Harwell*), Barry Primus (*Paul Wilson*), Mary Kay Place (*Bernice*), Georgie Auld (*Frankie Harte*), George Memmoli (*Nicky*), Dick Miller (*Palm Club owner*), Murray Moston (*Horace Morris*), Lenny Gaines (*Artie Kirks*), Clarence Clemons (*Cecil Powell*), Kathy McGinnis (*Ellen Flannery*), Norman Palmer (*desk clerk*), Adam David Winkler (*Jimmy Doyle, Jr*), Dimitri Logothetis (*desk clerk*), Frank Silvera (*Eddie di Muzio*), Diahnne Abbott (*Harlem Club singer*), Margo Winkler (*argumentative woman*), Steven Prince (*record producer*), Don Calfa (*Gilbert*), Bernie Ruby (*justice of the peace*), Selma

Archerd (*wife of justice of the peace*), Bill Baldwin (*announcer in Moonlight Terrace*), Mary Lindsay (*hatcheck girl in Meadows*), Jon Cutler (*musician in Frankie Harte's band*), Nicky Blair (*cab driver*), Casey Kasem (*DJ*), Jay Salerno (*bus driver*), William Tole (*Tommy Dorsey*), Sydney Guilaroff (*hairdresser*), Peter Savage (*Horace Morris's assistant*), Gene Castle (*dancing sailor*), Louie Guss (*Fowler*), Shera Danese (*Doyle's girl in Major Chord*), Bill McMillan (*DJ*), David Nichols (*Arnold Trench*), Harry Northup (*Alabama*)
Original release version, 136 mins; re-release version, 163 mins

1978

The Last Waltz
Thanksgiving Day, 1976, Winterland, San Francisco. The Band give a farewell concert after sixteen years on the road, with a host of rock legends performing their own songs. Intercut with the stage acts, Scorsese interviews the members of The Band about their lives and music.

Production company: United Artists
Producer: Robbie Robertson
Cinematography (colour): Michael Chapman, Laszlo Kovacs, Vilmos Zsigmond, David Myers, Bobby Byrne, Michael Watkins, Hiro Narita
Editors: Yeu-Bun Yee, Jan Roblee
Songs: 'Don't Do It', 'Theme from the Last Waltz', 'Up On Cripple Creek', 'Shape I'm In', 'It Makes No Difference', 'Stagefright', 'The Night They Drove Old Dixie Down', 'Chest Fever', 'Ophelia', 'Evangeline', 'Old Time Religion', 'Genetic Method', 'Sip The Wine' (The Band); with The Band 'The Weight' (The Staples), 'Evangeline' (Emmylou Harris); 'Who Do You Love' (Ronnie Hawkins); 'Such A Night' (Dr John); 'Helpless' (Neil Young); 'Dry Your Eyes' (Neil Diamond); 'Mystery Train' (Paul Butterfield); 'Coyote' (Joni Mitchell); 'Mannish Boy' (Muddy Waters); 'Further On Up the Road' (Eric Clapton); 'Caravan' (Van Morrison); 'Forever Young', 'Baby Let Me Follow You Down' (Bob Dylan); 'I Shall Be Released' (Bob Dylan, Ringo Starr, Ron Wood et al.)
Poems: Introduction to Chaucer's *The Canterbury Tales* read by Michael McClure; 'Loud Prayer' read by Lawrence Ferlinghetti
Production designer: Boris Leven
Cast: The Band (Robbie Robertson, Rick Danko, Levon Helm, Garth Hudson, Richard Manuel), Paul Butterfield, Eric Clapton, Neil Diamond, Bob Dylan, Emmylou Harris, Ronnie Hawkins, Dr John, Joni Mitchell, Van Morrison, The Staples, Ringo Starr, Muddy Waters, Ron Wood, Neil Young, Martin Scorsese, Michael McClure, Lawrence Ferlinghetti
117 mins

American Boy: A Profile of Steven Prince
At George Memmoli's Hollywood home, Scorsese and friends are entertained by Steven Prince's stories (intercut with home movies) about his middle-class Jewish childhood, working as a road manager for Neil Diamond, his experience with drugs and guns, and his relationship with his father.

Production company: New Empire Films/Scorsese Films
Producer: Bertram Lovitt
Treatment: Mardik Martin, Julia Cameron
Cinematography (colour): Michael Chapman

Editors: Amy Jones, Bertram Lovitt
Song: 'Time Fades Away' (Neil Young)
Cast: Steven Prince, Martin Scorsese, George Memmoli, Mardik Martin, Julia Cameron, Kathy McGinnis
55 mins

1980
Raging Bull
New York, 1941. Middleweight boxer Jake La Motta, managed by his brother Joey, forsakes his wife when he falls for teenager Vickie, whom he marries but treats with constant jealous suspicion. By following underworld advice, La Motta becomes world champion when he beats Marcel Cerdan in 1949. La Motta's increasing weight problem and obsessional rages lead him to beat up his wife and Joey, believing both to have been unfaithful. After a brutal defeat by 'Sugar' Ray Robinson, La Motta opens a night-club in 1956. Vickie finally leaves him, and he is arrested for soliciting minors and sent to jail. Back in New York in 1958, he unsuccessfully attempts to make up with his brother, and six years later is found giving recitations in a club.

Production company: United Artists
Producers: Irwin Winkler, Robert Chartoff in association with Peter Savage
Screenplay: Paul Schrader, Mardik Martin, from the book *Raging Bull* by Jake La Motta with Joseph Carter and Peter Savage
Cinematography (black and white/colour): Michael Chapman
Editor: Thelma Schoonmaker
Music: 'At Last', 'A New Kind of Love', 'Webster Hall' (arranged by Robbie Robertson, performed by Garth Hudson, Richard Manuel, Larry Klein and Dale Turner)
Other Music: Intermezzo from *Cavalleria Rusticana*, Barcarolle from *Silvano* by Pietro Mascagni
Songs: 'Stornelli Fiorentini' (Carlo Buti); 'Scapricciatiello' (Renato Carosone); 'Turi Giuliano' (Orazio Strano); 'Cow Cow Boogie' (Ella Fitzgerald and The Ink Spots); 'Whispering Grass', 'Do I Worry' (The Ink Spots); 'Stone Cold Dead in the Market' (Ella Fitzgerald and Louis Jordan); 'Till Then' (The Mills Brothers); 'Big Noise from Winnetka' (Bob Crosby and The Bobcats); 'Heartaches' (Ted Weems); 'Blue Velvet' (Tony Bennett); 'Flash', 'Two O'Clock Jump', 'All or Nothing at All' (Harry James); 'Drum Boogie' (Gene Krupa); 'Jersey Bounce' (Benny Goodman); 'Come Fly With Me', 'Mona Lisa' (Nat King Cole); 'I Ain't Got Nobody' (Louis Prima, Keely Smith); 'Nao Tenho Lagrimas' (Patricio Teixera); 'Prisoner of Love' (Perry Como); 'Prisoner of Love' (Russ Colombo); 'Frenesi' (Artie Shaw); 'My Reverie' (Larry Clinton and his Orchestra); 'Just One More Chance', 'That's My Desire' (Frankie Laine); 'Bye, Bye, Baby' (Marilyn Monroe); 'Lonely Nights (The Hearts)'; 'Tell the Truth' (Ray Charles)
Production designer: Gene Rudolf
Cast: Robert De Niro (*Jake La Motta*), Cathy Moriarty (*Vickie La Motta*), Joe Pesci (*Joey La Motta*), Frank Vincent (*Salvy*), Nicholas Colasanto (*Tommy Como*), Theresa Saldana (*Lenore*), Mario Gallo (*Mario*), Frank Adonis (*Patsy*), Joseph Bono (*Guido*), Frank Topham (*Toppy*), Lori Anne Flax (*Irma*), Charles Scorsese (*Charlie, man with Como*), Don Dunphy (*himself*), Bill Hanrahan (*Eddie Eagan*), Rita Bennett (*Emma, Miss 48's*), James V. Christy (*Dr Pinto*), Bernie Allen (*comedian*), Michael Badalucco (*soda fountain clerk*), Thomas Beansy Lobasso (*Beansy*), Paul Forrest (*Monsignor*), Peter Petrella (*Johnny*), Sal Serafino Thomassetti (*Webster Hall bouncer*), Geraldine Smith

(*Janet*), Mardik Martin (*Copa waiter*), Maryjane Lauria (*first girl*), Linda Artuso (*second girl*), Peter Savage (*Jackie Curtie*), Daniel P. Conte (*Detroit promoter*), Joe Malanga (*bodyguard*), Sabine Turco Jr, Steve Orlando, Silvio Garcia Jr (*bouncers at Copa*), John Arceri (*maître d'*), Joseph A. Morale (*first man at table*), James Dimodica (*second man at table*), Robert Uricola (*man outside cab*), Andrea Orlando (*woman in cab*), Allan Malamud (*reporter at Jake's house*), D. J. Blair (*State Attorney Bronson*), Laura James (*Mrs Bronson*), Richard McMurray (*J.R.*), Mary Albee (*underage ID girl*), Liza Katz (*woman with ID girl*), Candy Moore (*Linda*), Martin Scorsese (*Barbizon stagehand*), Johnny Barnes (*'Sugar' Ray Robinson*), Floyd Anderson (*Jimmy Reeves*), Eddie Mustafa Muhammad (*Billy Fox*), Louis Raftis (*Marcel Cerdan*), Johnny Turner (*Laurent Dauthuille*)
129 mins

1982

The King of Comedy

Having tricked his way into the limo of his idol TV chat show host Jerry Langford, hopeful stand-up comic Rupert Pupkin deludes himself that Langford wants him on his show, and even fantasizes about replacing Langford. Continually fobbed off by Langford's staff, Pupkin plots with crazy fellow fan Masha to kidnap Langford. The plan succeeds, and Pupkin wins his chance to perform his act on television. Following his brief jail sentence, Pupkin appears to have succeeded in becoming a major television celebrity.

Production company: Twentieth Century–Fox
Producer: Arnon Milchan
Screenplay: Paul Zimmerman
Cinematography (colour): Fred Schuler
Editor: Thelma Schoonmaker
Music production: Robbie Robertson
Songs: 'Jerry Langford Theme', 'Rupert's Theme' (Bob James); 'Come Rain or Come Shine', 'Sweet Sixteen Bars' (Ray Charles); 'The Finer Things' (David Sanborn); 'Back on the Chain Gang' (The Pretenders); 'Fly Me to the Moon' (Frank Sinatra); 'Swamp' (Talking Heads); 'Rainbow Sleeves' (Ricki Lee Jones); 'Between Trains' (Robbie Robertson); 'T'Ain't Nobody's Buziness If I Do' (B. B. King); 'Steal the Night' (Ric Ocasek); 'The Best of Everything' (Tom Petty); 'Wonderful Remark' (Van Morrison)
Production designer: Boris Leven
Cast: Robert De Niro (*Rupert Pupkin*), Jerry Lewis (*Jerry Langford*), Diahnne Abbott (*Rita*), Sandra Bernhard (*Masha*), Ed Herlihy (*himself*), Lou Brown (*bandleader*), Loretta Tupper, Peter Potulski, Vinnie Gonzales (*stage door fans*), Whitey Ryan (*stage door guard*), Doc Lawless (*chauffeur*), Marta Heflin (*young girl*), Catherine Scorsese (*Rupert's mom*), Cathy Scorsese (*Dolores*), Chuck Low (*man in Chinese restaurant*), Margo Winkler (*receptionist*), Shelley Hack (*Cathy Long*), Mick Jones, Joe Strummer, Paul Simonon, Kosmo Vinyl, Ellen Foley, Pearl Harbor, Gabu Salter, Jerry Baxter-Worman, Don Letts (*street scum*), Fred de Cordova (*Bert Thomas*), Edgar J. Scherick (*Wilson Crockett*), Kim Chan (*Jonno*), Dr Joyce Brothers, Victor Borge, Tony Randall (*themselves*), Jay Julien (*Langford's lawyer*), Harry Ufland (*Langford's agent*), Martin Scorsese (*television director*), Charles Scorsese (*first man at bar*), Mardik Martin (*second man at bar*)
108 mins

1985

After Hours

A mild-mannered word-processor operator, Paul Hackett, falls into conversation with attractive Marcy Franklin in a diner, and is later invited to her SoHo loft that night. After losing all his money on the way, he finds a strange reception and abruptly leaves. Trying to borrow his subway fare home from a sympathetic barman, an increasingly bizarre series of events leads him back to the loft, where he discovers Marcy has died from an overdose. Finding himself accused by local residents of being a burglar, he escapes them only by being disguised as a papier-mâché statue, and is finally dumped in front of his office as a new morning begins.

Production company: Double Play/The Geffen Company
Producers: Amy Robinson, Griffin Dunne, Robert Colesberry
Screenplay: Joseph Minion
Cinematography (colour): Michael Ballhaus
Editor: Thelma Schoonmaker
Music: Howard Shore
Other Music: Symphony in D Major, K 73n by Wolfgang Amadeus Mozart; Air from Suite no. 3 by Johann Sebastian Bach
Songs: 'En la Cueva' (Cuadro Flamenco); 'Sevillanas' (Manitas de Plata); 'Night and Day'; 'Body and Soul'; 'Quando, Quando, Quando'; 'Someone to Watch Over Me', 'You're Mine', 'We Belong Together' (Robert and Johnnie); 'Angel Baby' (Rosie and the Orginals); 'Last Train to Clarksville' (The Monkees); 'Chelsea Morning', 'I Don't Know Where I Stand' (Joni Mitchell); 'Over the Mountain and Across the Sea' (Johnnie and Joe); 'One Summer Night' (The Danleers); 'Pay to Cum' (The Bad Brains); 'Is That All There Is?' (Peggy Lee)
Production designer: Jeffrey Townsend
Cast: Griffin Dunne (*Paul Hackett*), Rosanna Arquette (*Marcy*), Verna Bloom (*June*), Thomas Chong (*Pepe*), Linda Fiorentino (*Kiki*), Teri Garr (*Julie*), John Heard (*Tom, the bartender*), Cheech Marin (*Neil*), Catherine O'Hara (*Gail*), Dick Miller (*waiter*), Will Patton (*Horst*), Robert Plunket (*Mark*), Bronson Pinchot (*Lloyd*), Rocco Sisto (*coffee-shop cashier*), Larry Block (*taxi driver*), Victor Argo (*dinner cashier*), Murray Moston (*subway attendant*), John P. Codiglia (*transit cop*), Clarke Evans (*first neighbour*), Victor Bumbalo (*second neighbour*), Bill Elvermann (*third neighbour*), Joel Jason (*first biker*), Clarence Felder (*bouncer*), Henry Baker (*Jett*), Margo Winkler (*women with gun*), Robin Johnson (*punk girl*), Stephen J. Lim (*Club Berlin bartender*), Frank Aquilino, Maree Catalano, Paula Raflo, Rockets Redglare (*angry mob members*), Martin Scorsese (*man with spotlight*)
97 mins

Mirror, Mirror

(episode in 'Amazing Stories' TV series)
After appearing on a TV chat show, highly successful horror fiction author Jordan returns home, where, as he prepares for bed, he sees a phantom in the mirror. This vision continues to haunt him until he descends into a paranoid state beyond human reassurance. Finally he turns into the phantom and throws himself out of the window.

Production company: Amblin
Producer: David E. Vogel
Screenplay: Joseph Minion, from a story by Steven Spielberg

Cinematography (colour): Robert Stevens
Editor: Joe Ann Fogle
Music: Michael Kamen
Production designer: Rick Carter
Cast: Sam Waterston (*Jordan*), Helen Shaver (*Karen*), Dick Cavett (*himself*), Tim Robbins (*Jordan's phantom*), Dana Gladstone (*producer*), Valerie Grear (*host*), Michael C. Gwynne (*jail attendant*), Peter Iacangelo (*limo driver*), Jonathan Luria (*cameraman*), Harry Northup (*security guard*), Glenn Scarpelli (*Jeffrey Gelb*), Jack Thibeau (*tough guy*)
24 mins

1986
The Color of Money
Former pool hustler 'Fast' Eddie Felson, now making a living selling liquor, is impressed by young pool player Vincent Lauria. Taking Lauria and his shrewd girlfriend Carmen on the road, Felson has a difficult time persuading the young man not to show off and not to win every game. Finally Felson himself takes up the cue again, but is beaten by a hustler. Felson tells Lauria to go his own way, and they meet up again as competitors at the Atlantic City nine-ball tournament. Felson wins the match, but later Lauria says he lost deliberately. Felson tells Lauria that he's reached the top league, and, beginning a private re-match, that he must give him his best game.

Production company: Touchstone
Producers: Irving Axelrad, Barbara De Fina
Screenplay: Richard Price, based on the novel by Walter Tevis
Cinematography (colour): Michael Ballhaus
Editor: Thelma Schoonmaker
Music: Robbie Robertson
Other Music: 'Va Pensiero' from *Nabucco* by Giuseppe Verdi
Songs: 'Strangers in the Night'; 'I'll Never Smile Again'; 'Anema e Cora'; 'The Day the Rains Came'; 'The Girl from Ipanema'; 'I'll Remember April' (Charlie Parker); 'Feel Like Going Home' (The Del Lords); 'Walk on the Wild Side' (Jimmy Smith); 'Still a Fool' (Muddy Waters); 'My Baby's in Love with Another Guy', 'Let Yourself in for It' (Robert Palmer); 'She's Fine – She's Mine' (Bo Diddley); 'It's My Life, Baby' (Eric Clapton and the Big Town Playboys); 'Who Owns This Place?' (Don Henley); 'It's in the Way You Use It' (Eric Clapton); 'Two Brothers and a Stranger' (Mark Knopfler); 'Don't Tell Me Nothin'' (Willie Dixon); 'Standing on the Edge' (B. B. King); 'One More Night' (Phil Collins); 'Still the Night' (Bodeans); 'Werewolves of London' (Warren Zevon); 'Out of Left Field' (Percy Sledge)
Production designer: Boris Leven
Cast: Paul Newman (*'Fast' Eddie Felson*), Tom Cruise (*Vincent Lauria*), Mary Elizabeth Mastrantonio (*Carmen*), Helen Shaver (*Janelle*), John Turtorro (*Julian*), Bill Cobbs (*Orvis*), Keith McCready (*Grady Seasons*), Robert Agins (*Earl at Chalkies*), Alvin Anastasia (*Kennedy*), Elizabeth Bracco (*Diane at bar*), Joe Guastaferro (*Chuck the bartender*), Grady Matthews (*Dud*), Steve Mizerak (*Duke, Eddie's first opponent*), Jerry Piller (*Tom*), Forest Whitaker (*Amos*), Bruce A. Young (*Moselle*), Vito D'Ambrosio (*Lou in Child World*), Randall Arney (*first Child World customer*), Lisa Dodson (*second Child World customer*), Ernest Perry Jr (*eye doctor*), Iggy Pop (*skinny player on road*), Richard Price (*guy who calls Dud*), Alex Ross (*bartender who bets*), Charles Scorsese (*first high roller*), Fred Squillo (*second high roller*)
119 mins

Armani Commercial (1)
In bed, a young woman teaches a young man some Italian words.

Production company: Emporio Armani
Producer: Barbara De Fina
Treatment: Martin Scorsese
Cinematography (black and white): Nestor Almendros
Cast: Christophe Bouquin, Christina Marsilach
30 secs

1987

Bad
Extended promo for Michael Jackson song
Returning home from his privileged school, Daryl is taunted by his friends in Harlem. Irritated by their posturing, he takes them down to the subway to show who's really 'bad'. Suddenly he's surrounded by his own fantasy gang, who perform an aggressive song and dance to prove he can give as good a show of 'doing wrong' as anyone.

Production company: Optimum Productions
Producers: Quincy Jones, Barbara De Fina
Screenplay: Richard Price
Cinematography (black and white/colour): Michael Chapman
Editor: Thelma Schoonmaker
Choreography: Michael Jackson, Gregg Burge, Jeffrey Daniel
Cast: Michael Jackson (*Daryl*), Adam Nathan (*Tip*), Pedro Sanchez (*Nelson*), Webley Sniper (*Mini Max*), Greg Holtz Jr (*Cowboy*), Jaime Perry (*Ski*), Paul Calderon (*dealer*), Alberto Alejandrino (*Hispanic man*), Horace Daily (*street bum*), Marvin Foster (*crack customer*), Roberta Flack (*Daryl's mother*)
16 mins

1988

Somewhere Down the Crazy River
Promo for Robbie Robertson song
Robbie Robertson sings to camera, and then is joined by a young woman for a passionate embrace.

Production company: Limelight
Producers: Amanda Pirie, Tim Clawson
Treatment: Martin Scorsese
Cinematography (colour): Mark Plummer
Production designer: Marina Levikova
Cast: Robbie Robertson, Sammy BoDean, Maria McKee
4½ mins

The Last Temptation of Christ
Jesus of Nazareth, whose carpentry skills are put to making crosses for the occupying Roman force, is tormented by visions of a special purpose in His life. Reviled for His weakness by Judas, a Zealot, and Mary Magdalene, a prostitute who was a childhood friend, Jesus sees manifestations of Satan and is convinced He should now preach God's message. Joined by Judas, then Mary, and then more disciples, He delivers the Sermon on

the Mount, but John the Baptist tells Him He must go into the desert to speak with God. After resisting temptation, Jesus returns with a new anger, performs miracles, raises Lazarus from the dead, and leads an assault on the Temple in Jerusalem. Telling Judas he must betray Him, Jesus is arrested by the Romans and crucified. On the cross, an angel appears, tells Him God has spared Him, and apparently offers Jesus a normal life as a family man. But when Paul tells Him about the crucifixion and resurrection, and Judas accuses Him of failing the cause, Jesus accepts His destiny and crawls His painful way back on to the cross.

Production company: Universal Pictures
Producer: Barbara De Fina
Screenplay: Paul Schrader, based on the novel by Nikos Kazantzakis
Cinematography (colour): Michael Ballhaus
Editor: Thelma Schoonmaker
Music: Peter Gabriel
Production designer: John Beard
Cast: Willem Dafoe (*Jesus*), Harvey Keitel (*Judas*), Paul Greco (*Zealot*), Steven Shill (*Centurion*), Verna Bloom (*Mary Mother of Jesus*), Barbara Hershey (*Mary Magdalene*), Roberts Blossom (*Aged Master*), Barry Miller (*Jeroboam*), Gary Basaraba (*Andrew Apostle*), Irvin Kershner (*Zebedee*), Victor Argo (*Peter Apostle*), Michael Been (*John Apostle*), Paul Herman (*Philip Apostle*), John Lurie (*James Apostle*), Leo Burmeister (*Nathaniel Apostle*), André Gregory (*John the Baptist*), Peggy Gormley (*Martha, sister of Lazarus*), Randy Danson (*Mary, sister of Lazarus*), Thomas Arana (*Lazarus*), Alan Rosenberg (*Thomas Apostle*), Del Russel (*money-changer*), Nehemiah Persoff (*Rabbi*), Donald Hodson (*Sadducee*), Harry Dean Stanton (*Saul/Paul*), Peter Berling (*beggar*), David Bowie (*Pontius Pilate*), Juliette Caton (*girl angel*)
163 mins

Armani Commercial (2)

Watched by a young man, a young woman looks for him in his apartment. Undiscovered, he leaves, knocking over a perfume bottle.

Production company: Emporio Armani
Producer: Barbara De Fina
Treatment: Martin Scorsese
Cinematography (colour): Michael Ballhaus
Cast: Jens Peter, Elisabetha Ranella
20 secs

1989

New York Stories: Life Lessons

Episode in three-part film; other parts – *Oedipus Wrecks*, directed by Woody Allen, and *Life without Zoe*, directed by Francis Coppola.

Successful painter Lionel Dobie is distracted from the need to produce work for his upcoming one-man show by his troubled relationship with his live-in girlfriend, aspiring painter Paulette. Angry when ditched after a brief affair with a performance artist, Paulette tries to move out of Dobie's studio. But Dobie's continuing erotic obsession with Paulette leads him to plead with her to stay, despite her fling with another artist. Paulette though, exasperated by Dobie's outbursts at both her recent suitors, finally does move out. At the private view of his new exhibition, Dobie meets another young aspiring painter, and offers her the chance to take Paulette's place with the promise of invaluable 'life lessons'.

Production company: Touchstone
Producers: Barbara De Fina, Robert Greenhut
Screenplay: Richard Price
Cinematography (colour): Nestor Almendros
Editor: Thelma Schoonmaker
Music: 'Nessun Dorma' from *Turandot* by Giacomo Puccini
Songs: 'Whiter Shade of Pale', 'Conquistador' (Procal Harum); 'Politician' (Cream); 'The Right Time' (Ray Charles); 'Like a Rolling Stone' (Bob Dylan and The Band); 'It Could Happen to You'; 'That Old Black Magic'; 'Stella by Starlight'; 'Sex Kick' (Transvision Vamp); 'What Is This Thing Called Love?', 'Bolero De Django' (Hot Club of France Quintet)
Paintings: Chuck Connelley
Production designer: Kristi Zea
Cast: Nick Nolte (*Lionel Dobie*), Rosanna Arquette (*Paulette*), Patrick O'Neal (*Philip Fowler*), Jesse Borrego (*Reuben Toro*), Steve Buscemi (*Gregory Stark*), Phil Harper (*Businessman*), Gregorij von Leitis (*Kurt Bloom*), Illeana Douglas (*Paulette's friend*), Kenneth J. McGregor, David Cryer, Paul Geier (*Suits*), Peter Gabriel, Richard Price, Michael Powell (*gallery patrons*)
44 mins

1990

GoodFellas

In East Brooklyn in 1955, teenage Henry Hill dreams of becoming a gangster while running errands for the local mobsters. He earns the respect of his mentor Jimmy Conway by refusing to testify when arrested for smuggling cigarettes. Adopted by the local godfather Paulie Cicero, Henry grows up to get rich on a series of money-making scams. In 1963 he joins forces with Jimmy and Tommy DeVito in robbing Idlewild airport. Henry marries a middle-class Jewish girl, Karen, who is at first innocent of his true profession; when she discovers he has a mistress, the marriage almost breaks up, but Paulie insists Henry patches things up. Henry and Jimmy are jailed for ten years for beating up a debtor, and inside prison Henry becomes involved in drug deals. Paroled after four years, he promises Paulie to drop the drugs, and in 1980 he joins forces with Jimmy and Tommy again on a $6 million airport hijack. With the FBI moving in, the minor participants in the team are eliminated by the trio. But when Tommy's murder in 1970 of 'made' man Billy Batts resurfaces, Paulie has him taken out. Henry begins to fear he is next in line for execution, and turns himself in to the FBI to join the Witness Protection Program. He then retires into anonymity with his wife and children.

Production company: Warner Brothers
Producer: Irwin Winkler
Executive producer: Barbara De Fina
Screenplay: Nicholas Pileggi, Martin Scorsese, based on the book *Wise Guy* by Pileggi
Cinematography (colour): Michael Ballhaus
Editor: Thelma Schoonmaker
Songs: 'Rags to Riches', 'The Boulevard of Broken Dreams' (Tony Bennett); 'Can't We Be Sweethearts' (The Cleftones); 'Heart of Stone' (Otis Williams and The Charms);

'Sincerely' (The Moonglows); 'Firenze Sogna', 'Parlami d'Amore Mariu' (Giuseppe di Stefano); 'Speedo' (The Cadillacs); 'Stardust' (Billy Ward and His Dominoes); 'This World We Live In (Il Cielo in Una Stanza)' (Mina); 'Playboy' (The Marvelettes); 'It's Not for Me to Say' (Johnny Mathis); 'I Will Follow Him' (Betty Curtis); 'Then He Kissed Me', 'He's Sure the Boy I Love' (The Crystals); 'Look in My Eyes' (The Chantells); 'Roses are Red' (Bobby Vinton); 'Life Is But a Dream' (The Harptones); 'Leader of the Pack', 'Remember (Walkin' in the Sand)' (The Shangri-Las); 'Toot Toot Tootsie Goodbye'; 'Happy Birthday To You; 'Ain't That a Kick in the Head' (Dean Martin); 'Atlantis' (Donovan); 'Pretend You Don't See Her' (Jerry Vale); 'Baby I Love You' (Aretha Franklin); 'Beyond the Sea' (Bobby Darin); 'Gimme Shelter', 'Monkey Man', 'Memo from Turner' (The Rolling Stones); 'Wives and Lovers' (Jack Jones); 'Frosty the Snowman' (The Ronettes); 'Christmas (Baby Please Come Home)' (Darlene Love); 'The Bells of St Mary's' (The Drifters); 'Unchained Melody' (Vito and the Salutations); 'Danny Boy'; 'Sunshine of Your Love' (Cream); 'Layla' (Derek and the Dominos); 'Jump Into the Fire' (Harry Nilsson); 'The Magic Bus' (The Who); 'What Is Life?' (George Harrison); 'Mannish Boy' (Muddy Waters); 'My Way' (Sid Vicious)

Production designer: Kristi Zea
Cast: Ray Liotta (*Henry Hill*), Lorraine Bracco (*Karen Hill*), Robert De Niro (*James Conway*), Joe Pesci (*Tommy De Vito*), Paul Sorvino (*Paul Vario*), Frank Sivero (*Frankie Carbone*), Tony Darrow (*Sonny Bunz*), Mike Starr (*Frenchy*), Frank Vincent (*Billy Batts*), Chuck Low (*Morrie Kessler*), Frank Dileo (*Tuddy Cicero*), Gina Mastrogiacomo (*Janice Rossi*), Debi Mazar (*Sandy*), Catherine Scorsese (*Tommy's mother*), Charles Scorsese (*Vinnie*), Suzanne Shepherd (*Karen's mother*), Margo Winkler (*Belle Kessler*), Welker White (*Louis Bird*), Julie Garfield (*Mickey Conway*), Christopher Serrone (*young Henry*), Ealine Kagan (*Henry's mother*), Beau Starr (*Henry's father*), Kevin Corrigan (*Michael Hill*), Michael Imperioli (*Spider*), John Williams (*Johnny Roastbeef*)
146 mins

Made In Milan

As he prepares for a show, fashion designer Giorgio Armani discusses his principles of fashion, his family history and the city of Milan.

Production company: Emporio Armani
Producer: Barbara De Fina
Screenplay: Jay Cocks
Cinematography (colour): Nestor Almendros
Editor: Thelma Schoonmaker
Music: Howard Shore
20 mins

1991

Cape Fear

New Essex, North Carolina. While in prison serving fourteen years for raping and beating a teenage girl, Max Cady learns the law and discovers that prosecuting lawyer Sam Bowden suppressed evidence of the victim's past promiscuity. On release Cady tracks down the Bowden family, and refuses Sam's offer of money to stop harassing them. Cady picks up Sam's mistress, Lori, and brutally rapes her, but she refuses to testify against him. Fearing for his wife, Leigh, and teenage daugher, Danielle, whom Cady has approached at school, Sam employs a private detective, Claude Kersek. When

Kersek fails to scare Cady off with violence, and Cady gets a restraining order put on Sam, Kersek suggests laying a trap for him at the Bowden home. When this goes wrong and Cady kills Kersek, Sam panics and takes his family off to their houseboat at Cape Fear, unaware that Cady has hidden underneath their car. During a storm, Cady ties up Sam and menaces both Leigh and Danielle. Danielle throws lighter fuel in Cady's face and sets him on fire, but he continues to threaten them until a storm throws everyone overboard. Sam manages to attack Cady with a rock, and he finally drowns in the river, leaving the Bowden family huddled together on the shore.

Production company: Universal Pictures
Producer: Barbara De Fina
Executive producers: Kathleen Kennedy, Frank Marshall
Screenplay: Wesley Strick, based on James R. Webb's screenplay and John D. Macdonald's novel *The Executioners*
Cinematography (colour/scope): Freddie Francis
Editor: Thelma Schoonmaker
Music: Bernard Herrmann, adapted by Elmer Bernstein
Songs: 'Tipitina' (Professor Longhair); 'Patience' (Guns N' Roses); 'Do Right Woman – Do Right Man' (Aretha Franklin); 'The Bog' (Bigod 20); 'Been Caught Stealing' (Jane's Addiction); 'The Creature From the Black Leather Lagoon' (The Cramps)
Production designer: Henry Bumstead
Cast: Robert De Niro (*Max Cady*), Nick Nolte (*Sam Bowden*), Jessica Lange (*Leigh Bowden*), Juliette Lewis (*Danielle Bowden*), Joe Don Baker (*Claude Kersek*), Robert Mitchum (*Lt. Elgart*), Gregory Peck (*Lee Heller*), Martin Balsam (*Judge*), Illeana Douglas (*Lori Davis*), Fred Dalton Thompson (*Tom Broadbent*), Zully Montero (*Graciella*)
128 mins

1993

The Age of Innocence
New York City, the 1870s. Lawyer Newland Archer, engaged to May Welland of the wealthy Mingott family, is frustrated when their marriage is delayed by her mother's insistence on observing the proper formalities. He becomes distracted by the arrival of May's cousin Ellen Olenska, who is escaping a disastrous marriage to a philandering Polish count. After successfully persuading the influential Van der Luydens to establish Ellen in society, Newland is irritated to find that womanizing Julius Beaufort is paying her close attention. In his official position, Newland dissuades Ellen from seeking a divorce; increasingly drawn to her, he takes the opportunity when May is on holiday to visit Ellen more often. When he finally declares his love for Ellen, a letter arrives from May saying that her marriage to Newland can be brought forward. Eighteen months after the wedding, Newland is still obsessed with Ellen and he sees her in Boston, where he begs her not to return to her husband in Europe. When Mrs Mingott suffers a stroke, Ellen joins her in New York, but just as Newland and Ellen agree on an assignation, May brings news to him that Ellen has in fact decided to leave for Europe. Desolated by the realization that all New York knows his true feelings, he tells May he wants to travel, but she reveals that she is pregnant, and that she told Ellen of her pregnancy two weeks before. Many years later, when May has died Newland is told by his son in Paris that May had always known of his love for Ellen. Newland has the chance to visit Ellen at her Paris home, but after standing outside her window, he turns and walks away.

Production company: Columbia Pictures
Producer: Barbara De Fina
Screenplay: Martin Scorsese, Jay Cocks, based on the novel by Edith Wharton
Cinematography (colour/scope): Michael Ballhaus
Editor: Thelma Schoonmaker
Music: Elmer Bernstein
Other Music: Scene from Act III of *Faust* by Charles Gounod; Piano Sonata no. 8 in C Minor, op. 13 ('Pathétique') by Ludwig van Beethoven; 'Radetzky' March by Johann Strauss I; 'Emperor' Waltz, 'Tales from the Vienna Woods', 'An Artist's Life' by Johann Strauss II; 3rd Movement from Quintet in B Flat, op. 87 by Felix Mendelssohn-Bartholdy
Song: 'Marble Halls' (Enya)
Production designer: Dante Ferretti
Cast: Daniel Day-Lewis (*Newland Archer*), Michelle Pfeiffer (*Ellen Olenska*), Winona Ryder (*May Welland*), Miriam Margolyes (*Mrs Mingott*), Richard E. Grant (*Larry Lefferts*), Alec McCowan (*Sillerton Jackson*), Geraldine Chaplin (*Mrs Welland*), Mary Beth Hurt (*Regina Beaufort*), Stuart Wilson (*Julius Beaufort*), Sian Phillips (*Mrs Archer*), Caroline Farina (*Janie*), Michael Gough (*Henry van der Luyden*), Alexis Smith (*Louisa van der Luyden*), Norman Lloyd (*Mr Letterblair*), Jonathan Pryce (*Riviere*), Domenica Scorsese (*Katie Blinker*), Robert Sean Leonard (*Ted Archer*), Cristina Pronzati (*Italian maid*), Joanne Woodward (*Narrator*)
136 mins

1995

A Century of Cinema – A Personal Journey with Martin Scorsese through American Movies

An extended documentary on the history of American cinema, made as part of a series celebrating the centenary of cinema in which leading film-makers were invited to give their personal viewpoint on the films produced in their respective countries. Occasionally seen in vision, but more often in voice-over, Scorsese narrates a vast array of film clips to illustrate his perspective as a director, operating within the Hollywood studio system like so many in America.

Part One: The Director's Dilemma; The Director as Storyteller; The Western; The Gangster Film; The Musical
Part Two: The Director as Illusionist; The Director as Smuggler
Part Three: The Director as Smuggler; The Director as Iconoclast

Production company: British Film Institute TV
Producer: Florence Dauman
Script: Martin Scorsese, Michael Henry Wilson
Cinematography (colour): Jean Yves Escoffier
Supervising editor: Thelma Schoonmaker
Music: Elmer Bernstein
With: Martin Scorsese, Billy Wilder, Gregory Peck, André De Toth, Sam Fuller, Arthur Penn, Clint Eastwood, George Lucas, Francis Coppola, Brian De Palma, Fritz Lang, Howard Hawks, King Vidor, Douglas Sirk, Nicholas Ray, Orson Welles, Elia Kazan, John Cassavetes, Frank Capra, John Ford
Part One: 73 mins; Part Two: 80 mins; Part Three: 74 mins

Casino

Las Vegas, 1973. With the casinos in the hands of the Teamsters' Union, the glamour and popularity of the gambling city, attracting billions of dollars a year, is a huge temptation to organized crime. Sam 'Ace' Rothstein, a skilled bookie who has risen through the ranks of the Midwestern mob, is picked by the bosses to front their operation to skim money from the casinos. Despite not having a licence appropriate to his actual authority, he takes charge of the Tangiers casino to ensure money is quietly taken out while it is counted, and to keep cheats and hustlers from operating at the tables. He is at the height of his success when he encounters a dazzling chip hustler, Ginger McKenna, and he becomes infatuated with her. She agrees to marry him when he proposes a deposit of a million dollars' worth of jewellery in a bank vault, which will become hers in the event of their separation. Together they have a daughter, and Sam becomes a respectable family man who is welcomed into the local country club.

Meanwhile his childhood friend Nicky Santoro, a ruthless hit man, takes refuge in Las Vegas and initially helps deal with potential threats to Sam's operation. But the dream begins to go sour when a bored Ginger turns more and more to drugs and drink, looking to her old pimp boyfriend Lester Diamond for help. At the same time, Nicky's increasingly violent methods force him out of Vegas. When Ginger tries to escape with her bounty to Europe in the company of Lester, Sam intervenes and brings her back, but she then takes solace in an affair with Nicky. Sam, already embarrassed by his association with Nicky, is further threatened when his dismissal of a casino employee with local connections leads to the refusal of his licence. He is reinstated by the mob as an entertainments director, making public appearances on local television, but the situation spirals further out of control and the FBI finally moves in to expose the rackets. Ginger, by now a physical wreck, leaves Sam and dies from drug abuse. The mob decides to take evasive action and murder anyone it suspects as unreliable, including Nicky. Their attempt to kill Sam with a car bomb leaves him only slightly injured.

By the early 1980s, Sam has returned to his life as bookie, and the casinos in Las Vegas are taken over by the big corporations, with the gambling now only one aspect of what has become a family resort.

Production company: Universal Pictures
Producer: Barbara De Fina
Screenplay: Nicholas Pileggi, Martin Scorsese based on the book *Casino* by Nicholas Pileggi
Cinematography (colour/scope): Bob Richardson
Editor: Thelma Schoonmaker
Music: Final Chorus from *St Matthew Passion* by J. S. Bach; Prelude from *Also Sprach Zarathustra* by Richard Strauss; *Flight of the Bumblebee* by Nicolai Rimsky-Korsakov; 'Theme de Camille' from *Le Mepris* by Georges Delerue
Songs: 'Angelina', 'Zooma Zooma', 'Sing, Sing, Sing (with a Swing)', 'Basin Street Blues/ When It's Sleepy Time Down South' (Louis Prima); 'Moonglow'/Love Theme from *Picnic*; 'You're Nobody (Till Somebody Loves You)' (Dean Martin); '7–11 (aka Mambo #5)' (The Gone All Stars); 'Hoochie Coochie Man' (Willie Dixon); 'Fa-Fa-Fa-Fa-Fa' (Sad Song)' (Otis Redding); 'Long Long While', '(I Can't Get No) Satisfaction', 'Heart of Stone', 'Sweet Virginia', 'Can't You Hear Me Knocking', 'Gimme Shelter' (The Rolling Stones); 'The "In" Crowd' (Ramsey Lewis); 'The "In" Crowd' (Dobie Gray), 'Compared to What' (Les McCann & Eddie Harris); 'Slippin' and Slidin' ' (Little Richard); 'Love Is Strange' (Mickey & Sylvia); 'Love Is the Drug' (Roxy Music); 'Nel Blu Dipinto Di Blu

(Volare)' (Domenico Modugno); 'Takes Two To Tango' (Ray Charles and Betty Carter); 'How High the Moon' (Les Paul and Mary Ford); 'I Ain't Superstitious' (Jeff Beck); 'Happy Birthday to You'; 'Unforgettable', 'What a Difference a Day Makes' (Dinah Washington); 'Working in the Coal Mine' (Lee Dorsey); 'Stardust'; 'I'll Take You There' (The Staple Singers); 'Love Me the Way I Love You' (Jerry Vale); 'Let's Start All Over Again' (The Paragons); 'Stella by Starlight' (Ray Charles); 'Boogaloo Down Broadway' (The Fantastic Johnny C.); 'Sweet Dreams' (Emmylou Harris); 'Toad', 'Those Were the Days' (Cream); 'Hurt'; 'The Glory of Love' (The Velvetones); 'Nights in White Satin' (The Moody Blues); 'Walk on the Wild Side' (Jimmy Smith); 'EEE-O Eleven' (Sammy Davis Jr); 'I'll Walk Alone' (Don Cornell); 'That's the Way I Like It'; 'Venus'; 'Whip It', '(I Can't Get No) Satisfaction (Devo); 'Go Your Own Way' (Fleetwood Mac); 'The Thrill Is Gone' (B. B. King); 'I'm Confessin' (That I Love You)' (Louis Prima and Keely Smith); 'Who Can I Turn To (When Nobody Needs Me)' (Tony Bennett); 'The House of the Rising Sun' (The Animals); 'Harbour Lights' (The Platters); 'Stardust' (Hoagy Carmichael)

Production designer: Dante Ferretti

Cast: Robert De Niro (*Sam 'Ace' Rothstein*), Joe Pesci (*Nicky Santoro*), Sharon Stone (*Ginger McKenna*), Don Rickles (*Billy Sherbert*), Kevin Pollack (*Phillip Green*), James Woods (*Lester Diamond*), Frank Vincent (*Franky Marino*), Alan King (*Andy Stone*), L. Q. Jones (*Pat Webb*), Dick Smothers (*Senator*), John Bloom (*Don Ward*), Pasquale Cajano (*Remo Gaggi*), Melissa Prophet (*Jennifer Santoro*), Bill Allison (*John Nance*), Vinny Vella (*Artie Piscano*), Oscar Goodman (*Himself*), Catherine Scorsese (*Piscano's Mother*), Phillip Suriano (*Dominick Santoro*), Erika Von Tagen (*Older Amy*), Frankie Avalon, Steve Allen, Jayne Meadows, Jerry Vale (*themselves*)

117 mins

As editor

1970

Woodstock

August 1969: the great rock festival featuring The Who, Jimi Hendrix, Joe Cocker, Sly and The Family Stone, Santana, Richie Havens, Joan Baez, Crosby, Stills and Nash, Jefferson Airplane, Ten Years After, Country Joe and The Fish, John Sebastian.

Production company: Warner Brothers
Director: Michael Wadleigh
Supervising editor: Martin Scorsese
184 mins

1971

Medicine Ball Caravan

(also released as *We Have Come for Your Daughters*)
Summer 1970: a touring rock roadshow including B. B. King, Alice Cooper, Doug Kershaw, Delaney and Bonnie, David Peel.

Production company: Warner Brothers
Director: François Reichenbach
Supervising editor: Martin Scorsese
88 mins

1972

Unholy Rollers

Behind-the-scenes life in a raunchy look at the roller derby phenomenon.

Production company: AIP
Director: Vernon Zimmerman
Supervising editor: Martin Scorsese
88 mins

Elvis on Tour

A record of Elvis Presley's last vital years on stage, intercut with old movie and TV clips.

Production company: MGM
Directors: Pierre Adidge, Robert Abel
Montage supervisor: Martin Scorsese
93 mins

As actor

1969

Who's That Knocking at My Door?

as gangster

1972

Boxcar Bertha

as client in brothel

1973

Mean Streets

as Shorty, Michael's hired killer

1974

Alice Doesn't Live Here Anymore

as patron at diner

1976

Taxi Driver

as man watching silhouette

1976

Cannonball

Directed by Paul Bartel
as mafioso

1980

Raging Bull

as Barbizon stagehand

1981

Il Pap'occhio (In the Eye of the Pope)
Directed by Renzo Arbore
as television director

1982

The King of Comedy
as television director

Pavlova – A Woman for All Time
Directed by Emil Lotianou
as Gatti-Cassaza, director of the Metropolitan Opera House

1985

After Hours
as man with spotlight

94 Scorsese as the passenger in *Taxi Driver*.

1986
Round Midnight
Directed by Bertrand Tavernier
as Goodley, the manager of Birdland

1989
Dreams
Directed by Akira Kurosawa
as Vincent Van Gogh

1991
Guilty By Suspicion
Directed by Irwin Winkler
as Joe Lesser, film director

1994
Quiz Show
Directed by Robert Redford
as sponsor

1995
Search and Destroy
Directed by David Salle
as IRS accountant

As Producer

1990
The Grifters

Director: Stephen Frears
Production company: Cineplex Odeon Films
Producers: Martin Scorsese, Robert Harris, James Painten
Executive producer: Barbara De Fina
Screenplay: Donald Westlake, based on the novel by Jim Thompson
Cast: Anjelica Huston (*Lily Dillon*), John Cusack (*Roy Dillon*), Annette Bening (*Myra Langtry*), Pat Hingle (*Bobo Justus*), Henry Jones (*Simms*), Michael Laskin (*Irv*), Eddie Jones (*Mints*), J. T. Walsh (*Cole*), Charles Napier (*Hebbing*)

1992
Mad Dog and Glory

Director: John McNaughton
Production company: Universal Pictures
Producers: Barbara De Fina, Martin Scorsese
Screenplay: Richard Price
Cast: Robert De Niro (*Wayne 'Mad Dog' Dobie*), Bill Murray (*Frank*), Uma Thurman (*Glory*), David Caruso (*Mike*), Mike Starr (*Harold*), Tom Towles (*Andrew*), Kathy Baker (*Lee*)

1994

Naked in New York

Director: Dan Algrant
Production company: Fine Line Productions
Producers: Fred Zollo, Carol Cuddy
Executive Producer: Martin Scorsese
Screenplay: Dan Algrant, John Wareen
Cast: Eric Stoltz (*Jake*), Mary Louise Parker (*Joanne*), Ralph Macchio (*Chris*), Jill Clayburgh (*Jake's mother*), Kathleen Turner (*Dana Coles*), Tony Curtis (*Carl Fisher*), Timothy Dalton (*Elliot Price*)

1995

Search and Destroy

Director: David Salle
Production company: New Image
Producers: Ruth Charny, Dan Lupovitz, Elie Cohn
Executive Producer: Martin Scorsese
Screenplay: Michael Almereyda, based on the play by Howard Korder
Cast: Griffin Dunne (*Martin Mirkheim*), Illeana Douglas (*Marie Davenport*), Christopher Walken (*Kim Ulander*), Dennis Hopper (*Dr Waxling*), John Turturro (*Ron*), Ethan Hawke (*Roger*), Rosanna Arquette (*Lauren Mirkheim*)

Clockers

Director: Spike Lee
Producers: Martin Scorsese, Spike Lee, Jon Kilik

Grace of My Heart

Director: Allison Anders
Executive Producer: Martin Scorsese

Martin Scorsese Presents

The following films have been released or re-released in the USA with Scorsese's support

1992

The Golden Coach (Italy, 1952)
Director: Jean Renoir
Distributor: Interama

Rocco and his Brothers (Italy, 1960)
Director: Luchino Visconti
Distributor: Milestone

Intervista (Italy, 1987)
Director: Federico Fellini
Distributor: Castle Hill

1993

Les Orgueilleux/The Proud Ones (France, 1953)
Director: Yves Allegret
Distributor: Interama

La Strada (Italy, 1954)
Director: Federico Fellini
Distributor: Kino

El Cid (USA, 1961)
Director: Anthony Mann
Distributor: Miramax

1995

I Am Cuba (Cuba, 1963)
Director: Mikhail Kalatozov
Distributor: Milestone

Mamma Roma (Italy, 1962)
Director: Pier Paolo Pasolini
Distributor: Milestone

A Matter of Life and Death (Britain, 1946)
Directors: Michael Powell, Emeric Pressburger
Distributor: Sony-Columbia

Belle de Jour (France, 1967)
Director: Luis Buñuel
Distributor: Miramax

The following Republic titles have been released on videocassette with Scorsese's support

Pursued (USA, 1947)
Director: Raoul Walsh

A Double Life (USA, 1947)
Director: George Cukor

Johnny Guitar (USA, 1954)
Director: Nicholas Ray

Force of Evil (USA, 1948)
Director: Abraham Polonsky

The following film was released in Italy with Scorsese's support

Con Gli Occhi Chiusi (Italy, 1994)
Director: Francesca Archibugi

Bibliography

Bliss, Michael, *Martin Scorsese and Michael Cimino*, The Scarecrow Press Inc., Metuchen, New Jersey, and London (1985)

Cocks, Jay and Scorsese, Martin, *The Age of Innocence*, ed. Robin Standefer, Newmarket Press, New York (1993)

Ehrenstein, David, *The Scorsese Picture*, Birch Lane Press, New York (1992)

Hickenlooper, George, *Reel Conversations*, Citadel Press, New York (1991)

Jacobs, Diane, *Hollywood Renaissance: Altman, Cassavetes, Coppola, Mazursky, Scorsese and others*, A. S. Barnes, New York; Tantivy Press, London (1977)

Kelly, Mary Pat, *Martin Scorsese: The First Decade*, Redgrave Publishing Company, Pleasantville, New York (1980)

– *Martin Scorsese: A Journey*, Thunder's Mouth Press, New York (1991)

Keyser, Les, *Martin Scorsese*, Twayne Publishers, New York (1992)

Kolker, Robert Phillip, *A Cinema of Loneliness: Penn, Kubrick, Scorsese, Spielberg, Altman*, Oxford University Press, Oxford and New York (1980, revised edition 1988)

Monaco, James, *American Film Now*, New York, Zoetrope (1979, revised edition 1984)

Phillips, Julia, *You'll Never Eat Lunch in this Town Again*, Random House, New York (1991)

Pileggi, Nicholas and Scorsese, Martin, *GoodFellas*, ed. David Thompson, Faber and Faber, London (1990)

Pye, Michael and Myles, Lynda, *The Movie Brats: How the film generation took over Hollywood*, Holt, Rinehart & Winston, New York; Faber & Faber Ltd, London (1979)

Schrader, Paul, *Schrader on Schrader*, ed. Kevin Jackson, Faber and Faber, London (1990)

– *Taxi Driver*, Faber and Faber, London (1990)

Scorsese, Martin, *In the Streets* (Once a Catholic, ed. Peter Occhiogrosso), Houghton Mifflin Company, Boston (1987)

Stern, Lesley, *The Scorsese Connection*, British Film Institute, London (1995)

Taylor, Bella, *Martin Scorsese* (Close-up: The Contemporary Director series, ed. Jon Tuska), The Scarecrow Press Inc., Metuchen, New Jersey, and London (1981)

Weiss, Marion, *Martin Scorsese: A guide to references and resources*, G. K. Hall & Co., Boston, Massachusetts (1987)

Selected Interviews/Articles

1973

Sight and Sound, Vol. 43, No. 1, Winter 1973/4
Article on *Mean Streets* by David Denby

1975

Film Comment, Vol. 11, No. 5, March 1975
Interview, mainly on *Alice Doesn't Live Here Anymore*, by Marjorie Rosen

Film Heritage, Vol. 10, Spring 1975
Interview, mainly on *Alice Doesn't Live Here Anymore*, by F. Anthony Macklin

1976

Film Comment, Vol. 12, No. 2, March/April 1976
Interview with Paul Schrader on *Taxi Driver* by Richard Thompson

Sight and Sound, Vol. 45, No. 3, Summer 1976
Article on Wertmuller's *Seven Beauties* and *Taxi Driver* by Colin L. Westerbeck and
Interview with Robert Getchell by Richard Thompson

Focus on Film, No. 25, Summer–Autumn 1976
Interview, mainly on *Taxi Driver*, by Carmie Amata

1977

Film Comment, Vol. 13, No. 4, July/August 1977
Interview, mainly on *New York, New York*, by Jonathan Kaplan

Sight and Sound, Vol. 47, No. 1, Winter 1977/8
Interview, mainly on documentary making, by Richard Combs and Louise Sweet

1978

Film Comment, Vol. 14, No. 5, September/October 1978
Scorsese selects his 'Guilty Pleasures'

1980

American Film, Vol. 6, No. 2, November 1980
Interview, mainly on *Raging Bull*, by Thomas Wiener

1981

Sight and Sound, Vol. 50, No. 2, Spring 1981
Article on Cassavetes's *Gloria* and *Raging Bull* by Richard Combs

1982

American Film, Vol. 8, No. 2, November 1982
On the set and in post-production of *The King of Comedy* by Carrie Rickey

1983

Sight and Sound, Vol. 52, No. 3, Summer 1983
Analysis of *The King of Comedy* by Terrence Rafferty

Film Comment, Vol. 19, No. 6, November/December 1983
Article on Scorsese's teaching methods at NYU by Allan Arkush

1985

Film Comment, Vol. 21, No. 2, March/April 1985
Jay Cocks and Scorsese talk about Rosanna Arquette

Film Comment, Vol. 21, No. 4, July/August 1985
Article on five American directors including Scorsese by Stephen Farber

1986

Film Quarterly, Vol. 39, No. 3, Spring 1986
Article on Italian–American directors Coppola, De Palma and Scorsese, by Leo Braudy

Movie, No. 31/32, Winter 1986
Article on five Scorsese films, from *Mean Streets* to *The King of Comedy*, by Bryan Bruce, Richard Lippe, Lez Cooke and Robin Wood

American Film, Vol. 12, No. 2, November 1986
Interview with Scorsese and Richard Price on *The Color of Money* by Peter Biskind and Susan Linfield

1987

Interview, Vol. 17, No. 1, January 1987
Interview with Scorsese by David Ansen

The Face, February 1987
Interview with Scorsese by James Truman

1988

Film Comment, Vol. 24, No. 5, September/October 1988
Article and interview on *The Last Temptation of Christ* by Richard Corliss

1989

American Film, Vol. 14, No. 5, March 1989
Interview with Scorsese, mainly on *New York Stories*, by Chris Hodenfield

1990

Village Voice, 18 September 1990
Interview with Scorsese, mainly on *GoodFellas*, by Amy Taubin

Film Comment, Vol. 26, No. 5, September/October 1990
Interview with Scorsese, mainly on *GoodFellas*, by Gavin Smith

Rolling Stone, 1 November 1990
Interview with Scorsese, mainly on *GoodFellas*, by Anthony De Curtis

Cinema Papers, No. 81, December 1990
Interview with Scorsese by Ana Maria Bahiana

1991

Playboy April 1991
Interview with Scorsese by David Rensin

Blitz, No. 103, September 1991
Interview with Scorsese on the set of *Cape Fear* by David Morgan

American Cinematographer, Vol. 72, No. 10, October 1991
Interview with Freddie Francis on *Cape Fear* by David Morgan

Première, Vol. 5, No. 3, November 1991
Interview with Scorsese by Peter Biskind

Interview, Vol. 21, No. 11, November 1991
Interview with Scorsese, mainly on *Cape Fear*, by Graham Fuller

Entertainment Weekly, 6 December 1991
Interview with Scorsese by Owen Gleiberman

1992

Sight and Sound, Vol. 1, No. 10, February 1992
Articles on *Cape Fear* by J. Hoberman and Jenny Diski

1993

Première, Vol. 7, No. 2, October 1993
Interview with Scorsese, mainly on *The Age of Innocence*, by Daphne Merkin

American Cinematographer, Vol. 74, No. 10, October 1993
Interviews with Michael Ballhaus and Thelma Schoonmaker Powell, mainly on *The Age of Innocence*, by Stephen Pizzello

Interview, Vol. 23, No. 10, October 1993
Interview with Scorsese, mainly on *The Age of Innocence*, by Graham Fuller

Vanity Fair, October 1993
Scorsese does the Proust Questionnaire

Film Comment, Vol. 29, No. 6, November/December 1993
Interview with Scorsese, mainly on *The Age of Innocence*, by Gavin Smith

Films In Review, Vol. 44, Nos. 11/12, November/December 1993
Interview with Scorsese, mainly on *The Age of Innocence*, by Kenneth M. Chanko

Sight and Sound, Vol. 3, No. 12, December 1993
Article on *The Age of Innocence* by Amy Taubin

1994

Time Out, 12–19 January 1994
Interview with Scorsese, mainly on *The Age of Innocence*, by Geoff Andrew

Sight and Sound, Vol. 4, No. 2, February 1994
Interview with Scorsese, mainly on *The Age of Innocence*, by Ian Christie

Esquire, February 1994
Interview with Scorsese by Marcelle Clements

Empire, No. 56, February 1994
Interview with Scorsese, mainly on *The Age of Innocence*, by Chris Heath

1995

Sight and Sound, Vol. 5, No. 6, July 1995
Article on *A Personal Journey* by Raymond Durgnat

Notes on the Editors

David Thompson

After graduating from the University of Cambridge in 1978, David Thompson worked in film distribution and exhibition (the Electric Cinema in Portobello Road, London), before joining BBC Television as a film programmer in 1983. Following 'The Film Club' series, he has gone on to produce and direct numerous documentaries on cinema subjects, including Roberto Rossellini, Peter Greenaway, Michael Powell, Jean Renoir, Josef von Sternberg and Quentin Tarantino. He has also programmed seasons at the National Film Theatre, worked as a freelance journalist for *Time Out* and *Sight and Sound*, and was the editor of *Levinson on Levinson* and co-editor of *Jean Renoir: Letters*.

Ian Christie

Ian Christie is a fellow of Magdalen College and Visiting Lecturer in Film at Oxford University, as well as Associate Editor of *Sight and Sound*. He was formerly Head of Distribution and of Special Projects at the British Film Institute, for which he wrote and co-produced a BBC series on early cinema with Terry Gilliam, *The Last Machine*. He lectures and broadcasts regularly on cinema history, and his books include *Arrows of Desire: The Films of Michael Powell and Emeric Pressburger* and *Eisenstein Rediscovered*.

Index

Page numbers in italics refer to illustrations